The Mandy Money High School Textbook: Financial Literacy for Yea

Authored by Barbara van der Merwe and the Mandy Money Team
Published by Mandy Education Pty Ltd
Melbourne, 3000
Australia

ISBN: [ISBN Number]

For permissions, requests, or other inquiries, please contact:
Email: hello@mandymoney.com.au
Website: mandymoney.com.au

Disclaimer: Educational-Only Financial Content

The content within this textbook, is provided for educational purposes only. It is important to note that the information presented herein is not intended to provide any specific financial advice or recommendations. Every individual's financial situation is unique, and any decisions or actions taken based on the information presented should be done so at your own discretion and risk.

Efforts have been made to ensure that the content provided is accurate, reliable, and up to date. However, no guarantee or warranty is given regarding the completeness, accuracy, or reliability of the information. Furthermore, the content may not cover all aspects or considerations of a particular financial topic or scenario.

It is strongly advised that you consult with a qualified financial professional or advisor before making any financial decisions or implementing any strategies discussed in this content. Financial matters are complex and can involve various factors and risks, which may not be adequately addressed solely through educational content.

Any examples or hypothetical scenarios provided are for illustrative purposes only and do not reflect actual financial situations or guarantees of future outcomes. Past performance is not indicative of future results, and investments or financial strategies discussed may involve risks and potential losses.

The creators and publishers of this content shall not be held responsible or liable for any losses, damages, or expenses that may arise from the use of or reliance on the information presented herein. By accessing and using this content, you acknowledge and agree to hold harmless the creators and publishers from any such claims.

Please be aware that laws, regulations, and financial practices can change over time, and the information provided may become outdated. It is your responsibility to seek the most current and relevant information before making any financial decisions.
In conclusion, this content is intended solely for educational purposes and does not constitute financial advice. You should consult with a qualified professional and conduct your own research before making any financial decisions.

Acknowledgement of Country

Our HQ is situated on the stolen lands of the Wurundjeri People of the Kulin Nation. We would like to show our respects to the Traditional Custodians, to Elders past, present and emerging. We recognise their great knowledge and care of the lands and waterways we work and live on. Always was, always will be, Aboriginal land.

Hello!

Welcome to the Complete Personal Finance TextBook for Australian High Schoolers! In this Mandy Money textbook, you'll find (pretty much) every single thing you need to know about your money before you leave school.

Why is it worth your time?

We could throw the stats at you, but the bottom line is that not-knowing about money has disastrous consequences. Mental health implications, downgraded quality of life, impact on your happiness, health and overall well-being. In serious cases, not having financial literacy can keep you trapped in physically dangerous environments!

On the flip side, being financially literate and applying this knowledge can lead to confidence, empowerment, upgraded quality of life, and a position of safety and security. The biggest win, however, is freedom... And you can't put a price on that!

Much of what you're learning here, might not feel immediately relevant. That's ok. It's about soaking in as much as you can, so that when it does become relevant... You know where to start! Becoming 'good' at your money takes practice, and these micro-credentials are the best place to start.

Invest in education to gift yourself the power of good decision-making!

You will need:

Something to **write** with

Something to **access** quiz materials with

Something to **research** with...

Something to **motivate** you *(what's your Why?)*

My why: _____

Something to keep you on **track**

Calendar events

I, _____, am committing to completing ____ pages every _____

Signed:

X_____   X_____

Person about to get in the know about their dough

Accountability partner

Someone to keep you **accountable**

Contents

SMART FOUNDATIONS
micro credential

Collect all three Mandy Money resume badges!

The Big Question... What Actually Is Money?

First things first! Let's dive into the concept of what money is, where it came from, and the role it plays in our world. First of all, let's take a moment to try and understand what money really is.

It's a bit of an illusive concept. Think about it:

- Money is a physical object - but you can also transfer it online without anyone ever touching it.
- Every country has their own currency, but you can use your own money to buy money from other countries.
- A dollar is a dollar is a dollar, but the value of what you can buy with a dollar will change over time.

Confusing, right? Don't worry — Mandy's here to help you understand how it works!

Let's take it back 40,000 years.

You have

Scientists have tracked exchange and trade over the millenia, and the invention of money represented a major leap forward for humans. Before money came along, people had to resort to bartering, which refers to trading something you have, for something you want.

You want

The problem was...

if you had a goat, and you wanted some shoes, you had to rely on the shoemaker next door also wanting a goat. Even if you got lucky, you had to agree on how many pairs of shoes a goat is worth... and what happens if you don't want this many shoes?

#yeehaw

Money solved these problems, because goat farmers, shoemakers, and everyone else believed in its ability to store value. Our ancestors no longer had to try and guess what shoemakers wanted in return for their shoes, because everyone wanted money!

This made trading so much easier, and therefore helped to stabilise communities. Why would you need to invade your neighbouring kingdom to take their resources if you could come in peace and secure a long-term trading relationship?

Of course, money isn't a perfect tool, and if we leap back to the present day, much of today's global inequality can be linked to the formalisation and distribution of money. We humans haven't worked everything out yet, but we're getting there!

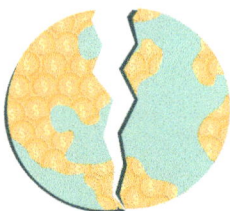

Overall, if we zoom out, money is an important economic, political, and social tool. Zooming back in, though, money plays a big role in dictating your lifestyle, your freedoms, and your quality of life. How much you have is one part of the equation, but how you use it, perceive it, and deal with it is equally as important.

That's a short summary of where money has come from and why we use it. Understanding this, and how it works, will help you make better decisions and ultimately have a better relationship with it.

Money and You

Your **money story** is the culmination of factors and influences in your life that create the way that you think, feel and behave in regards to money. Understanding your own money story will help you actively shape your money attitudes and behaviours in ways that benefit your financial and overall future.

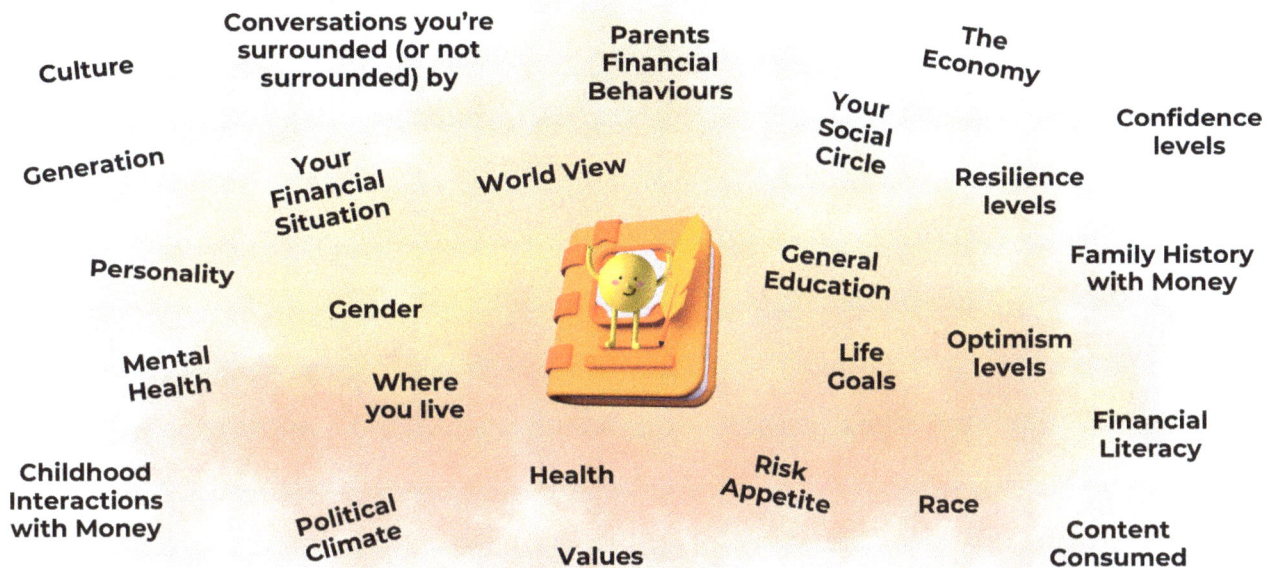

Culture

Conversations you're surrounded (or not surrounded) by

Parents Financial Behaviours

The Economy

Confidence levels

Generation

Your Financial Situation

World View

Your Social Circle

Resilience levels

Personality

Gender

General Education

Family History with Money

Mental Health

Where you live

Life Goals

Optimism levels

Financial Literacy

Childhood Interactions with Money

Political Climate

Health

Risk Appetite

Race

Content Consumed

Values

A Spotlight on Money and Culture!

We can't talk about money without talking about culture. Every culture has different ways of viewing personal finances. Even within one culture, you might find that there are different ways that money is discussed or used. And as the world becomes increasingly connected, being aware of... and making space for cultural nuances will make you a more respectful and empathetic individual. Let's explore a few fascinating examples form around the world...

Germany uses cash

Unlike almost all developed regions, Germany is a cash society. Germans use cash for about 80 percent of their purchases, staying away from both credit cards and personal debt.

Pakistan makes charity obligatory

They have what is referred to as Zakat, which is a rather generous giving practice. in Pakistan it's mandated by law. The principle requires everyone to donate at least 2.5% of their income to charities and those who are less fortunate.

Kenya has community based credit

In countries where getting loans to invest in a business can be next to impossible, communities have started to form their own systems of credit. In Kenya, harambee, a community-led initiative whereby participants pool their money together and use it for a project the community needs.

Islam forbids charging interest

Our next journey is not to another country, but to a religious nuance... In Islamic beliefs, the interest rate is forbidden. This means, that unlike a typical loan where you pay a fee for being able to borrow that money, many muslims rely on community based or alternative forms of financing for big purchases.

These examples don't even scratch the surface of how money & culture interact, yet they are fascinating examples to get you thinking about your money story.

A Chance To Reflect On Your Story...

For each of these factors, explore how they have each impacted your relationship with money!

Culture	World View
Personality	Risk Appetite
Life Goals	Gender
Your Financial Situation	Race
General Education	The Economy
Conversations you're surrounded by	Content Consumed
Parents Financial Behaviours	Generation
Your Social Circle	Health
Financial Literacy	Where you live
Your Values	Childhood Interactions with Money
Optimism/ Confidence / Resilience levels	Political Climate
Family History with Money	Mental Health

Writing your new story...

This is your chance to design what you want your relationship with money to be! How would you like to feel, think and act when it comes to money? Come back to this over your journey.

Money & Me
Our story...

ESSENTIAL SYSTEMS
micro-credential

BUDGETING

Learn how to manage your money, design your financial ecosystem, and build strong saving skills!

Lesson 1
Building a Budget

- ☐ **1** Elements of a successful budget
- ☐ **2** Personal Financial Ecosystem
- ☐ **3** Budget Building Steps
- ☐ **4** Basic Budgeting Maths

Lesson 2
Budgeting in the Real World

- ☐ **1** Long Term Budgeting
- ☐ **2** Budget Logistics
- ☐ **3** Tech Tools & Budgeting
- ☐ **4** Budgeting in a Nutshell

Lesson 3
Introduction to Saving

- ☐ **1** Financial Freedom Rationale
- ☐ **2** Maths Behinds Savings Goals
- ☐ **3** Building Savings Into Your Budget
- ☐ **4** Psychology of Budgeting

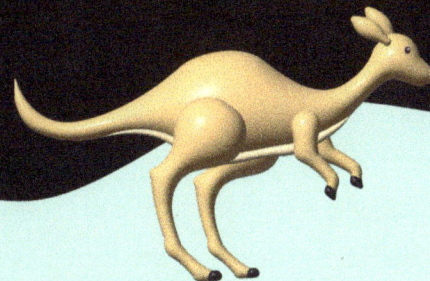

The Key Elements Of A Budget

Learning to manage a budget is one of the key ingredients in the recipe to financial wellbeing. In this chapter, we'll help you understand the core elements of what makes a successful budget.

Income
- Job Payment
- Side Hustle
- Centrelink
- Investment Profit

Expenses
- Bills
- Essentials
- Debt Repayments
- Donations
- Lifestyle

Savings
- Long Term Savings
- Short Term Savings
- Emergency Funds
- Investments

The first major component is your **income**. This is all the money coming into your financial ecosystem. It can include everything from job payments... to birthday money from your lovely nana... to welfare money and even investment income. An understanding of how much money is coming into your bank account will help you allocate it accordingly.

The second component, **expenses**, is all the money that goes towards your expenses. It can consist of bills, essentials, debt repayments, donations, and of course a little for lifestyle and fun. Basically, it's all of the money that leaves your account. We also call these "Outflows", and it's really important to learn how to manage these well!

Finally, we have **savings**. This is all the money going towards general or specific savings goals, emergency funds or investments. It's all the money you earn, but don't spend! It's key to have dedicated savings location(s) to make sure that you don't accidentally mix up your accounts and spend your savings.

Where does each component 'live'?

Now, the key is to be smart about where each of these components lives. In other words... which products, accounts or locations will you be using to house the money for each component? Let's start with a cash example to give you a tangible example of this. In this case, your income, expenses, and savings buckets might take the form of physical locations. For example...
- All your **income** might go in a cash tin
- Your **spending** money or expenses might go in your wallet
- Your **savings** might go in a jar with a really tightly closed lid

Cash isn't very realistic in a today's world where your money is managed through a phone or computer. You'll likely want to convert these physical locations into digital ones at some point.
- This might mean your **income** lives in one bank account
- Your **spending** money lives in another account
- Your **savings** lives in a third account (or investment)

From here is where you design your financial ecosystem, linking these locations together and designing how your money flows into, through and out of your ecosystem. As you get older, your budgeting may get more complex, but by and large, these are the major three components that the complexity will be shaped around.

Basic Bank Accounts

There are many different locations you can choose for your digital money to live. Here's a quick intro to the two most common types of bank accounts you have available to you.

Everyday / Transaction Account
This is an account that stores your money, gives you instant access to manage it, and comes with a debit card to pay for things.

Savings Account
This is an account that stores your money, and allows you to earn 'interest'. You can't pay for anything from this account.

B1.1.1

Looking at your unique situation...
Decide on the best locations for each of your budget components! It doesn't need to be a complex product, but make sure to be specific!

Where is your income
going to land?

Where is your spending
money going to be based?

Where will your
savings live?

Mapping Out Your Personal Financial Ecosystem

Step number one of building a budget is to visually map out your financial ecosystem. Why is it important? Well, money in our modern world lives in our phones, and we can feel really out of touch with its movements and whereabouts. This makes it really tricky to manage and deal with. Treating it like a tangible object, and being able to understand where it flows is pretty essential. The first part is to map out all of your locations (flip back to the previous page to focus on this). The second part is to connect each of these locations to show how money flows around.

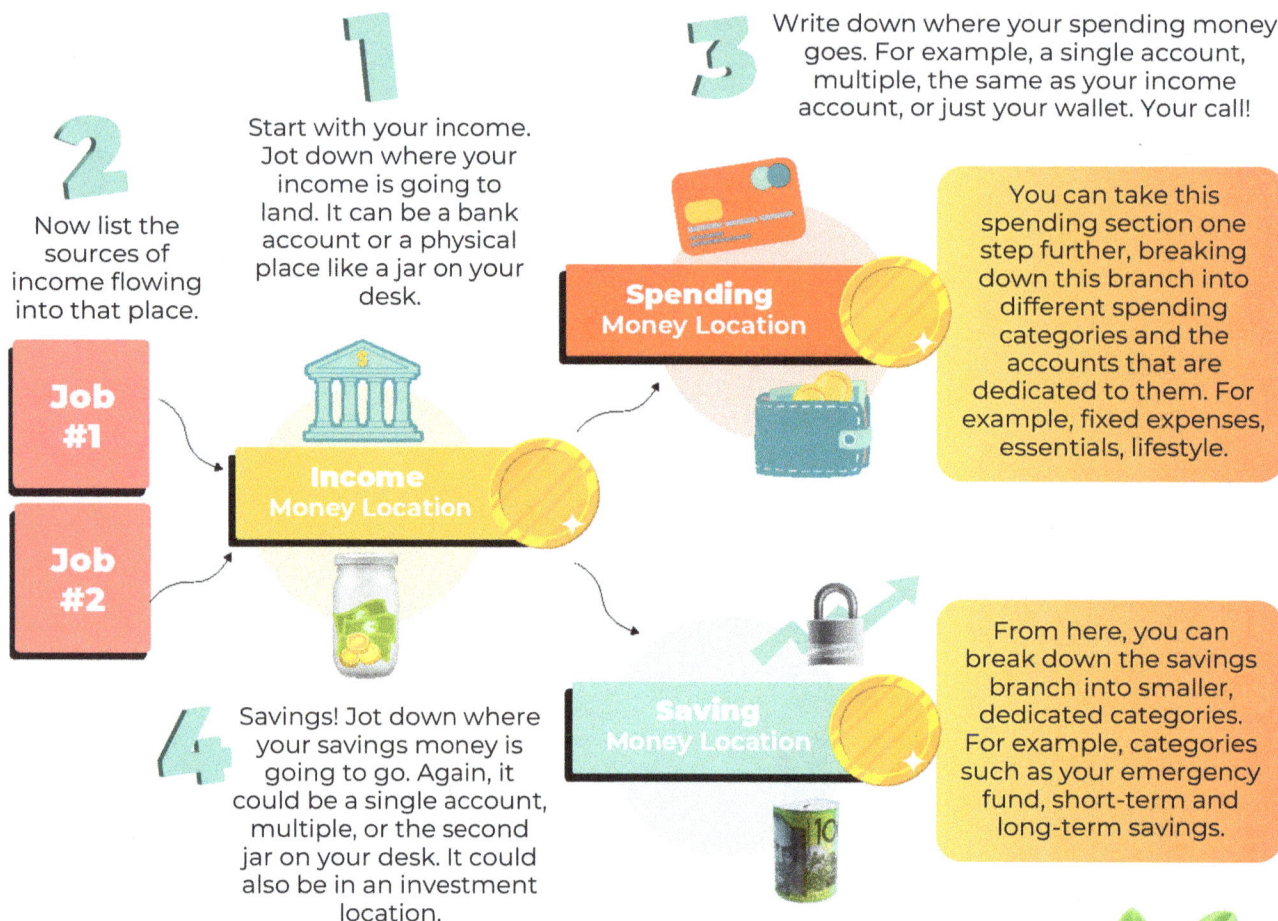

1 Start with your income. Jot down where your income is going to land. It can be a bank account or a physical place like a jar on your desk.

2 Now list the sources of income flowing into that place.

3 Write down where your spending money goes. For example, a single account, multiple, the same as your income account, or just your wallet. Your call!

Job #1

Job #2

Income Money Location

Spending Money Location

You can take this spending section one step further, breaking down this branch into different spending categories and the accounts that are dedicated to them. For example, fixed expenses, essentials, lifestyle.

Saving Money Location

From here, you can break down the savings branch into smaller, dedicated categories. For example, categories such as your emergency fund, short-term and long-term savings.

4 Savings! Jot down where your savings money is going to go. Again, it could be a single account, multiple, or the second jar on your desk. It could also be in an investment location.

5 Finally, now that you have identified each of your locations, finish by connecting them however best it works for you. This diagram allows you to visualise where your money is flowing and how to deal with it efficiently. Eventually, you can step it up by making some of those flows automatic with automatic transfers.

How can you draw your own?

Start at the very beginning and put on your visualisation cap...
- First, visualise all the different types of income. How are they flowing into your ecosystem?
- Next, think about all your different expenses and how you would pay for them (card, transfer etc) and how the money leaves your ecosystem.
- Then, consider all your different savings and investment products, how does money end up in those?
- Once you have all your locations laid out and organised, draw arrows between all your key points and show how money flows, into, through and out of your system.

Mapping out your ecosystem isn't necessary for each and every budget, but it helps you figure out what's going on behind the scenes. In any case, it's an excuse to get creative! It doesn't need to be complicated (in fact, the simpler, the better), but it does need to clear.

Design your own ecosystem...
Using your decided locations, map out your own money flow and ecosystem. As long as you include your three primary components and show where income is flowing into, your ecosystem can be as simple or complicated as you like!

Structuring A Basic Budget

Building a budget isn't rocket science, but there is a logic to it that you need to learn to make it work. Let's build one together! The very first thing you'll have to decide, is what period of time your budget is for! This might be a week, a month, or even a specific period such as a holiday.

1 Prepare the framework

You'll see here, we've just taken out ecosystem diagram and tilted it vertically to create our headings!

- **Income** is listed at the top
- **Expenses**, **Savings** and other umbrella categories will go in the middle
- We've added a T**otal** at the bottom to keep track of numbers

5 Double-check

Once you've allocated your amounts, check two things...

- Firstly, that your **Income** is equal or greater to your **Total** amount allocated to spending and saving.
- Secondly, making sure that what you've generally allocated and then specifically planned for each category is the same.

	Plan	Actual
Income	**$500**	**$450**
Spending	**$300**	**$250**
Fun	$50	$25
Bills	$150	$150
Food	$100	$75
	$300	$250
Saving	**$200**	**$200**
Emergency Fund	$50	$50
Car Goal	$150	$150
	$200	$200
Total	**$500**	**$450**

2 Add your line items

Within each element, you'll have specific line items to list. This is to help you break down your plan to understand it better. Don't worry too much at this stage about what these are, we'll get to that in the next chapter!

3 Add Numbers

In the middle column, we'll input your numbers!

- The **Income** number tells you how much money you're expecting to receive into your account
- The big **Spending** number tells you how much in total you're planning on spending
  - Each Spending line item is simply is a breakdown of where exactly you'll be spending you're money
- The big **Saving** number tells you how much in total you're planning on sending to your savings.
  - Each Saving line item is simply a breakdown of how exactly you'll allocate your savings amount.
- The big **Total** number is your savings and spending added together... This number has to be the same or less than your income number!

4 Review column

The final column is for the end of the budget period, to review what actually happened. The first half is all planning, but you also want to record what did or didn't end up happening.

- For example, you expected to earn $500, but only ended up with $450.
- So, you took your spending allocation down to $250 but kept your savings allocation the same at $300

Looking at the above process in simple terms... We started by looking at how your money flow is structured and then changed the shape into a vertical layout. Next, we input real numbers into the framework (more on this in the next chapter). Finally, we tied it all together by looking at what happened, to make sure we started next month's budget on the right foot!

B1.3.1

Design a budget structure...
Using the Budgeting System as inspiration, practise structuring a basic budget, before converting your personal ecosystem into your personal budget!

Organise each of these scrambled elements into a budget structure!

Bills   **Total**

Cafe Job Income

Plan   *Short Term Goal*

Fun   **Saving**

Retail Job Income

Actual   *Food*

Spending   **July**

Long Term Goal

Income   *Transport*

Emergency Fund

Referring back to your ecosystem flow, organise it into a budget structure! If the way we've designed ours doesn't make logical sense to you... Try designing it in a way that you understand. There is no right or wrong here!

Basic Budgeting Maths

The maths involved to build a budget isn't particularly complex, but there are four key steps to follow., which come together into the easy-to-remember acronym **S.A.V.E!** Sum, Allocate, Validate, Execute.

1 Sum your Income, Expenses & Savings

List all your types of Income, Expenses, and Savings... how often you'll encounter them, and your total for that expense. In this example, we're building a budget for a **month**!

Income	Amount	Frequency	Total (Month)
Job #1	$20 Hourly	10 Hours	$200
Job #2	$20 Hourly	15 Hours	$300
Expense			
Movie Tickets	$10	2	$20
Hobby Supplies	$30	1	$30
Gym Membership	$50	1	$50
Transport Ticket	$5	20	$100
Canteen Lunches	$10	8	$80
Hot Chocolates	$5	4	$20
Savings			
Emergency Fund	$12.50 Weekly	4 weeks	$50
Car Goal	$37.50 Weekly	4 Weeks	$150

2 Allocate into your individual buckets

Remember the categories from before? Allocate each of these line items into your buckets!

Income	
Job #1	$200
Job #2	$300
Expense	
Movie Tickets	$20
Hobby Supplies	$30
Gym Membership	$50
Transport Ticket	$100
Canteen Lunches	$80
Hot Chocolates	$20
Savings	
Emergency Fund	$50
Car Goal	$150

Income — **$500**

Spending — **$300**
Fun — $50
Bills — $150
Food — $100
$300

Saving — **$200**
Emergency Fund — $50
Car Goal — $150
$200

You can choose to list every single expense, instead of grouping them into buckets. But! This can make the process overly complex. Instead of tracking general bucket categories, you would have to track and note down every specific purchase. This can be time-consuming and also make your budget inflexible to change.

3 Validate that these numbers work

Once you've built the budget... Do the numbers add up? Check these key questions:
- Does your income cover your expenses and savings? If not, adjust them!
- Are your expenses realistic? Will be able to stick within your spending budget?
- Do your savings allocations keep you on track to meet your savings goals?

4 Execute your budget!

Once you've got your budget built, now is the time to figure out a plan of action to make sure you don't veer off track. This could be: Using a budgeting app and notifications to help keep track of your spending, saving your budget as a screensaver, or keeping a copy of your budget handy in your diary. Creating your budget is a logical process... Sticking to it is a mental game.

. When putting together your budget maths, remember to be as detailed as possible. Consider every expense, no matter how little. Try to build in some conservative 'padding' to be safe!

B1.4.1 — Loletta and her snail farm...

Use this template budget to build a weekly budget for Loletta

monday
- Feed the Snails (5c per snail)
- Snail party in the city

tuesday
- Feed the Snails
- Wash the Snails (10c per snail)

wednesday
- Feed the Snails

thursday
- Feed the Snails
- Take the snails to the Cinemas to watch the slug of wall street

friday
- Feed the Snails
- Wash the Snails

saturday
- Feed the Snails
- Take the snails to the snail polish salon (10c per snail)

sunday
- Feed the Snails

- Her weekly income is $283.
- She has 200 snails.
- It costs 5c per snail each time she feeds them.
- She needs to drive to and from the party on Monday!
- She's considering buying a present or a new outfit for the party. Does she have budget for this?
- Every time Loletta uses her truck, it costs her $5 in fuel (one way).
- Her entire snail herd fits into one $20 cinema seat.
- Loletta is saving for a VIP $300 snail masseuse to buy in 8 weeks.
- She has a long term goal she needs to save $10 a week for.
- She wants to put $10 a week into her emergency fund.

Level up by making this budget on excel!

Start with the maths, calculating individual elements!

Income	Amount	Frequency	Total

Expense	Amount	Frequency	Total

Savings	Amount	Frequency	Total

Then transfer it into a formal budget plan

Week Budget Plan

	$
	$
	$
	$
	$
	$
	$
	$
	$
	$
	$
	$
	$
	$

Working out space

mandy

19

How To Build Your Budget For The Long Term

Building a single budget helps you plan out your next week or month... But how can you make longer term plans, especially when your income and spending is irregular and you have long-term goals to hit? The real magic happens when you can flesh out that planning as part of a long term strategy.

Let's turn a short term budget into a long term one

There is quite literally only one step to make this happen. Simply take your singular period budgets (our example is a monthly budget), and place them side-by-side in a straight line. The final product should look close to this, where...

- All your budgeting periods (Jul, Aug, Sept...) are listed across the top of the page.
- Your categories (income, expenses, totals...) are down the left-hand side.

Now you have a view of your budgeting plan for the next few weeks, months or years!

	Jul	Aug	Sep	Oct	Nov
Income	$500	$400	$600	$500	$500
Spending	$300	$300	$300	$300	$300
Fun	$50	$50	$50	$50	$50
Bills	$150	$150	$150	$150	$150
Food	$100	$100	$100	$100	$100
	$300	$300	$300	$300	$300
Saving	$200	$100	$300	$200	$200
Surfboard Goal	$50	$50	$50	$50	$50
Emergency Fund	$150	$50	$250	$150	$150
	$200	$200	$200	$200	$200
Total	$500	$400	$600	$500	$500

This layout will allow you to do three specific things...

1 Number one, you will be able to connect all your flows. Maybe your income is expected to be lower than usual for one month because you're taking some time off. But thanks to your smart budgeting calendar, you will be able to adjust your future spending and plan your money allocations strategically.

	Jul	Aug	Sep	Oct	Nov
Income	$500	**$400**	**$600**	$500	$500

Earn $100 less, *So to compensate...* **...Plan $100 extra income**

$250 surfboard in time for summer!

Surfboard Goal	$50	$50	$50	$50	$50

2 Number two, it will help you to work towards your savings goals efficiently. For example, it might help you to visualise that if you could save fifty dollars each month for six months, that new surfboard is totally within reach!

3 Finally, at number three, you will begin to notice certain trends, ESPECIALLY the spending trends. You'll start to notice where maybe you're splurging a bit unnecessarily and where you could cut back. Or see your total income and be motivated to find another income stream.

	Jul	Aug	Sep	Oct	Nov
Spending	$300	$300	$300	$300	$300
Fun	$50	$50	$50	$50	$50
Bills	$150	$150	$150	$150	$150
Food	$100	$100	$100	$100	$100

Spending way too much on bills across a 5 month period, should I look for cheaper deals?

Now that you know how to plan your long term budgets, that first car or even first house could be yours a whole lot quicker.

B1.5.1 Fix your budget!

It's July and you realised you've overspent on fun this month ($100 spent, instead of $50). You now don't have enough money to put $50 into your Surfboard savings. Because you have a long-term view, what are *three* adjustments you could make to your future budget to get back on track with your surfboard goal?

	Jul	Aug	Sep	Oct	Nov
Income	$500	$400	$600	$500	$500
Spending	$300	$300	$300	$300	$300
Fun	~~$50~~ $100	$50	$50	$50	$50
Bills	$150	$150	$150	$150	$150
Food	$100	$100	$100	$100	$100
	$300	$300	$300	$300	$300
Saving	$200	$100	$300	$200	$200
Surfboard Goal	~~$50~~	$50	$50	$50	$50
Emergency Fund	$150	$50	$250	$150	$150
	$200	$200	$200	$200	$200
Total	$500	$400	$600	$500	$500

Solution 1

Solution 2

Solution 3

Can you sketch out a budget plan for your own next 4 weeks or months?

Two Key Elements Of A Functioning Budget

Think of a budget as a snapshot of a point in time; it's static. We want to develop it into something that can adapt to changes in your lifestyle, something that keeps up with you and your spending! In this chapter, we'll explain the two components of a working budget...

1 "Foundation" Planner

This is your "foundation", where you plan your budget. It's what you'll keep coming back to create and review your plans and track your progress. It can be a piece of paper, Excel document or an App.

2 "Data" Tracker

This is a tool that helps you FIND the inputs that go into this foundational budget. It's something that gives you data about each of your budget categories. It could simply be your banking app!

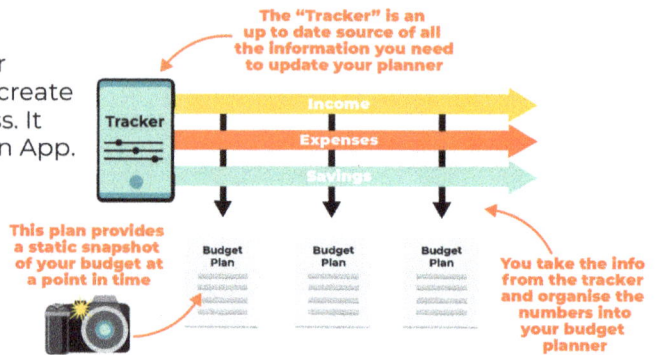

The "Tracker" is an up to date source of all the information you need to update your planner

Tracker → Income → Expenses → Savings

This plan provides a static snapshot of your budget at a point in time

Budget Plan | Budget Plan | Budget Plan

You take the info from the tracker and organise the numbers into your budget planner

Let's put two and two together. Each period (month or week), you want to construct a classic budget. It's a snapshot of your plan for the month or week ahead. At the end of the period, you want to review this plan and write down what actually happened. This is where the tracker data comes in handy. It tells you what actually happened... How much you actually earned, spent and saved.

An Example!

Firstly, **income**! You want to be able to see how much has actually entered during the budget period. Note that refunds and transfers from friends don't count as income!

Next, **expenses**. You want to see how much you have spent, and ideally how much on your different spending categories.

Lastly, **savings**. It could be that you have several savings accounts or investments. You'll want something to tell you how much you have sent to savings (or withdrawn from savings).

	Plan	Actual
Income	**$500**	**$450**
Spending	**$300**	**$225**
Fun	$50	$25
Bills	$150	$150
Food	$100	$50
	$300	$225
Saving	**$200**	**$225**
Emergency Fund	$50	$75
Car Goal	$150	$150
	$200	$225
Total	**$500**	**$450**

Income
How much did you actually earn this week?
$450

Expenses
How much have you spent this week?
How much per category?
$225
Fun: $25
Bills: $150
Food: $50

Savings
How much have you sent to your savings / investments?
$225

Tracker

It sounds more complicated than in reality. Call it what you like, at the end of the day, you simply want to decide:
- Where you'll construct your budget (Planner)
- Where you'll find the real numbers to review & update it (Tracker)

Don't over complicate it!

Your planner could simply be a piece of paper or an excel sheet. Your tracker could be your banking app or a budgeting app.

B1.6.1 Budgeting Hazards!

The concept of a 'planner' and 'tracker' can seem complicated. In your own words, let's recap each of them and their purpose.

In your own words, what exactly is a 'Planner' and why do you need one?

In your own words, what exactly is a 'Tracker' and why is it important?

One of the key reasons we need to use a 'Tracker' to be able to reflect and update our planner, is because there are so many unexpected expenses that come your way. The better you can predict these expenses, the more accurate you will be able plan. List as many (expected and unexpected) expenses as you can!!

1.	26.	51.	76.
2.	27.	52.	77.
3.	28.	53.	78.
4.	29.	54.	79.
5.	30.	55.	80.
6.	31.	56.	81.
7.	32.	57.	82.
8.	33.	58.	83.
9.	34.	59.	84.
10.	35.	60.	85.
11.	36.	61.	86.
12.	37.	62.	87.
13.	38.	63.	88.
14.	39.	64.	89.
15.	40.	65.	90.
16.	41.	66.	91.
17.	42.	67.	92.
18.	43.	68.	93.
19.	44.	69.	94.
20.	45.	70.	95.
21.	46.	71.	96.
22.	47.	72.	97.
23.	48.	73.	98.
24.	49.	74.	99.
25.	50.	75.	100.

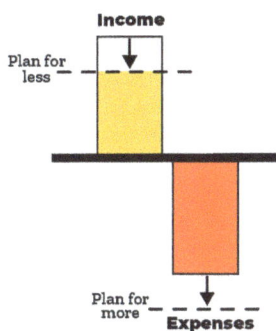

Income
Plan for less
Plan for more
Expenses

In relation to building your budget planner, what does this diagram recommend? Do you agree?

Tools, Technology And Your Budget

Budgeting can range from being a manual pen & paper exercise to one that takes place entirely on your phone or computer. Referring back to the two components of a functioning budget (Planner & Tracker), here are some tech options to explore, and a look at how to understand your banking app!

1 Constructing your "Foundation" Planner (aka. budget)

Budgeting App
There are many apps to help you plan your budget. Some of these apps can even access your live banking data to update the budget in real time. Make sure to find one that fits you!

Excel Sheet
The program, 'Excel', is a powerful and customisable tool to build budgets of any shape and size. It can seem complicated, but is an infinitely useful tool to learn how to use!

Digital Document
Not a fan of apps and not ready for excel? Simply using word or canva to write out your budget can work! Use the 'table' feature to create your budget layout and go from there!

2 Understanding your "Data" Tracker (aka. Banking App)

Using your banking app to manage your money can be the trickiest part of budgeting! Here's an example of how to interpret your account activity (this example ecosystem has 3 bank accounts).

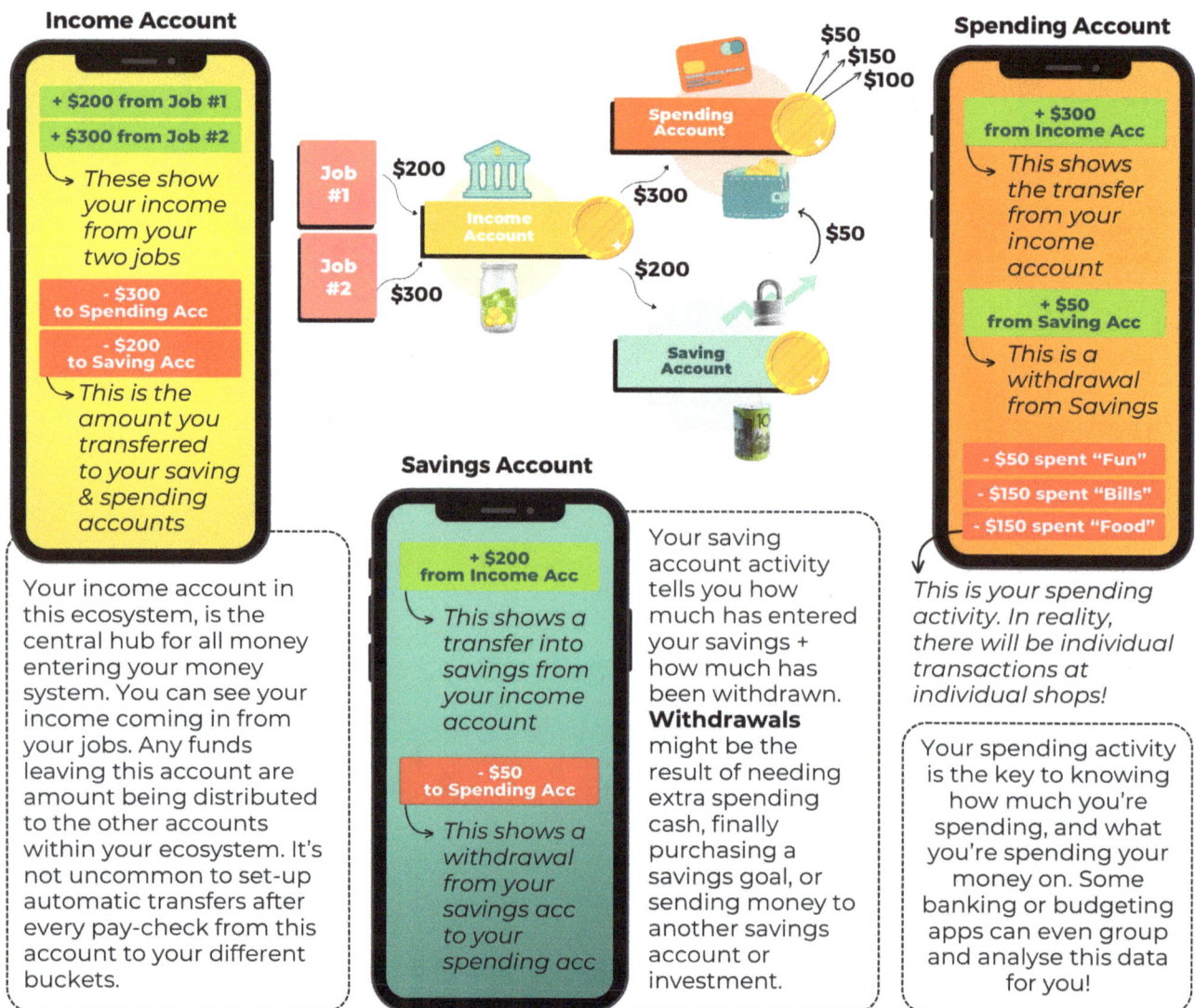

Income Account

+ $200 from Job #1
+ $300 from Job #2

↳ *These show your income from your two jobs*

- $300 to Spending Acc
- $200 to Saving Acc

↳ *This is the amount you transferred to your saving & spending accounts*

Job #1 — $200
Job #2 — $300

Income Account

$300
$200
$50

Spending Account → $50 $150 $100

Saving Account

Your income account in this ecosystem, is the central hub for all money entering your money system. You can see your income coming in from your jobs. Any funds leaving this account are amount being distributed to the other accounts within your ecosystem. It's not uncommon to set-up automatic transfers after every pay-check from this account to your different buckets.

Savings Account

+ $200 from Income Acc

↳ *This shows a transfer into savings from your income account*

- $50 to Spending Acc

↳ *This shows a withdrawal from your savings acc to your spending acc*

Your saving account activity tells you how much has entered your savings + how much has been withdrawn. **Withdrawals** might be the result of needing extra spending cash, finally purchasing a savings goal, or sending money to another savings account or investment.

Spending Account

+ $300 from Income Acc

↳ *This shows the transfer from your income account*

+ $50 from Saving Acc

↳ *This is a withdrawal from Savings*

- $50 spent "Fun"
- $150 spent "Bills"
- $150 spent "Food"

This is your spending activity. In reality, there will be individual transactions at individual shops!

Your spending activity is the key to knowing how much you're spending, and what you're spending your money on. Some banking or budgeting apps can even group and analyse this data for you!

Analyse these banking app activity feeds!
Use the "tracker" information below (screenshots of your banking app) to construct a budget with categories and figures.

Income
Account Activity

+ $100 from Job

- $100 to Spending Acc

+ $200 from Job

- $100 to Spending Acc

- $100 to Savings Acc

Spending
Account Activity

+ $100 from Income Acc

- $100 on food

+ $100 from Income Acc

- $100 on Bills

+ $10 food refund

- $100 on fun

+ $10 from Savings Acc

- $10 on fun

Savings
Account Activity

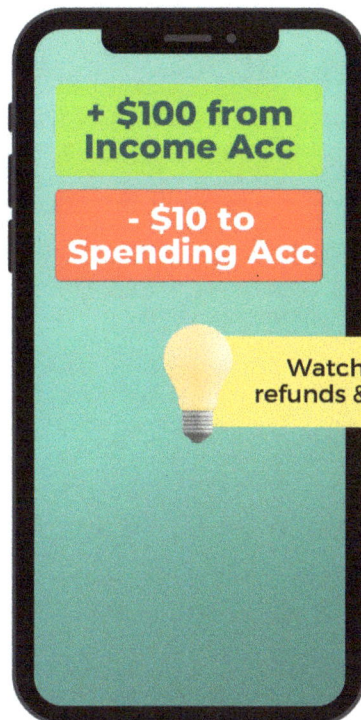

+ $100 from Income Acc

- $10 to Spending Acc

Watch out for refunds & transfers!

INTERPRET this activity tracker data to create a budget which summarises what happened during the week!

Income	
Spending	
Saving	
Total	

Looking at your own situation... What will work for you as a "planner"?

Looking at your own situation... What will work for you as a "tracker"?

The Budgeting Process In A Nutshell

Budgeting can seem difficult, complicated and overwhelming. Yet in reality, keeping it simple is the key to making it a sustainable and enjoyable practise... There are a few key steps to take, and the rest is just bells & whistles! Here are the key steps, recapped...

1 Sort out your Ecosystem

This is all about understanding the layout of your financial ecosystem, answering questions like...
- In which locations does your money live?
- Which financial products will you be using for each of these locations? ie. A bank account, savings account, investment product etc.
- How does money flow into, between and from these locations?

Being able to sketch this out will help you visualise and understand how your money works. It helps keep it all organised!

2 Create your Planner + Tracker

Next, it's about planning the tools and logistics.
- For your planning document, will you be using an excel document, a notebook, a folder, or a page in your diary?
- For your tracking tools, where will you find the up-to-date data needed to update your planning document? Will you be checking individual banking/investment platforms, or will you be using an app that collates a lot of this info?

3 Input your numbers (Short & Long Term)

Time to build your 'planner' budget & input your numbers! Whether you plan for the week, month or year, make sure to think long term.
- Will you be able to hit savings goals?
- Will your income cover all your expenses?
- Will you be able to contribute to your emergency fund?

	Jul	Aug	Sep	Oct	Nov
Income	$500	$400	$600	$500	$500
Spending	$300	$300	$300	$300	$300
Fun	$50	$50	$50	$50	$50
Bills	$150	$150	$150	$150	$150
Food	$100	$100	$100	$100	$100
	$300	$300	$300	$300	$300
Saving	$200	$100	$300	$200	$200
Surfboard Goal	$50	$50	$50	$50	$50
Emergency Fund	$150	$50	$250	$150	$150
	$200	$200	$200	$200	$200
Total	$500	$400	$600	$500	$500

4 Execute & Review

Once you've built your budget, now you must follow it through, and review it at the end of the budget period!

Consider...
- Can you automate any transfers?
- How can you keep your budget targets front of mind?
- How can you make sure you stick to your budget plan?

Use the F.A.C.T.S acronym to help stick to and execute your budget plan!

Flexibility
Remember to build in the 'human factor'

Accountability
Find an accountability partner!

Consistency
Set a time each period to review & reset!

Tools
Get tech and the right tools on your side!

Sympathy
Be kind to yourself, budgeting is tricky!

From start to finish...
Complete this budgeting process top to bottom!

Step 1: Label this Ecosystem using the facts on the left!

- You have two jobs, paid monthly.
- Each month you earn $200 from the first job and $100 from the second.
- You dedicate $210 to spending
- $90 of your spending allocation goes towards bills, paid directly from your income account (transfers).
- The remaining $120 is broken down equally into three other spending categories (Essentials, Food, Fun).
- You dedicate $45 to each of your two savings goals (Short Term, Long Term)

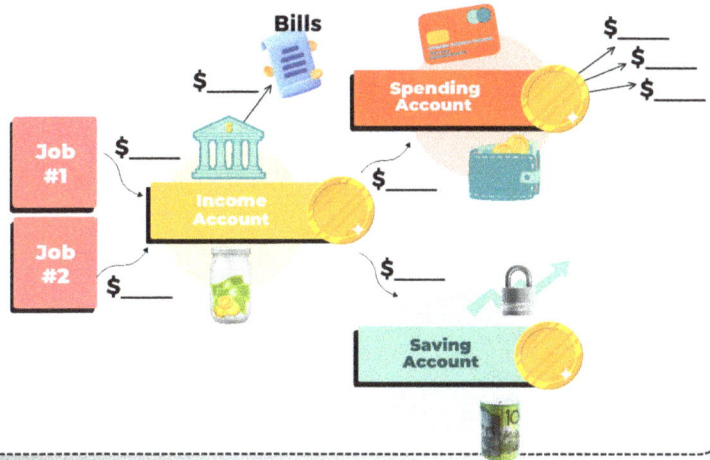

Bills

$____

$____
$____
$____

Spending Account

Job #1 $____

Job #2 $____

Income Account

$____

$____

Saving Account

Step 2: Create a 'Long-Term' budget

Based on the above facts, convert the labelled ecosystem into a 3-month budget plan! We've created the basic framework for you, and you can assume each month is exactly the same.

	Month 1	Month 2	Month 3
Income			
Spending			
Saving			
Total			

Step 3: Review Month 1

Based on screenshots from each of your accounts, what *actually* happened during the first month?

Income Account
- + $100 from Job
- + $190 from Job
- - $90 on Bills
- - $120 to Spending Acc
- - $80 to Spending Acc

Spending Account
- + $120 from Income Acc
- - $40 Essentials
- - $40 on Food
- - $40 on fun
- + $5 food refund

Savings Account
- + $80 from Income Acc

	Month 1
Income	
Spending	
Saving	
Total	

Step 4: Adjust Long-Term Budget

Re-write next two monthly plans to ensure you stay on track with your savings goals.

	Month 1	Month 2	Month 3
Income			
Spending			
Saving			
Total			

Are you on track with your saving goals?

→ $90 ☐
→ $90 ☐

Why Does Saving Even Matter?

Saving can be an uninspiring topic. It involves giving up money today, for a future version of you to spend. But! there's a much bigger picture that sits behind it... The picture of financial freedom. In this chapter, we'll explore the different sides to saving and what financial freedom actually means.

There are two sides to saving...

Firstly, it enables you to fix or avoid rainy-day situations where something goes terribly wrong in life.

&

Secondly, it gives you the freedom to enjoy the sunny days, like taking that opportunity, or spending money on experiences and things you like.

Focusing on optimising both of these sides, allows you to work towards financial freedom. By this, we don't mean swimming pools full of cash (although power to you if this is what financial freedom looks like to you!). We like to think of there being are six levels of financial freedom...

Start at Level 1 and work up!

Quality Retirement

Level Six is the tip-top of financial freedom (excluding outliers like Melanie Perkins or Elon Musk). This is where you have enough to retire with a good standard of living - maybe even with beaches, coconuts and the Bahamas if you're that way inclined. For most people, though, if you're doing well and are happy with your current standard of living, it's more about having the funds to sustain this way of life during retirement.

Retirement

Level Five is all about having enough money for a basic retirement. Remember, if you're planning on living to blow out 100 candles, retirement can potentially be forty years or more!

Time Freedom

Level Four is the freedom to reclaim your time. Almost everyone wants more flexibility with their schedules in their hectic lives, whether that's to follow their passion, spend time with family, or just take a day off whenever you feel like it.

Material Freedom

Level Three is having the money to enjoy some of the finer things in life, while still consistently having enough left over to save and be responsible with your finances.

Job Pause

Level Two is having the freedom to quit your job, at least for a couple of months! Saving enough money to quit your job forever is a big undertaking, but saving enough to take even a small amount of time off is a really liberating experience. Financial freedom is all about adding an element of optionality into your work life.

Cashflow Flexibility

Level One is the first rung on the financial freedom ladder, and it simply refers to not living paycheck to paycheck. This means working towards building some emergency funds and having cash flow flexibility.

Financial freedom isn't about private jets or having enough cash to fill your swimming pool. It's more about gaining the freedom, safety, and choice to create the life you want to live. Having the freedom to say no to things you don't want to do, and say yes to things you do want to do. This is different for everyone, so the next step is to figure out what you want and what financial freedom looks like to you!

The sky is the limit!
What does financial freedom look like to you? Draw a landscape with all the things you want for your future. Make it as real as possible, labelling key objects and getting specific about details.

The Maths Behind Your Savings Goals

In order to save effectively, you need to know what exactly you're saving towards, whether it's for your first car, an early retirement, or something small yet essential. In this chapter, we'll help you define your personal saving goals.

While having a generic savings allocation isn't the worst way to do things, you'll be much better off when your saving strategy includes a particular end goal. It doesn't have to be fancy, just defined. There are multiple ways you could decide how much to send to savings. Maybe it's percentage of your income, or any money left over after expenses. The most straight-forward method, however, is figuring out a set amount per week / month. Here's the maths...

1 How Much? (How much do you need?)

2 By When? (When is the goal due?)

3 Time? (Between now and the due date, how much time do you have?)

It's a pretty simple exercise, but ask yourself these questions and your savings dream just became a savings strategy.

An Example

You want:
- $1000 saved in your emergency fund
- By December 31st,
- Which is six months away.

From here, it's a pretty simple calculation to determine how much you need to save each pay period, either weekly or monthly—making it easier to prioritise the savings you'll need to make every time your pay packet comes through the door. That's $42 a week.

1 How Much? $1000

2 By When? Dec 31st

3 Time? 6 months

$1000

42 42 42 42	42 42 42 42	42 42 42 42	42 42 42 42	42 42 42 42	42 42 42 42
Jul	Aug	Sep	Oct	Nov	Dec

Let's say you have multiple goals at once, a short and a long term goal. Here are a few things to keep in mind for that multi-goal maze.

1 Stay focused with only 2-3 goals

Firstly, too many goals means you risk splitting your focus. Two to three are probably as many as you should have at a time. To begin, even having just one is perfect!

2 Diversity of Goals

Secondly, make sure your goals are for both sunny and rainy days! Saving for a holiday is sweet, but it won't hurt to have extra cash in the bank for when your cat accidentally swallows a balloon and needs an emergency vet visit.

3 Be conservative and realistic!

Finally, be conservative! Aim for more savings than you might necessarily need (or a longer time period). This will give your budget a little bit of flexibility and room to absorb unexpected occurences.

The trick with learning to save is not about the actual number you are putting into savings, but the act of putting it in there. Don't worry if your numbers are smaller than you would like. Simply focus on building a good habit. And at the end of the day, it comes down to following through with your strategy. The less complex and more realistic, the more likely you are to stick to your strategy!

Design your own personal savings goals!
Decide on 3 things you would like to save for. Figure out how much you will need to save weekly/monthly to achieve these goals!

Goal 1: _____

1 How Much?
2 By When?
3 Time?

$_____ a week / month

Goal 1: _____

1 How Much?
2 By When?
3 Time?

$_____ a week / month

Goal 1: _____

1 How Much?
2 By When?
3 Time?

$_____ a week / month

Building Savings Into Your Budget

Creating a savings goal and figuring out a strategy towards meeting that goal is half of the effort. The final part of the process is building that strategy into your budget, and executing it! Here's how:

1 Figure out your savings numbers

The first step is to figure out your savings goals, and how much you need to dedicate to those goals each week or month. Whether it's a fixed number (like the chapter before) or a percentage, it's important to get clear on the numbers.

What are your Savings Goals?
- Short Term Goal
- Medium Term Goal
- Long Term Goal

Due in...	Goal	$ per week
6 months	Summer Holiday Spending	$10
2 Years	Car Purchase	$25
5 Years	Moving Out	$20

How much are you contributing per week?

2 Create space within your budget

These savings goals aren't going to magically reach themselves. A goal without a plan is just a dream. The 'Plan' that you need in the case of savings goal, is a budget. It doesn't need to be complicated, but your budget does need to accomodate for your weekly savings contributions.

Month 1

Income

Spending

Saving

		Progress
Summer Holiday Spending	$10	$10 / $200
Car Purchase	$25	$25 / $1000
Moving Out	$20	$20 / $5000

It's up to you how you like to set-up your budget. In our budget, savings lives in its own category.
- You might be sending each of these goal amounts to a single savings location.
- Sometimes you could be sending each of these amounts to different places (multiple savings accounts, or other investment types).

Another useful feature is to note down how far along your goal you will be if you follow through with your budget plan. This helps keep you up to date with where you are at.

One last thing to note... Make sure the total of your savings allocations + your expenses, equal the same or less than your income coming in.

3 Create a framework to Execute your Savings

Making a plan is one thing, following through with it is another! There are three parts to making sure you successfully follow through with your budget plan...

Decide when and how the transfers happen

Once you've made your budget, you actually have to make the transfer(s) from your income account into your savings location(s). The easiest time to do this is right after you get paid. If this is the same and amount each time, think about setting up auto-transfers!

Book in a time to review and track progress

Set a date with yourself to check-in with your savings!
- How much did you end up transferring into savings?
- Did you withdraw anything?
- Are you on track to meet your goals?
  - Do you need to adjust your savings amounts each week or month?

Put measures in place to avoid dipping into savings

Transferring money into your savings is half of the savings game... Keeping it there is the other half! Your bank likely has a feature which lets you lock your savings accounts. Or you might consider an investment product which doesn't give you immediate access to your savings.

Savings simulation
Build these goals into your budget & track your progress!

You've just set up three brand new savings goals, starting with $0 for each.
- Short term goal: a camping holiday, $20 a month (Total Goal: $200)
- Long term goal: a car, $20 a month (Total Goal: $8,000)
- Emergency Fund: $20 a month (Total Goal: $3000)

Income	$200
Spending	
Essentials	$60
Clothes	$50
Fun	$30
Saving	
Total	$200

Step 1: Build these savings goals into your budget

Step 2: Complete this progress Tracker

Progress: Month 1
$ / $
$ / $
$ / $

You had a successful first **two** months, saving planned amounts! It's now the end of the third month and you've had a wonky month. You have only saved...
- $10 for your Short term goal
- $10 for your Long term goal
- $15 for your Emergency Fund

What's more! You also had to dip into your emergency fund to take out $5.

	Plan	Actual
Income	$200	$200
Spending		
Essentials	$60	$60
Clothes	$50	$50
Fun	$30	$30
Saving		
Total	$200	

Step 1: Write Month three's 'planned figures' and 'actual figures'

Step 2: Complete this progress Tracker for month three

Progress: Month 3
$ / $
$ / $
$ / $

Getting Your Brain Onboard The Savings Train

Saving is both an art and a science. Science... Because there are processes and technical numbers involved. Art... Because because you have to find creative ways to get your brain onboard the savings train! Here's an assortment of techniques to help you at each stage of the savings process.

First, set a strong foundation...

Start with figuring out your **'why'. In other words,** the 'Purpose' behind your goals. *There are two distinct concepts here:*

- **Purpose**: your purpose, or "why", is the north star, the guiding visualisation of things yet to be achieved - motivating you to keep moving forward in the right direction.
- **Goal**: Goals themselves, are your "how", the individual, actionable steps that move you closer to your destination.

> If you know the bigger **'why'** behind your goals, you're less likely to be swayed by short term distractions or hurdles that pop up between you and your goals.

Techniques to Incentivise your Savings

1. Reward your savings efforts

Using the savings ladder technique, break down your goals into smaller checkpoints with a reward at each point!

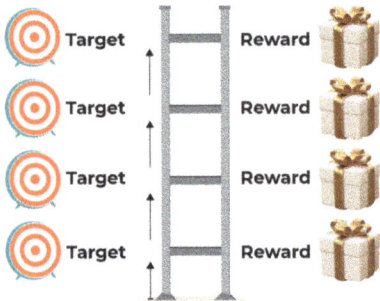

Target — Reward
Target — Reward
Target — Reward
Target — Reward

2. Accountability Buddy

Whether it's a friend, parent or even teacher... Find someone to keep you accountable! This could mean checking-in once every month to see how you are progressing along your goals. They could also be someone to chat about any troubles you are facing to reach them!

3. Make A Goal Chart

Make a chart to track how far along you are to your goals. Having this visible can be motivating!

Goal Progress
Short Term Goal
Medium Term Goal
Long Term Goal

4. Make a Vision Board

The best way to keep your goal or purpose front-of-mind is to have it visually available to you. A vision board is place to put inspiration pictures, phrases and anything else that might help motivate your efforts.

5. "Round up" your Purchases

Sometimes making big contributions can feel intimidating or unachievable. Start getting in the habit of moving funds into your savings by transferring a few dollars every week. Or, tap into features available in your banking, budgeting or investing apps. A key feature is call "Round up" sends a few cents or dollars to your savings each time you buy something. It all adds up!

6. Automate what you can...

Savings can be tricky to take care of consistently *There are two ways you can achieve this consistency...*

- **Automate** your transfers. If you get paid on the same day each week or month, set up a transfer to happen straight after it.
- Set up a **reminder** in your calendar to manually do this transfer if you have a less consistent situation. Transferring straight away means that you're less likely to confuse it as spending money!

Start small, start imperfectly... The key is to start! The emphasis is on building the habit, just like building a muscle. Start with one tiny savings habit and build this up over time. You've got this!

Savings reflection
Apply the savings strategies to your own situation!

What is your bigger "purpose" that will feature on your vision board?

Which goals will feature on your goal chart?

Who will be your accountability buddy and what will you ask them to do?

Doing some research, which banking app or investment app can you use to be able to use a round-up feature?

Is this something you would use? Why / why not?

Looking at your savings situation, when is the best date each week or month to organise a savings transfer?

Build your own savings ladder! Choose one of your savings goals from a previous chapter, and turn it into a step-by-step challenge with rewards.

Savings Step Goals

Step Reward

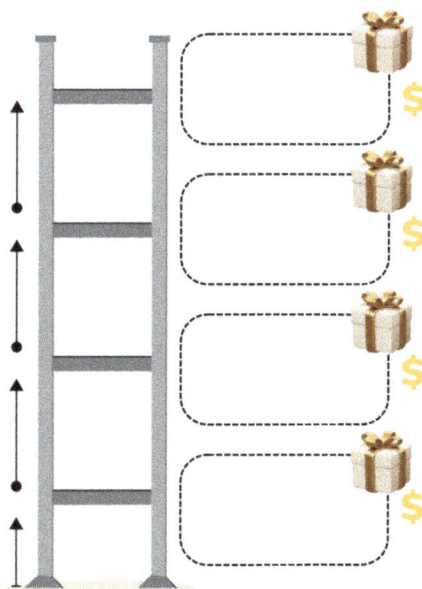

Total Savings

$

$

$

$

= $

= $

= $

= $

BUDGETING ✨

A space for your notes, questions, plans!

SUPER

Learn about Australia's Super system, your part in it and how to invest your retirement funds!

Lesson 1
Super Fundamentals

- **1** Super Basics
- **2** The Role Of Super In Australia
- **3** Calculating The Super Guarantee
- **4** The Super Controversy

Lesson 2
How Superfunds Works

- **1** Super Fund Basics
- **2** Super Fund Investment Basics
- **3** Returns And Fees
- **4** Interpreting Super Fund Performance

Lesson 3
Application Of Superannuation

- **1** Researching Your Super Fund
- **2** Comparing Super Funds
- **3** Applying For A New Super Fund
- **4** Super Fund Investment Options

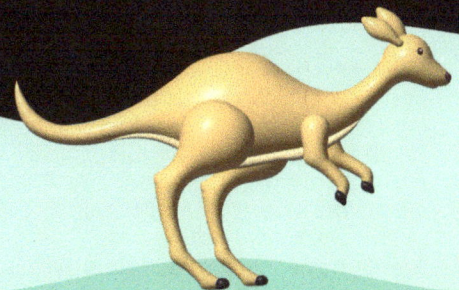

Welcome To Australia's Superannuation System!

Superannuation for long, super for short. Super is all about making the most of your retirement, so you can keep the lifestyle you want long after you stop working. Here's the basic theory explaining how it works! It's quite a simplistic way to look at a complex system, and there are lots of factors it doesn't take into account, however it's a good visual to get you started!

1 Running horizontally, we have the base line for money that you need to survive over your life.

On the left side is when you're born...

which runs across to the...

...Right side is when you reach the end of your life

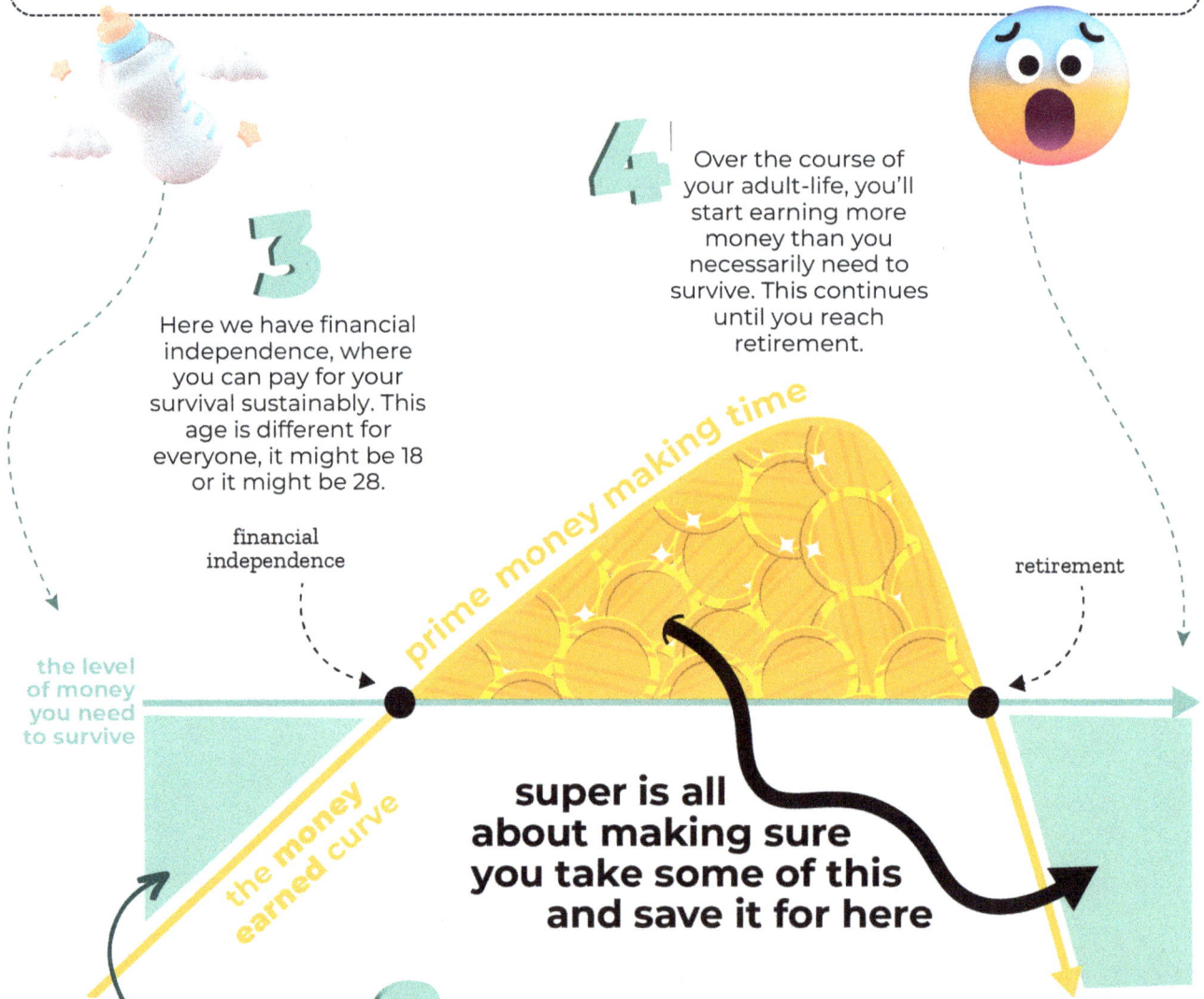

3 Here we have financial independence, where you can pay for your survival sustainably. This age is different for everyone, it might be 18 or it might be 28.

financial independence

4 Over the course of your adult-life, you'll start earning more money than you necessarily need to survive. This continues until you reach retirement.

retirement

prime money making time

the level of money you need to survive

the money earned curve

super is all about making sure you take some of this and save it for here

2 Now, when you're a child you don't have a big income (you don't come out of the womb with a salary plus benefits). Luckily, usually your parents or guardians will cover your survival expenses during this time, and maybe you even earn a bit of pocket money too.

5 Super is all about taking some of the money you earn over your life and smoothing it out to reach your retirement. This helps ensure you can maintain your lifestyle once you stop working.

The super system (and this model) are not perfect. Many retirees still end up relying on the pension. But! It's a system which has long-term objectives for both individuals and the country's economy.

What age bracket are you typically here?

What milestone is this?

What milestone is this?

prime money making time

the level of money you need to survive

What does this line represent?

super is all about making sure you take some of this and save it for here

What period is this?

This theory ignores lots of real-life factors. Not everyone follows this curve exactly. What are three flaws in this economic theory? When might it not be accurate?

Flaw #1	Flaw #2	Flaw #3

Introducing The Super Guarantee

The Super guarantee is just a fancy way to describe your employer's responsibility within the Super system. What this means is that your employer is legally bound to pay to a certain percentage of your wage, on TOP of what you earn, into your retirement super fund account.

"The superannuation guarantee (SG), dictates the minimum percentage of your earnings your employer needs to pay into your super fund"

Moneysmart, 2020

Super funds!

We'll get into this in more detail in the Level 2 lesson, but it's handy to know that a super fund is basically the dedicated investment fund which looks after your super until you retire.

This is YOUR money, totally your own. But you can't access it yet, as it's locked away by your Superfund until you reach retirement age. There are a few exceptions which allow you to take out your super before you retire, but it's pretty rare that a person qualifies for them.

Check out some key concepts below!

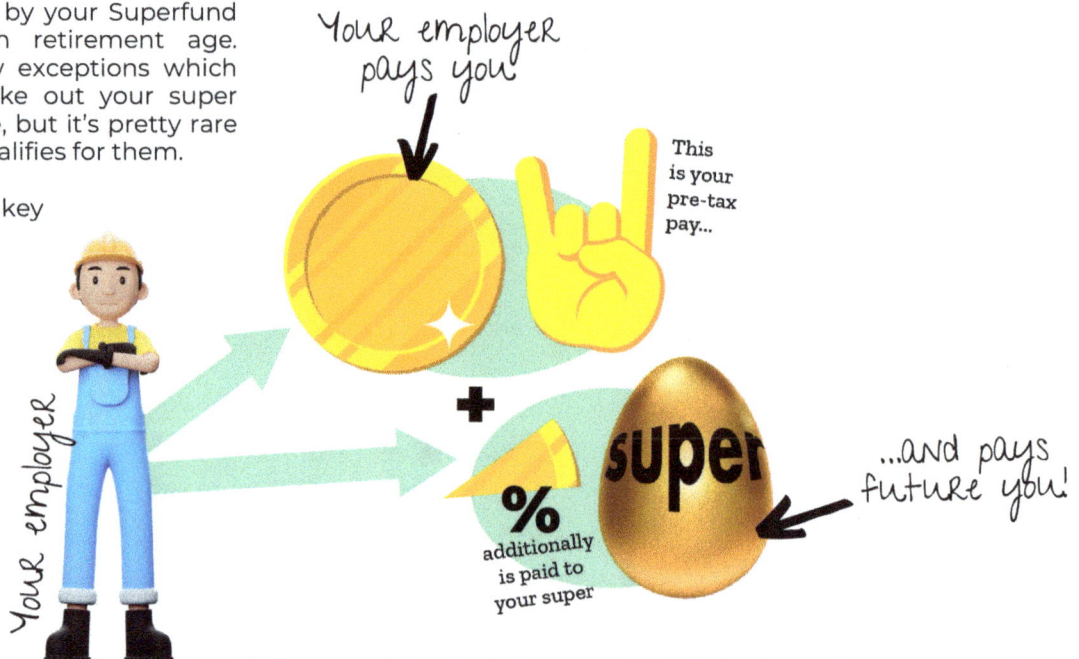

Your employer pays you

This is your pre-tax pay...

Your employer

%
additionally is paid to your super

...and pays future you!

Retirement age

There are two concepts to understand here: **Retirement** age and **Preservation** age.

Retirement age: The age you retire. You can choose to retire at any age, but this doesn't mean you can access your super yet (except in certain cases).

Preservation age: The age you can access your super. This age depends on the year you were born! Your retirement status impacts how you can access your super.

Eligibility

If you are under 18, it's actually quite tricky to qualify for Super! You need to work almost full time to be eligible. This criteria changes time to time, search for up-to-date criteria!

If you are over 18, you have to earn a certain (very low) amount per month to qualify. Search for up-to-date criteria to be sure! Your employment status, whether it's full-time, part-time, or casual, has no impact on your eligibility.

Withdrawal exceptions

There are a handful of early withdrawal criteria. Broadly...

- Compassionate grounds (Health related reasons)
- Severe financial hardship (when you are struggling financially and meet criteria for this set-out by the government)
- First home super saver scheme (to help pay for your first home!)

...Amongst a few others!

Using your research skills...
Find answers to below questions from *reliable* online sources.

What is the current Super Guarantee Rate?
Is it predicted to change?

What age, regardless of your **retirement status** *(whether you're working or not)* or **preservation age** *(the age where you can access your super IF you are not working)*, can you access your super?

What are 3 reasons you can you access your Super *before* preservation age?

If you're under 18, are you guaranteed Super? Why / why not?

If you're over 18, in what two situations might you not get paid Super?

Doing The Super Guarantee Maths

The maths behind super is very straight forward. It's simply requires you to know the up-to-date super guarantee percentage and the amount you are getting paid. That's it!

How is super calculated

Super is simply your earnings (for example $100) **times** the super rate (for example, 10%) and voila, your super amount.
- Let's say the super rate is 10% and your pre-tax earnings are $100
- 10% x $100 = $10
- $10 is sent to super!
- $100 is then taxed and the rest is yours to keep.

The cool thing about super is this is calculated ON TOP of your earnings! So you just brought home $110 (well, $10 of that you'll be using to play bingo on a retirement cruise somewhere)

Do your Research!

The Superannuation guarantee percentage changes from time to time. Do a quick search to see what the current super guarantee percentage is!

Inclusive or Exclusive?

Super is legally calculated as a percentage of your salary and paid additionally to this (exclusive).

- **$100 wage + $10 super = $110 total compensation.**

But, some employers might informally quote your wage and include your super in this (inclusive).

- **$90.90 wage + $9.10 super = $100 total compensation.**

This could be to make your pay look better than it actually is. Simply check your contract!

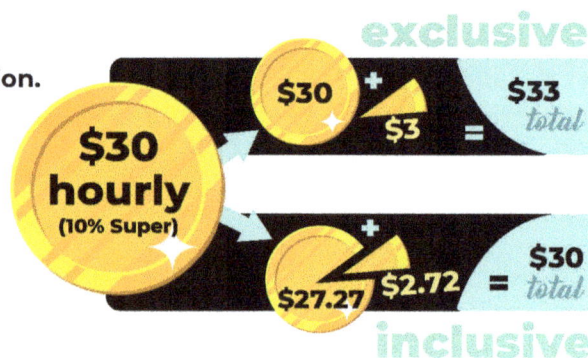

$30 hourly (10% Super)

exclusive
$30 + $3 = $33 *total*

inclusive
$27.27 + $2.72 = $30 *total*

The paper trail?

So you may be wondering how do you know how much super your employer is paying you and where you find this info... The answer lies in your payslip, or the document your employer gives you every time they pay you.

You may have noticed a part on your payslip from work which has the title "super guarantee". The amount of money that's noted here is what your employer is sending to your super.

Payslip

Pay Period: June 2022
Pay Date: July 1st

Employer: Mandy Money
ABN: 123 456 789
Employee name: Alex Simon
Employee status: Part-Time

Earnings:

	Unit	Rate	Total
Hours Worked Week 1	40	$20	$800
Hours Worked Week 2	20	$20	$400
Hours Worked Week 3	40	$20	$800
Hours Worked Week 4	20	$20	$400
Gross Monthly Payment			$2400

Super Contribution:

Superannuation <10%>	$240

Deductions:

Taxation (PAYG)	$168

Net Payment	**$2232**

Super & Tax

Super is paid to you as a before tax payment So, your super amount doesn't get included in your taxable income amount (woohoo!).

But, this doesn't mean super is tax free! There's lots of nuance to when, how and how much super is taxed... But the most relevant tax you need to know about is the 15% tax rate which gets applied to the super your employer contributes as part of the superannuation guarantee.

Complete these payslip questions!
Assume there's a super rate of 10%

Payslip

Pay Period:	May
Date of Payment:	31st May

Employer:	Mandy Money
ABN:	123456789
Employee Name:	Mandy
Employment Status:	Part Time

Earnings

	Unit	Rate	Total
Hours Worked Week 1	10	$25	$250
Hours Worked Week 2	8	$25	$200
Hours Worked Week 3	5	$25	$125
Hours Worked Week 4	10	$25	$250
Gross Fortnightly Payment		$ 825	

Super Contribution

Superannuation <10% additional>	$

Deductions

Taxation (PAYG)	$23.75

Net Payment

Net Payment	$

> How much is the net payment? (amount that ends up in your bank account)

> How much is this payslip's Super contribution?

> How much money did you earn from this pay (incl. super?)

Do the maths!

If you're on a $60,000 annual salary, inclusive of 10% super...

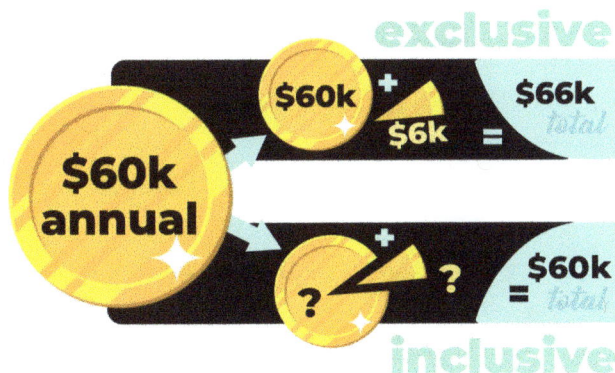

exclusive

$60k + $6k = $66k total

$60k annual

? + ? = $60k total

inclusive

How much super are you earning?

How much are you getting paid (before tax)?

The Pros And Cons of Super In Australia

Let's wrap our heads around where super came from and why it came about. The actual concept of Super has been around for a while, but was generally limited to a minority of workers, such as higher-paid executives, public servants and members of the Defence Force. When 1970 came around, it became more widely available as more industries started adopting it formally.

So when did it become a guarantee and a nationwide formality?

The year was 1992, Terminator 2 had just come out in cinemas, the Fresh Prince of Bel-Air was on tv, and Superannuation was first introduced in Australia. There are a few reasons why it came about, but it primarily stemmed from the fact that we have an "aging population"

"Aging population"

An aging population means that proportionally, the ratio of old people to young people in a population is getting bigger. More older people (because people are living older) and less younger (people because birth rates are decreasing).

- Because old people work less (or not at all), they pay little to no tax....
- This means that younger and working people are responsible for majority of tax revenue...
- And with less young people, there's less and less tax revenue being collected...
- And because tax revenue is important to support communities and pay pensions for oldies...
- There are more old people needing financial support, but less tax revenue to provide it.
- See the dilemma?

You can see here population prediction trends towards an older population (Institute of Health & Welfare, 2019)

So, Super is a way of making sure that people are able to support their own retirement while lessening pressure on government support.

Another reason, quite simply, is that people have lots of other things to focus their spending and saving on, which means that most people simply forget to save for their retirement which is probably still FIFTY years away from now. That's a long time, so to make sure you do have some cash when you retire on those sandy beaches, your employer steps in and handles it for you.

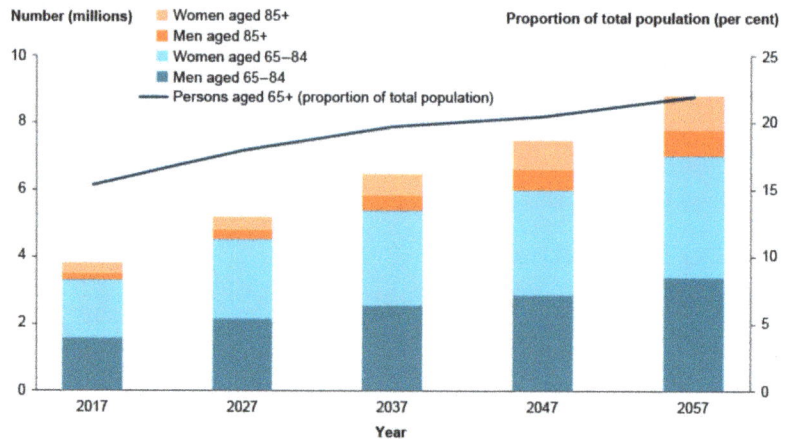

Number (millions) / **Proportion of total population (per cent)**

- Women aged 85+
- Men aged 85+
- Women aged 65–84
- Men aged 65–84
- Persons aged 65+ (proportion of total population)

(Years: 2017, 2027, 2037, 2047, 2057)

But! When super came out it was a bit controversial

Some common arguments FOR super are that it:

- Spreads out the burden of retirement saving across your lifetime
- Provides relief on the Australian pension system
- Gives your money lots of time to be invested and grow across your lifetime

Some common arguments AGAINST super are:

- It can be an extra burden for small business to pay a percentage on top of salary
- Some costs of super funds can be quite expensive
- The system isn't always effective for people who take time off, such as for childcare, leading to a large gap in super balance between men and women

S2.4.1 **Should Super be Compulsory?**
Give your reasons for 'Why' and 'Why not'

Why?

Reason 1

Reason 2

Reason 3

Why not?

Reason 1

Reason 2

Reason 3

What are three ways Australia can tackle the gender inequality dilemma?

Solution Idea 1

Solution Idea 2

Solution Idea 3

What Actually Is A Super Fund?

In simple terms, a super fund is a business that looks after your superannuation investment, and manages your contributions on your behalf. Much like how a fish 'n' chip shop specialises in fish 'n' chips, a super fund specialises in maintaining your super.

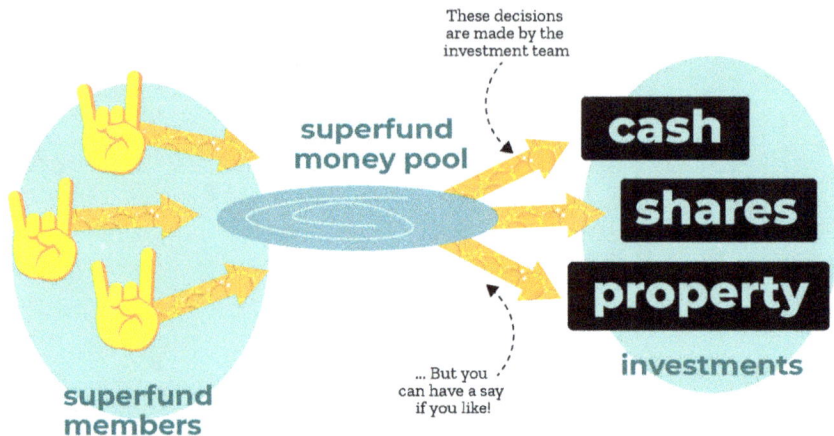

your **super fund**
pool cleaner

your **super**
pool

Investing your money for growth
Keeping your money secure
Insurance Options
General Advice
Draw Down

Zooming out to the big picture, you sign up to be a member of a fund, your employer pays your Super contribution into your super fund, where the super fund looks after that money, and invests it with the aim of making it grow for your retirement.

These decisions are made by the investment team

superfund money pool

cash

shares

property

investments

... But you can have a say if you like!

superfund members

Why does my super fund charge fees?

Super funds are an interesting type of business. They are run like any other business - they have employees who work for them, and have to do business-y things like attract new customers and charge people for their services. Their main job is to manage the 'fund' in which your money is invested.

However, super funds are also controlled by rules and regulations set in place by government bodies (notably, APRA) and the fund's board of trustees. The rules are designed to protect your interests and make sure investments stay within strict guidelines.

Super Fund Rules

3 types of super funds

1 Retail fund

You might choose a retail fund – the sort that your bank or financial institution offers. These super funds invest your money and generates a return on your behalf. They then takes a portion as a fee and for their own profits.

2 Industry fund

Or, you might choose an industry fund, which is owned by the fund members themselves. This means all the profits are passed to members. Each industry fund is usually dedicated to serving members that work in a particular industry (like healthcare or education).

3 Self-Managed fund

Or, thirdly, you can also do it yourself via a Self-Managed Fund. This is quite a serious endeavour. Unless your family already has an existing SMSF, it's not an option you have to worry about until later in life!

There is no obvious winner when it comes to best investment returns on your super. There are good, average and underperforming funds in each category.

Whichever you choose, it's always a good idea to keep in mind that where your money goes... That area grows. Going back to investment 101: when you invest in an industry or a business, the intent is to help that industry or business grow and flourish. **Super investment makes up almost half of Australia's investment landscape**. This means your choices in super fund can make a difference in which businesses grow and flourish in Australia in the future.

Complete this summary...
Explaining the ins and outs of superfunds.

A super fund is....

...Which is similar to a "normal" business in the fact that...

1	2	3

...Except for the fact that...

There are three types of super funds to choose from:

1	2	3

Which have their defining features being....

1	2	3

How Does Super Fund Investment Work?

When you contribute money to your super fund, your super doesn't just sit there and wait for you to grow old... Your money is put to work! In this chapter, we'll explore exactly how super funds look after your money for you.

#SuperOld

The process...

These decisions are made by the investment team

superfund money pool

cash

shares

property

investments

... But you can have a say if you like!

superfund members

Once your employer contributes your money to the fund, your super fund adds your money to their big pool of funds. This is made up of all the members' money. They then invest your money across a range of categories, including:

- Australian shares
- International shares
- Government bonds; and
- Investments in commercial property or residential properties like apartment blocks.

Everyone has a choice as to where the fund puts their investment money, and this comes in the form of 'investment options'. Exactly how much control you have, will differ between providers. Some will offer you detailed percentage control, and others will simply provide broad investment "packages".

So now that your contribution has been pooled together, and invested into a wide variety of different financial products, this is where the waiting game begins.

Over time, some products will gain value, and others will drop - that's the nature of investing! What you want to keep an eye on however is the combined growth or loss of your super investment portfolio.

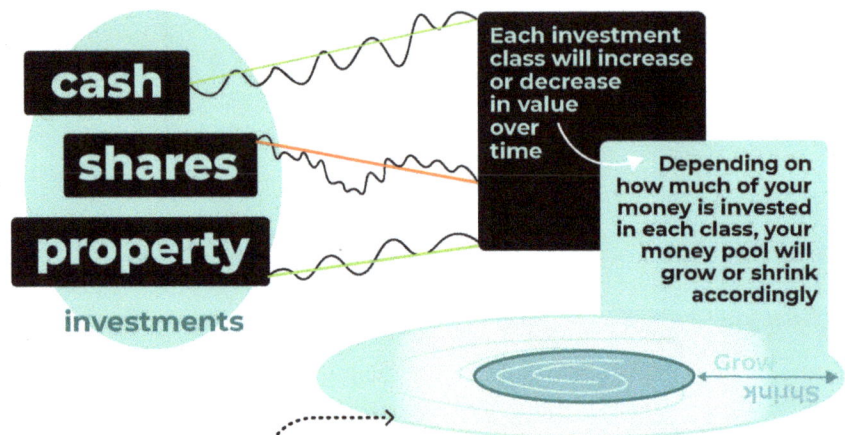

cash

shares

property

investments

Each investment class will increase or decrease in value over time

Depending on how much of your money is invested in each class, your money pool will grow or shrink accordingly

Grow

Shrink

superfund money pool

Via...

Lump Sum

Or

Money is distributed to members at retirement

Payment Plan

If the total amount of invested money grows over time, then you'll be cashing out more at retirement than you put in, and if it shrinks, then you'll be cashing out less. This is why it's important to choose a superfund that you trust will choose investments wisely and grow your retirement funds.

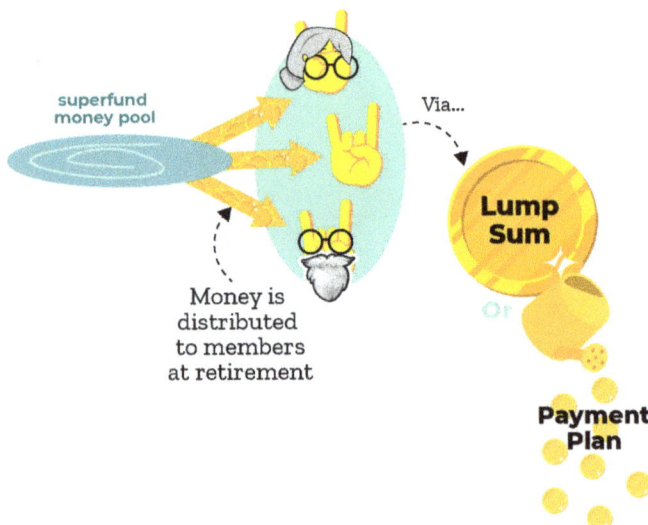

So we've invested, waited, and now it's time for retirement. When you do go to hang your boots up and retire, a proportion of the funds invested in the pool are given back to you.

This can be done either as a big sum of money all at once, or it can be paid out over time while the money left behind will continue to be invested.

S2.6.1

Using a combination of brainstorming and research...
Answer these question about super fund investment!

Why is it really important for super funds to have good investment strategies?

Why do you think super funds invest in a wide range of options?

Why might someone want their retirement money paid out
on a payment plan (as opposed to a lump sum)?

How Do Super Returns & Fees Impact My Super?

If you want to understand how your super is growing and performing, you'll need to stay on top of two important numbers: these are the **returns** on your investment and **fees** charged by your super fund. In this chapter, we'll help you understand both of these key metrics!

Returns

Firstly, returns. Returns are expressed as percentages, and what they do... is tell you how much money your investment might grow by when invested in a certain Superfund.

For **example**, if your super had a '6% annual return' last year, that means that every $100 you held in the fund for that year, would have ended up growing to $106. Bueno!

This is especially important, as it represents the growth in your savings, and how well your superfund is performing in comparison to others.

6% annual return

$100

For every $100 in your superfund...

$100 + $6

Additionally is earned!

$106

Every $100 is now worth $106 at the end of the year.

Sort of like how the supermarkets are competing with each other to offer the lowest prices to entice you in, super funds are in competition with each other to provide you with the best return on investment.

Fees

Fees are an important part of any fund to consider – they're an important part of allowing the fund to exist and be able to offer its services. They pay for things like admin, wages and taxes. Fees can be charged in two different ways, or a combination of the two...

The first is percentage-based, which means you get charged a set percentage of your investment balance as your fee (say, for example 0.5%). So if your balance is $10 000, that would mean your fees would be $50 a year. That's not much on an individual level, but with membership levels in the thousands it all adds up.

your **super** pool

your **superfund** pool cleaner

You have to pay the pool cleaner (superfund management) too

The other method is a fixed dollar fee. This could be, say, $90 a year for example. Now, in this case that is irrespective of the amount of money you've actually got invested, unlike the percentage amount.

Percentage Based

0.5% $50 FEE

$10,000 BALANCE

$90 ANNUAL FEE

Fixed Dollar Fee

Some super funds have a combination of the two fee settings – often they charge a small flat fee, in addition to a percentage depending on the size of the balance invested.

There's plenty to consider when you're investing your retirement money. The goal in the end is to maximise your investment returns and minimise the fees you pay – it could make the difference between being able to retire comfortably and live the life of your dreams, versus a retirement where you might need to make some compromises.

A bit of super maths...
Calculate the annual fee amounts for each of these scenarios!

How much is the total annual fee a super fund charges $3 a week fee in a year where $3500 is contributed to your super

ow much is the total annual fee a super fund charges 0.5% per annum on balance fee on a $15000 balance

Why do you think a Superfund that charges a fixed fee might not be ideal for a young person with a small super balance?

What Does Good Superfund Performance Look Like?

When you want to describe how well a super fund is doing, you look for something called 'net return'. Net return is a fancy way of talking about the actual money returns made by the superfund. It's calculated by taking the gross return, minus fees charged. In other terms, investment gains minus costs.

It's often said that the net returns are really what matters when you compare all the different super funds. This is because a net return allows you to look at all the funds on an equal playing field.

Some funds offer lower fees, but have lower expected returns. Some charge high fees but promise higher returns. Many sit somewhere in the middle!

Net Returns (NR) allow you to compare apples and apples, looking beyond superficial numbers. The NR percentage allows you to understand how much your super actually grew over the year compared to previous years and other superfunds.

Low Fees **Low Returns** **High Fees** **High Returns**

= **5%** Net Return

Example, you have a balance of $100 in your super

returns − **fees** − **net returns**

8% annual return **+$8**

$100

$108

0.01% annual balance fee **-$1.08**

$1 annual flat fee **-$1**

minus...

5.92% net return

$105.92

Every $100 is now worth $105.92 at the end of the year after fees.

Last year, your investment...
- Made a gross return of 8%
- Balance fee of 1% ($1.08)
- Flat fee of $1

Your net return would be...
- The $8 gross return
- Minus the $1.08 balance fee
- Minus the $1 flat fee

Which comes to $5.92 (or 5.92%).

In summary, first figure out the gross return, and then minus off the fees.

You might be asking - does this actually matter? Does it make a difference? The answer is that while in the short term you might not notice the difference, over the 40-50 years before you retire: it's a massive difference!

1 **Scenario 1:** You start with $100 in your super fund account, and then contribute $100 each month for the next 50 years. At an **8% net return***, you'll end up with a balance of $798,561

2 **Scenario 2:** where everything stays exactly the same, except due to excess fees, you have **7% net return***. In this scenario, you'll end up with a balance of $548,085.

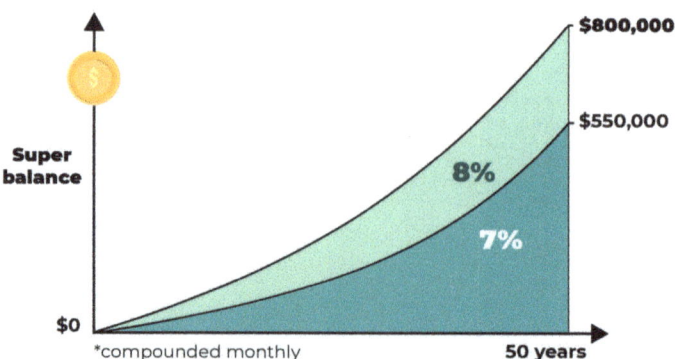

Super balance

$800,000

$550,000

8%

7%

$0

*compounded monthly

50 years

That's a $250,476 difference, from just a 1% difference in net return. While it might not feel like a big deal, paying attention to your super fund's net return can mean a big difference in your retirement standard.

S2.8.1

Calculate your net returns!
If you had a return of 6% on a balance of $1000, yet a $10 flat fee as well as a 0.02% annual fee, calculate:
- Your net return dollar value
- Your net return percentage

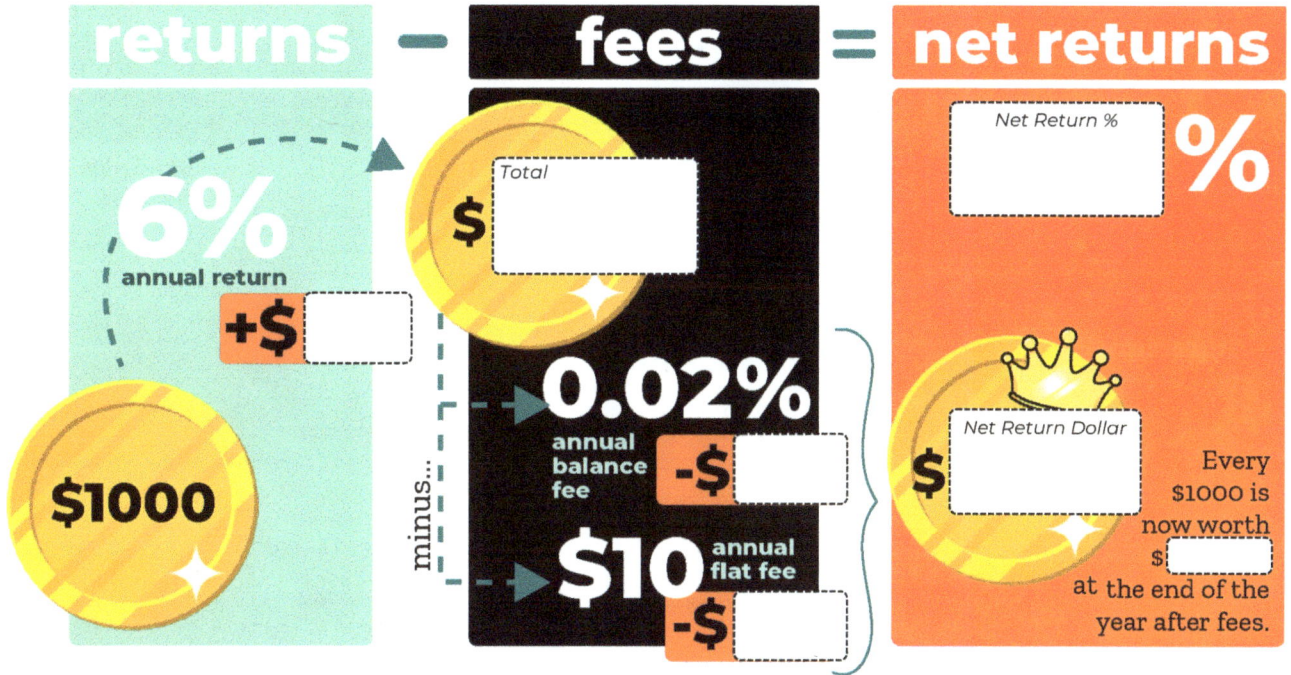

returns − **fees** = **net returns**

6%
annual return

$1000

+$ [____]

$ Total [____]

minus...

0.02%
annual balance fee −$ [____]

$10 annual flat fee
−$ [____]

Net Return % [____] **%**

Net Return Dollar
$ [____]

Every $1000 is now worth $[____] at the end of the year after fees.

Working out space

How To Research For Your Superfund

Researching super funds can be really confusing sometimes. So much choice, lots of information - it's really easy to get lost in it all. In this chapter, let's take a walk through super research park!

The most reliable place to look for information on a fund is in the fund's product disclosure statement, or PDS for short. BUT! Reading them can feel like you're watching paint dry. Despite this, a PDS will include virtually everything you will need to know about an investment fund. To find them, just Google the superfund's name and PDS. With a bit of algorithm luck, you'll find an official document amongst the top results. cool.

Product Disclosure Statement

Superfund PDS   Search

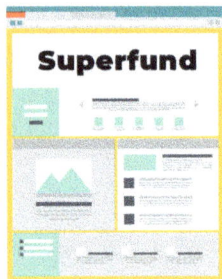

The next best option is to have a scroll through the fund's website. Most of the more-commonly-asked-for information will be found on there, and this can be a bit easier on the eyes.

Superfund

If you're just after the broad brush strokes, you can lean on a variety of comparison websites. They take bits of information from superfund sites and then put this all together to make it easier to compare your options side by side. These sites aren't always 100% accurate or reliable, so while they can be a great place to start your research, don't just finish there.

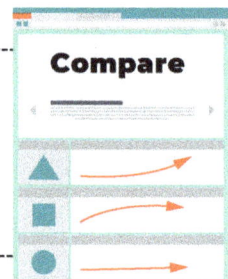

Compare

Key Research Criteria

When looking at any of these sources, you'll come across lots of information. Some of it is really important, but lots isn't... Don't let it overwhelm you! **There are four key things to look for:**

- Fund Performance
- Fund Fees
- Investment Options
- Insurance Options (and extra services)

Some factors might be more important to you than others. Consider all factors, but focus on what's most important to you.

Fund Performance (Returns)

Performance is the term for looking at how well a fund has performed previously. While it's never an indicator of future performance, it's a good starting place to contextualise yourself. One way you can determine the past performance of a fund is to look at an averaged total of the returns from the last 5 years.

Fund Fees

Now for fees, and it's useful to remember that these can differ wildly between providers, depending on their structure and service offerings. When comparing fees, it can be useful to imagine you have an account with $50 000 in it. Comparing the fees on such an account between providers will make things a lot clearer.

Investment Options

These basically mean that you have different types of investments to select from, depending on your requirements or wishes for how you want your money invested. Many funds will follow naming conventions, so 'conservative', 'balanced' or 'growth' funds might have similar characteristics. When comparing investment risks between funds, have a look at the different investment traits. This will lead you to the information you need.

Insurance and extras

Insurance and other services are often offered by fund providers as a bit of a side gig. Disability, Life and Income Protection Insurance are examples. To get info on a fund's insurance options, look at the fund website. Before signing up, consider whether you already have a particular insurance and whether it's the best option available to you.

Research and consider...
In your own words, answer the following factors testing whether you understand each of the research factors. Why are each of these important to consider when researching super funds?

Performance
- What exactly is meant by 'Performance' in context of a super fund?
- Why is 'performance' important to consider?

Fees
- What exactly are fees in context of a super fund?
- Why are fees important to consider?

Investment Options
- What exactly are investment options in the context of a super fund?
- Why are investment options important to consider?

Insurance
- What exactly is insurance in context of a super fund?
- Why are super fund insurance options important to consider?

How To Compare Superfunds

So, you want to choose your first ever superfund, or switch to a new super fund? That's a very normal and healthy part of super investing. You can have many reasons for wanting to switch Superfunds....

- Maybe you aren't happy with the fund you're with?
- Maybe you've outgrown your current super fund after reaching a different life stage.
- Maybe you have multiple accounts and want to combine them all into a single account.

Here's how to go about it...

1 Create a comparison grid, with four to five rows, and at least three columns.

2 Decide on your comparison categories. There are four key things people typically consider when comparing funds:

- Performance (returns)
- Fund fees
- Investment options
- Insurance & extra services.

List these in your rows.

3 Decide on which superfunds you will be comparing. You could compare two, or 100. Put the names of these superfunds in your columns.

	Superfund A	Superfund B	Superfund C
Returns	*Compare 'annualised returns' from the last 5 years for equivalent investment options*		
Fees	*Compare annual fees on a $50,000 account balance*		
Investment Options	*Compare investment options with the same name or similar traits*		
Extra Services	*Compare a list of extra services that might be offered.*		

You might also want to compare Net Returns calculated on your current account balance to get the true numbers

4 Go on your information hunt! Fill in the grid with as much detail as possible. When you're researching, you'll want to compare like-to-like. For example, compare conservative funds with other conservative funds – keep it apples to apples, not apples to oranges, or it'll drive you bananas!

5 Step five is to pick your top one or two, and go do exploratory research to find out the full picture. Go down the rabbit hole of exploring their...

- Investment ethics
- Customer Reviews
- Service options
- Team Values
- User experience.

From here, the ball is in your court to decide on your favourite!

	Superfund A	Superfund B	Superfund C
Returns	5%	6%	4%
Fees	$90 +1%	2%	$150
Investment Options	One Option	5 Options	DIY
Extra Services	Life Insurance	Ethical Option	24/7 customer service

Scrolling endless fund pages and documents to look for information can be painful. Not to worry, you can always look at fund comparison websites to get the big picture details. Just make sure that you've got your critical advertising eye on. Many of these websites accept sponsorship to promote certain products, and can therefore be biased towards the certain funds. You know the drill: Spot the snakes, and look out for #fakenews

Compare super funds!
Choose three superfunds to research and compare. Which superfund is your top pick, why?

Super fund comparison grid	Superfund A _____	Superfund B _____	Superfund C _____
Returns			
Fees			
Net Return on balance of $_____			
Investment Options			
Extra services + Preferences			
Comments etc			

Which is your favourite super fund? Why?

How To Apply For A New Superfund

So you've decided to open a new super fund, or switch over to another one? Cool beans! Knowing how to do this will be handy when the time comes. In this chapter we'll cover three key steps.

1 Open an account with the new super fund

The first step is to open a new account with the super fund you've chosen. This will require you to fill out a bit of personal info and letting the fund know a few preferences.

Most of what you'll need at this stage is pretty basic.
- Your name
- Birth date
- Email
- Postal address

You'll also need a couple of other details, including...
- Tax file number
- Australian Business Number (if you have one).

Some of these details you'll find on your MyGov Account.

Name
Birthday
Email
Address
Tax File number
Australian Business Number
Investment options
Beneficiaries

In terms of your preferences, some funds will also ask you...
- Which investment options you're after
- Who's receiving your super money if you were to pass away
- Whether you want any of the insurance policies that the fund might offer

You'll be given a membership number once your fund account has been set up. It's a good idea to have this written down or printed out and filed away in a safe location.

2 'Consolidate' your old and new account

Step number two is consolidation if you're combining more than one fund. This basically means you'll be transferring all your money into one fund... instead of being spread over multiple funds.

There are two ways to do this:
- One is to log onto your superfund's web portal, give the information you need to give about your other account, and let them do the heavy lifting.
- Alternatively, you can log onto MyGov and follow the process on there to do the same.

Via New Superfund

Via MyGov

3 Tell your employer

The last step is to inform your employer where to pay any super contributions. Without this last step, your super money won't be going into your new account!

The easiest way to do this is through a "standard choice form" where you give them your funds details. Ask your employer for this form, or download it online! Your new super fund might also have a pre-filled form you can send to your employer. Easy peasy, standard choice form squeezy.

Standard Choice Form

....and that's it! As with many superannuation processes, there are a few hoops to jump through, but once you know what the hoops are, it's a pretty simple exercise to work through.

When you set up a new superfund account, your employer will likely ask you to fill out the ATO's "standard choice form"

Do any of the words or concepts mentioned on the form confuse you and need further research?

Pick a super fund (feel free to use the super fund chosen in the previous activity) and research the details you would need to complete the form.

Australian Government
Australian Taxation Office
Superannuation Standard choice form

For use by employers when offering employees a choice of fund and by employees to advise their employer of their chosen fund.

Section A: Employee to complete

⚠ Where your super should be paid is your choice. From 1 November 2021, if you start a new job and you do not advise your employer of your choice of super fund by completing this form, most employers will need to check with the ATO if you have an existing super account to pay your super into.

1 Choice of superannuation (super) fund
I request that all my future super contributions be paid to: (place an X in one of the boxes below)

The APRA fund or retirement savings account (RSA) I nominate ☐ ▸ Complete items 2, 3 and 5

The self-managed super fund (SMSF) I nominate ☐ ▸ Complete items 2, 4 and 5

The super fund nominated by my employer (in section B) ☐ ▸ Complete items 2 and 5

2 Your details

Name

Employee identification number (if applicable)

Tax file number (TFN)

⚠ You do not have to quote your TFN but if you do not provide it, your contributions may be taxed at a higher rate. Your TFN also helps you keep track of your super and allows you to make personal contributions to your fund.

3 Nominating your APRA fund or RSA
You will need current details from your APRA regulated fund or RSA to complete this item. To do this you can contact your fund or RSA directly, or you can view your fund or RSA account details by logging into ATO online services via the ATO app or through myGov and selecting Super.

Fund ABN

Fund name

Fund address

Suburb/town   State/territory   Postcode

Fund phone

Unique superannuation identifier (USI)

Your account name (if applicable)

Your member number (if applicable)

Correct information about your super fund is needed for your employer to pay super contributions. Your employer **may choose not to accept** this form if you do not provide:
▪ all the information requested on this form
▪ a letter from your fund stating they are a complying fund and can accept contributions from your employer (some funds may have a copy of this compliance letter on their website. For other funds you will need to contact them for this information).

illustrative only, not representative of current or official superannuation documents

---

Fund name

Fund ABN (Australian Business Number)

Fund address

Fund phone number

Fund USI (Unique Superannuation Identifier)

How to Pick Your Superfund Investment Options

Your superfund works by investing your super money across a range of different types of investments with the goal of increasing its value. The cool part, is that you get a say. Here's how.

There are two parts to the investment process.
- First, is deciding the big picture asset classes (types of investments) and the rough breakdown of your portfolio.
- Next, within each of these classes, the specific investments.

You typically get a say in the first part.
- The rough portfolio breakdown, including the sorts of asset classes you want your money invested across.
- How much risk you're willing to take on.
Based on your selection and preferences, your fund will then figure out the investment details.

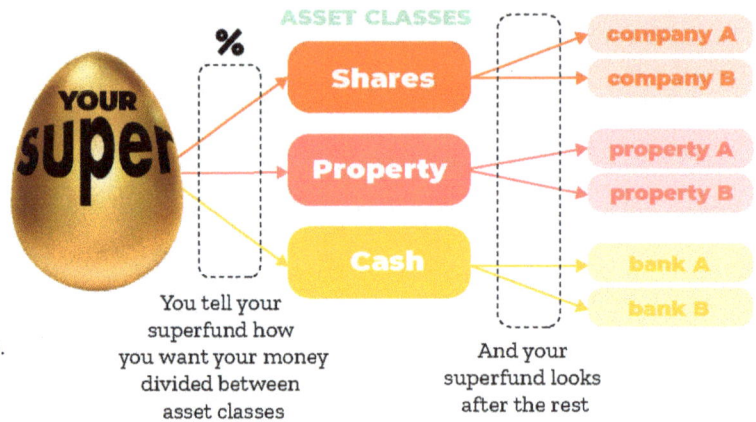

ASSET CLASSES

%

YOUR super

Shares → company A, company B

Property → property A, property B

Cash → bank A, bank B

You tell your superfund how you want your money divided between asset classes

And your superfund looks after the rest

While having these options great for some, simplicity is key for others! Many superfunds will offer you with preselected investment options. These are pre-selected portfolio options usually with different tiers of risk and reward. There are four main types of these.

Growth
If you are looking for **high growth** over the long term

>> majority invested in shares or property

>> aims for higher average returns over the long term (also means higher losses in bad years due to higher risk profile)

Conservative
If you are looking to **minimise risk**

>> highest percentage in fixed interest or cash, with roughly a third in shares and property

>> aims to reduce risk of loss and therefore accepts a lower return over the long term

Balanced
If you are looking for **reasonable growth**

>> highest percentage in shares and property, with roughly a third in fixed interest or cash

>> aims for reasonable returns but also to reduce risk of losses in bad years

Ethical
If you are looking to **invest ethically**

>> Similar investment fundamentals as conservative or balanced

>> Aims to include ethical investment options and exclude unethical options

Growth funds are those that target higher returns in the long run. They do this by investing in riskier options. In good times, these funds can be effective at generating a lot of growth in a short amount of time. However in bad times, they can come with quite large losses.

Conservative funds, on the other hand, prioritise minimising losses. On average, they'll tend to provide a lower return in the long-term because they're investing in less risky investments.

Balanced funds take inspiration from both growth funds and conservative funds. They aim for returns that are a bit lower than growth fund returns, but higher than conservative fund returns.

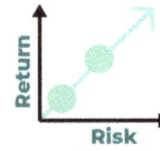

Ethical or sustainable funds are a bit unique. They often have the same fundamentals as a balanced or conservative fund. However, these funds have ethical investment guidelines. The definition of 'ethical' is complex, but as an example, they might look to invest in clean energy companies + avoid coal mining companies.

The option you'll choose depends on a few different factors, including...
- What kind of return are you looking for?
- What kind of risk are you willing to take on?
- What are your ethical preferences?

Through research and referring to the theory...
List key characteristics of the following investment options!

Growth

Pros: Cons:

At what stage in your life might you
consider this option? Why?

Conservative

Pros: Cons:

At what stage in your life might you
consider this option? Why?

Balanced

Pros: Cons:

At what stage in your life might you
consider this option? Why?

Ethical

Pros: Cons:

At what stage in your life might you
consider this option? Why?

Which option aligns most with your current investment objectives? Why?

SUPER

A space for your notes, questions, plans!

TAX

Learn about Australia's Taxation system, your part in it and how it impacts your working life

Lesson 1
Introduction to Tax

- [ ] 1 Tax Basics
- [ ] 2 Logistics Underpinning Tax
- [ ] 3 Tax As An Economic Tool
- [ ] 4 Opinion Formulation

Lesson 2
Tax And You

- [ ] 1 Income Tax
- [ ] 2 Tax And Employment
- [ ] 3 The Progressive Tax System
- [ ] 4 Employment Tax Documents

Lesson 3
Applications Of Tax

- [ ] 1 Tax Return Basics
- [ ] 2 Tax Deductions
- [ ] 3 Tax Bill vs Tax Return
- [ ] 4 Tax Return Execution

What Actually Is Tax?

Somebody wise once said, 'There are only two certainties in life: death and taxes.' Whether or not you agree, taxes are definitely something worth knowing more about! In this chapter, we'll cover what tax is and its role in society.

It's worth asking the question: what exactly is tax? Well put simply, a tax is a compulsory payment made to the government. There are many nuances surrounding what gets taxed and what doesn't, but as a general rule, it's paid when anybody earns or spends money.

Yours!

Tax

In Australia, there are four types of tax...

1 **Personal Tax**
First, personal tax, covering taxes you as an individual must pay on income and investments; things like your job wage, or any shares you might own.

2 **Business Tax**
Second, business taxes, covering the profits made by any business.

3 **Property Tax**
Third, property taxes, covering stamp duty and land tax paid by property owners.

4 **Consumption Tax**
And finally, consumption taxes, covering GST when you buy something or pay for a service, as well as extra taxes such as those on alcohol and petrol.

All of these taxes have different applications and purposes. Taxes are a useful lever to impact population behaviours, control the flow of money within an economy and help achieve economic and social outcomes. The world of tax is constantly changing and as you go through life, new taxes will become relevant to you. For now, personal tax is the only one that impacts your financial situation directly.

That's plenty of taxes to think about! You might be surprised at all the things your tax dollars go to: the road you're walking on was likely built thanks to tax revenue. The building you're in probably pays land tax. The clothes you're wearing might have cost you import taxes without you even realising! Every time you buy something, you're likely paying a Goods and Services Tax!

Now might ask, why do we need to help the government make money? Well, a country is a pretty expensive thing to run. We pay tax for the primary reason of raising funds. These funds, the government can use to provide the nation with essential goods and services, such as healthcare, welfare support, roads and public transport, schools, environment conservation etc. etc. **All really important things!**

Thinking about services such as healthcare and welfare, you can perhaps start to see that one of the purposes of tax is to redistribute money across an economy. This re-distribution provides more support to lower-income earners, funded by higher-income earners.

If you earn more, you typically pay more tax, helping to fund services and a healthy community for those who aren't in as fortunate a position. Taxes in theory are the Robin Hood of economic policy... Take to give!

Tax gets a bad rep, largely because some governments do a pretty bad job of putting it back into the community. There's a lot of incompetency and corruption that gets in the way of effective tax redistribution!

T3.12.1 **Through research and personal perspective...**
Answer these broad questions about Tax!

What do you think are the top 2 most important reasons tax exists?

List 3 things that would happen (good or bad) if tax didn't exist?

Can you research or think of examples of when a government (Australian or foreign) hasn't re-distributed tax effectively?

How Does Tax Work?

There's a bit wide world of taxes out there! Personal taxes, company taxes, income taxes, spending taxes, property taxes, investing taxes... lots of big words and the list goes on. If that wasn't enough, add to that the fact that each level of government has their own catalogue of taxes - federal, state and local - and you're in for a head-scratching ride! In this chapter, we'll focus on a specific part of the equation, walking you through each of the levels of government in Australia and the taxes that fall under their jurisdiction.

Local

The smallest level of government is your 'local' government, which you might also know as 'councils'. They have power to determine some smaller taxes such as those on building permits, as well as other collection activities such as traffic fines and animal licences for pets.

State

The next level up is your state government. They have a bit more authority over tax, and decide on their state's approach to taxes such as stamp duty, land tax, and taxes on gambling.

Federal

The largest level is the federal government, covering all of Australia. The federal government has the right to determine many of the larger taxes, such as income tax, company tax, GST, Medicare levies, customs duty on imports and departure tax at airports.

Most of these taxes happen in the background of your life... The only tax you have to think about right now is income tax!

Although it might seem like the federal (national) government is collecting most of the tax, they will also distribute a lot of federal revenue to state and local governments. They don't need it all... They simply collect it because it's easier to collect at a national level.

The **Federal Government** spends the most across **five** major buckets...

Welfare
Defence
Education
Health
Everything else

Some of this money is distributed to **State Governments** who spend on...

Health
Education
Environment
Safety and justice
Transport
Culture
Other

who then also pass **some onto Local Governments**

Waste management
Community services
Traffic management
Local business support

Who actually enforces all of these rules?

The tax you pay on your income comes out of your paycheck automatically, but many types of tax rely on people being honest about reporting their income, so somebody's got to keep people accountable.

In the context of local and state taxes, accountability and collection is usually the independent responsibility of each government. However, when it comes to federal taxes, this is where we introduce the Australian Tax Office. The ATO is the body in charge of the big task of collecting federal taxes and enacting Superannuation legislation. They're separate to the government, and therefore they don't determine tax rates and policies - that's done by your elected officials!

The Australian Taxation Office (ATO) is the principal revenue collection agency of the Australian Government.

source: ato.gov.au

In short, tax policies are set by different levels of government, and enforced by independent bodies.

Research and Sort!
Write a brief description of each type of 'tax' and then sort them into which level of government has jurisdiction over them!

Company Tax

Stamp Duty

Medicare Levies

Animal Licenses

Land Tax

Traffic fines

Gambling Tax

Building Permits

Departure Tax

Councils

State Government

Federal Government

How Is Tax Used In Economics

Tax is a really powerful economic tool. Looking around the world, every country has a unique economy, and will therefore have different preferences for how they manage that economy - particularly for how they earn and spend tax.

When it comes to earning and collecting tax, some countries rely on income tax as their primary source of revenue. Others have very few personal taxes and rely on other sources of revenue such as tourism or exports. When it comes to spending tax, some countries choose to re-invest back into the direct wellbeing of communities, while some decide to focus their spending on growing their economies and indirectly, the wellbeing of their communities. There are so many combinations of how to approach tax policy. Regardless of how it is collected, not collected, spent, or not spent, taxation is an important tool to shape a healthy society! Putting aside the high level theory, let's focus in on the logistics of how tax impacts lives and societies. The basic premise to understand is that... what is taxed versus not taxed, can discourage or encourage different behaviour. An example...

Tax Increase

If you increase the tax on vehicles, one possible outcome is that more people decide to take public transport!

+ Tax

you on public transport!

Tax Reducation

- Tax

Or, if you decrease tax on Electric vehicles, one possible outcome is that more people decide to buy electric cars!

you, in an EV

It might all sound really simple, but unfortunately tax isn't a 'magic lever' that governments can pull in order to get exactly the outcome they want. Tax is only one of many factors that influence people's behaviour. Sometimes a well-meant tax adjustment it will miss the target in the short or long term.

An Example

= increase wellbeing

TAX
- Childcare
- Aged-Care
- Housing
- Transport
- Renewables

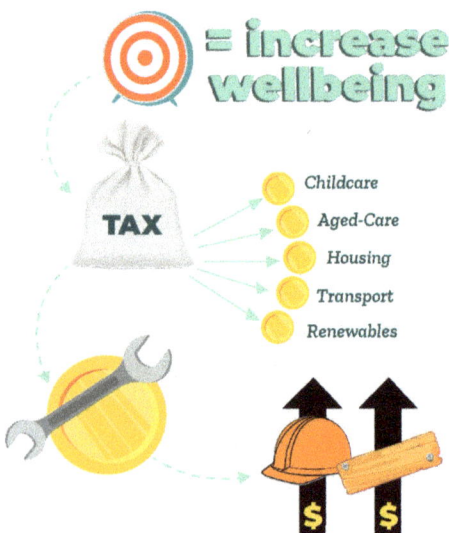

Let's imagine the Government decides to try and increase community wellbeing by making a sudden, increased investment into childcare, aged and disability care, public housing, transport and renewable energy. This is awesome... but at the same time, because so much money is suddenly being spent on materials and people to build those new things, it could mean that the increased demand could push up the price of labour and materials.

- Because labour is more expensive... Businesses might not be able to afford to employ people.
- Because materials are more expensive... People can't afford the cost of living.

Increased cost of living

Unemployment

Wellbeing

This example is quite dramatic and highly simplified, but hopefully you can start to understand some of the indirect, long-term impacts a decision on tax and spending can make. Ultimately, there's no one 'right' amount of tax for the government to collect or spend on public services. It's a powerful tool that's used to create powerful outcomes, when harnessed effectively. That's why we rely on economists to spend lots of time thinking hard about these decisions and predicting all the different outcomes.

M3.3.1

Get your research hat on!
Find examples of tax regulations attempting behaviour change.

Find 1x Example of a government successfully introducing a tax change to **discourage spending** on something

Find 1x Example of a government successfully introducing a tax change to **encourage spending** on something

What Are Your Thoughts On Tax?

Tax is possibly one of the most hotly debated issues in Australia. We're not special, either: people are fiercely discussing and debating it all around the world. Some people love it, and some people really, *really*, don't! Let's go through some of the pros and cons of tax so you can form your own opinions.

What are the pros of tax?

- When spent correctly, it can create a more equal society by distributing wealth across a society.
- It can to ensure safe and healthy communities, which in turn could leads to more people being able to work and support themselves.
- When people can support themselves, they're also typically much happier, healthier and motivated.

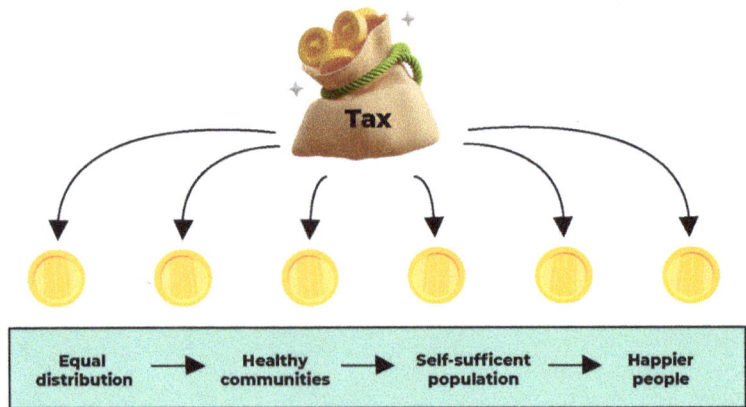

Smiles all round? Maybe not quite.

| Equal distribution | → | Healthy communities | → | Self-sufficent population | → | Happier people |

The cons of tax include...

- Some people feeling like they're being unfairly taxed, which could spark resentment towards governments and their decisions.
- Taxes can disincentive people to work. After all, if you're losing a chunk of your income to the government, why bother even going to work?
- There's also an argument that those who pay disproportionately high amounts of tax, don't see much of the benefit of some spending initiatives.

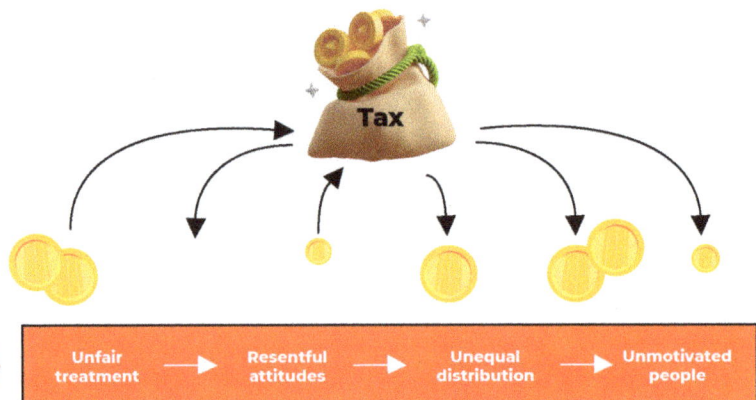

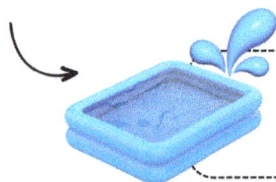

| Unfair treatment | → | Resentful attitudes | → | Unequal distribution | → | Unmotivated people |

For example, in the case of a local swimming pool, tax payers help pay for it, but if they don't swim or like going to the local pool, they don't necessarily get to enjoy it.

Make your vote count!

make an educated vote!

The most direct way to have your say in how you get taxed and how your tax money gets spent is to pay attention to politics (local, state and federal). The party and people that get elected have a reasonably big say in where your tax money gets spent. When looking at their campaigns, look at what tax changes their suggesting and which projects that will look to invest in.

Of course, there are lots of factors to take into consideration when voting. Tax is simply another factor to add in, where it guides you to consider a candidate or party who you believe is spending money in the areas you care about!

It's a crunchy problem, and as a society we haven't figured out the right answer just yet. Regardless of where you stand, though, tax is a fact of life, and it's worth understanding its complexities.

T3.4.1   **Your opinion?**
What are the pros and cons of high income taxes?

Why?

Reason 1

Reason 2

Reason 3

Why not?

Reason 1

Reason 2

Reason 3

What is your opinion on high income tax?

What is Income Tax?

There are many different types of tax that impacts your life in direct and indirect ways. The most relevant tax for the average person however, is called 'Income Tax'.

An important place to start with income tax is first of all understanding what exactly we mean when we say 'income'. As a general rule, 'income' simply refers to any money that you receive. This isn't just money that you get paid from your employer: it could also be from investments, welfare payments from the government, income from a business, and a whole range of other sources.

The interesting part... While most are, not all of these income sources are taxed. The ones that are, are referred to as 'taxable income'. During any given year, you'll earn a particular amount of 'taxable income'. This is all added up to find your 'total taxable income'. From there, your total tax for the year is calculated.

There are three main concepts you'll deal with as a tax-paying individual...

1 Tax File Number

The first concept is what's called a Tax File Number, or TFN. This is a unique 9-digit number that acts as your personal identifier in the tax and superannuation systems. Like a passport keeps track of your travel, a TFN keeps tabs on your tax records.

You're not legally obliged to have one, but without one, you might end up paying more tax than you need to. If you don't have one, simply visit the ATO's website and go from there. It's a relatively speedy process, and it's free!

> If you've lost your TFN, you can find it via your MyGov account!

> Keep it secret to avoid Identity theft, Tax Fraud, financial scams!

2 Financial Year & Tax Season

The second concept is the 'Financial Year'. You might have heard of a 'calendar year', which runs from January to December. The poor ATO staff and accountants don't want to be stuck doing all their end-of-year admin on New Years' Day, though, so the Financial Year runs in the middle of the year - from the start of July to the end of June, the following year. When talking about tax, it's always discussed and calculated according to the Financial Year.

To figure out how much tax you owe in one Financial Year, simply look at how much you earned starting July 1st of one year, all the way through to June 31st of the next. You'll make this calculation after the year is finished. Hence, the four months after the end of the Financial Year are what we like to call 'tax season'. This is when you'll do your tax return and settle your accounts for the year.

| July | Aug | Sept | Oct | Nov | Dec | Jan | Feb | Mar | Apr | May | Jun | July | Aug | Sept | Oct |

Financial Year   **Tax Season**

Time to complete tax obligations of the Financial Year just ended

3 Progressive Tax Season

The final concept is the **Progressive Tax System**. While there are a few tax collection systems, the Progressive Tax System is used for income tax in Australia. In simplicity, it means that the more you earn, the higher the percentage of tax you'll end up paying overall. It can make calculations a bit tricky, but the intention of this system is to help redistribute wealth from high earners to low earners. We'll explore into this concept later in the tax module!

Through Research and brainstorming...
Answer these questions about income tax.

List as many examples of Income as you can find! Are there any sources of income that aren't taxable?

Why is having a Tax File Number (TFN) important?

What is one reason Australia's financial year does not correspond with the calendar year?

What is one reason we use a Progressive Tax System and not just tax everyone the same?

How Does Tax Impact My Job?

Have you got your head around the basics of tax? That's awesome! Now, how much tax do you actually need to pay? That's a trickier question... and it depends on the kind of work you do. In this chapter, we'll dive into the relationship between tax and the different types of work you might do.

1 Employee

Let's start off with the most simple kind of structure, which is what you'll know as being an 'employee'. If you're working as an employee, your employer has to withhold your tax from your wages on your behalf and send it straight to the ATO. This system is called Pay As You Go, or PAYG withholding. Primo!

Payslip

Pay Period: June 2022
Pay Date: July 1st

Employer: Mandy Money
ABN: 123 456 789
Employee name: Alex Simon
Employee status: Part-Time

Earnings:

	Unit	Rate	Total
Hours Worked Week 1	40	$20	$800
Hours Worked Week 2	20	$20	$400
Hours Worked Week 3	40	$20	$800
Hours Worked Week 4	20	$20	$400
Gross Monthly Payment			**$2400**

Super Contribution:

Superannuation <10%>	$240

Deductions:

Taxation (PAYG)	$168

Net Payment	**$2232**

Every payslip, your employer calculates how much tax you owe...

...they send that to the ATO,

and pass your net pay onto you!

You can spot PAYG on your payslip!

In this situation, all you'll need to do is to complete the Tax File Number declaration when you start your job. They'll pay your tax on your behalf every time you get paid, whether this is weekly, fortnightly, or monthly.

The cool part is, when you receive money into your bank account, you know that your tax obligations have already been taken care of. The rest is all yours to spend or save as you please!

2 Contractor or Sole Trader

On the other hand, if you work as a contractor, sole trader, or any other type of working arrangement, you might work on a tax bill basis. This means you get paid in full every pay period, and it's then your responsibility to pass the tax on to the ATO. You can do this periodically, or as a lump sum at the end of the year. Not sure which bucket you fall into? Well, if you don't get any sort of payslip which refers to pay-as-you-go tax, you're probably in the second bucket. Either way, the amount of tax you need to pay isn't impacted!

Pay As You Go

tax · tax · tax

payslip 1 · payslip 2 · payslip 3

End of Financial Year...

Because you've been paying tax incrementally, you likely won't get hit with a big tax bill!

Pay At The End

payslip 1 · payslip 2 · payslip 3

tax

End of Financial Year...

You'll still be paying the same amount of tax, but in one big go at the end of the year!

You can see that in both scenarios, your total tax paid is the same, but just paid at different times of the year!

Now you understand why it's super important to check your work contract whenever you start a new position.

Understanding what your working relationship and tax obligations will help you avoid a sticky situation where you end up owing tax money but haven't budgeted for it!

Compare the pair!
Taking a look at these two "payslips",
answer the below questions...

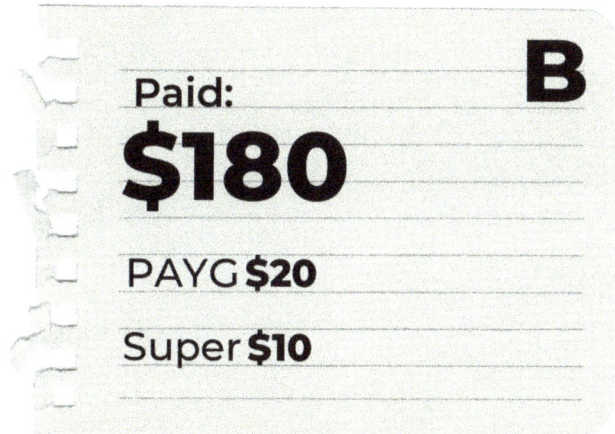

A

Paid:
$210

B

Paid:
$180

PAYG **$20**

Super **$10**

Which "payslip" is better, A or B? Why?

Which one belongs to an employee and which one
belongs to a contractor? How can you tell?

If you are a sole trader or contractor that needs to take care of paying your
own tax, what is one important thing to do to avoid a scary tax bill?

How Does The Progressive Tax System Work?

In this chapter, we'll cover what's known as the 'progressive tax system'. In this system, as an individual starts to earn more and more, they'll experience higher rates of tax on their earnings. This does not mean that their entire income will be taxed at a higher rate, but simply the part of their income that lands in the higher tax bracket! What's a tax bracket? It's simply describes a certain range of your income that has a certain tax rate attached to it.

"A progressive tax is a tax in which the tax rate increases as the taxable amount increases. "Progressive" refers to the way the tax rate progresses from low to high."

An Example

- Earnings between $0 - $20,000 land in Bracket #1
- Earnings between $20,000 - $50 000 land in Bracket #2

Each of these brackets has a percentage tax rate attached to them. Every dollar of someone's income that lands in each specific bracket, will have this percentage tax rate applied to it...
- Bracket 1, 0% tax rate
- Bracket 2, 20% tax rate

If you earn $50,000 in this system, parts of this income will fall in different brackets...
- $20,000 in Bracket 1
- $30,000 in Bracket 2

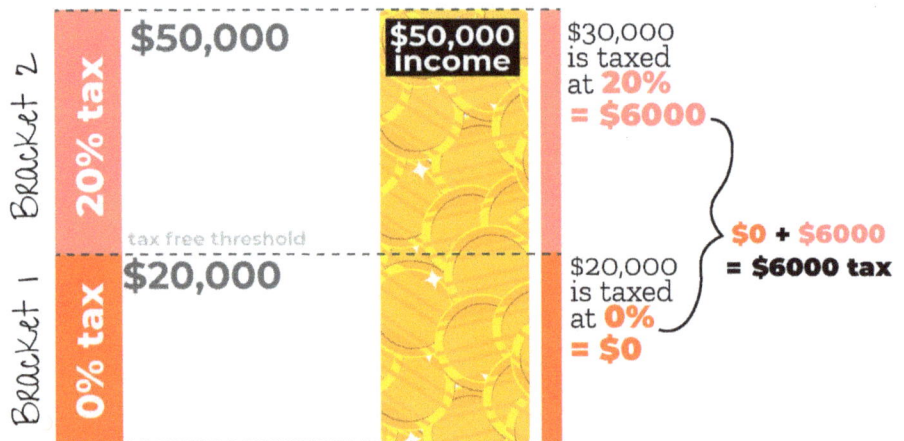

Bracket 2 — 20% tax — $50,000
Bracket 1 — 0% tax — $20,000 (tax free threshold)

$50,000 income

$30,000 is taxed at **20%** = **$6000**

$20,000 is taxed at **0%** = **$0**

$0 + $6000 = $6000 tax

Getting out our calculators, we'll therefore...
- Pay nothing in tax on the $20,000 in B1
- 20% of the $30,000 in B2

>>> Which comes to $6000 as our total tax bill

What is the Tax-Free Threshold?
You can see in this example that the first bracket charges no tax. Then, as we work our way into higher brackets, the income falling in each bracket is taxed at a higher percentage. This first bracket is what we like to call the "tax-free threshold". It's the amount of income that doesn't get taxed!

The Maths

To calculate your tax, you can use a formula. Note that these example brackets are different!

- First, determine your annual income and identify your tax bracket. For an example of $60,000, we fall in the third tax bracket.

- Next, take the lower end of the tax bracket – in this case it's $37,000 – and subtract that from your income. This step is to figure out how much income lands in the top bracket. Next, multiply that by the tax rate.

- Finally, take the amount just calculated and add it to the dollar tax given in the bracket... and that's your total tax figure!

Bracket	tax on this income
$0-$18,200	$0 + 0% over $0
$18,201 – $37,000	$0 + 19% over $18,200
$37,001 – $90,000	$3,572 + 32% over $37,000

Annual Income − Lower end of Bracket × Bracket Rate + Base Tax

$60,000 − $37,000 × 32% + $3,572

= $10,932

The bad news? As you earn more, there are more bits and pieces of tax that come out of your income, such as government healthcare levies and student loans. The good news? There are plenty of online calculators to help! Understanding the theory and the maths simply helps everything make sense.

Research and complete...
Australia's current tax brackets before calculating income tax amounts on different annual income amounts!

Bracket	tax on this income				
$0-$18,200	$0	+	0%	over	$0
$18,201 – $37,000	$0	+	19%	over	$18,200
___ – ___	$	+	%	over	$
___ – ___	$	+	%	over	$
___ – ___	$	+	%	over	$

$$\left(\text{Annual Income} - \text{Lower end of Bracket} \right) * \text{Bracket Rate} + \text{Base Tax}$$

Using this formula, how much income tax will someone earning **$50,000** pay, compared to someone earning **$100,000**?*

Not taking into consideration high earning tax complexities such as medicare, HECS, super.

There's a common misconception that all of your income is taxed at the highest tax bracket rate your income lands in. Why would this not work?

What Documents Do I Need To Sort My Tax?

If you understand how the taxation system works in general, the last piece of the puzzle before you're a tax whiz is to be able to apply it to your own employment situation. In this chapter, we'll explore the three key situations where you'll need to understand your tax situation and obligations.

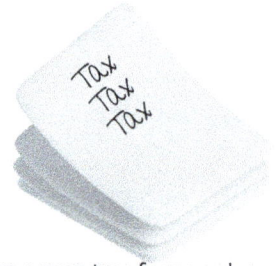

1 Starting a new job

The first is when you're starting a new job. In amongst all the questions on your tax form when you submit your tax file number, you'll be asked whether you'd like to 'claim the tax free threshold'. Most people get super confused by this, avoid it, and hope for the best!

The tax-free threshold simply refers to the first portion of your income which doesn't get taxed on your primary source of income.

There are only really two reasons you'd tick the box:
- If it's your primary job or the only job you've got for this financial year.
- If you're confident that your total income for the financial year (combining all your incomes) will be under this threshold.

If you have two jobs and you tick this box on both, you won't ultimately end up owing more tax at the end of the year, but you might underpay during the year and end up with a tax bill! Unless you're well under the threshold, ticking this box on only one main source of income every year could save you some admin time.

2 Getting Paid

The second is when you've been paid and you're looking at your payslip. Your payslip will tell you how much you were taxed during the period, and how much was sent to the Tax Office on your behalf. It's good to keep tabs to make sure the maths checks out.

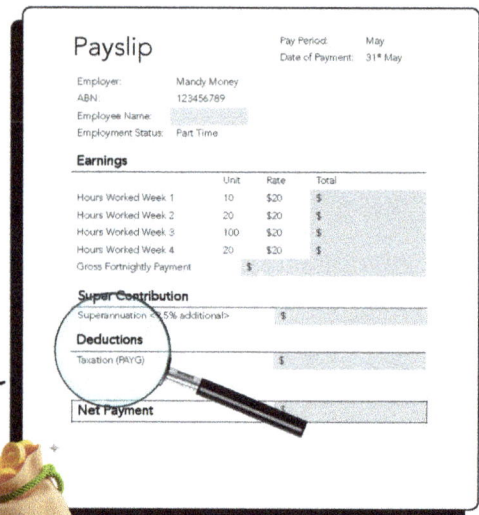

3 End Of Financial Year

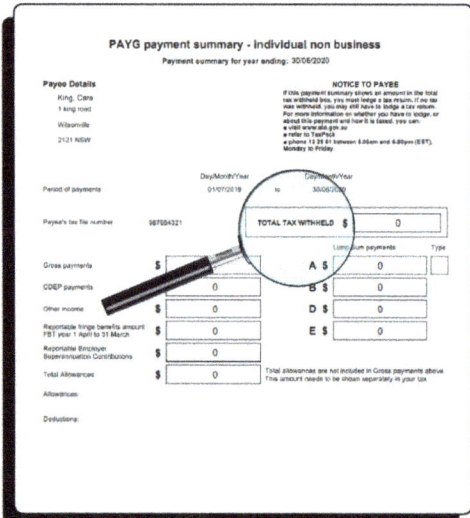

You might notice that this might result in you paying more tax than you should during the year! Not to fear - the third situation is when you receive your PayG summary form at the end of the tax year. This is the piece of paper you get telling you how much you earned that year, and how much your employer sent to the tax office for you.

Often your employer will submit this information to the tax office on your behalf, which makes it easier for you. Either way, you use this information to help you to understand your total tax for the year on your tax return.

When and when not?

When filling out a tax form after starting a new job, claiming the tax free threshold isn't always a good idea...

Within the magnified/highlighted section of the form:

Are you an Australian resident for tax purposes? ☐ Yes ☐ No
(ato.gov.au/residency to check)

8 Do you want to claim the tax-free threshold from this payer?

Only claim the tax-free threshold from one payer at a time, unless your total income from all sources for the financial year will be less than the tax-free threshold.

Answer no here and at question 10 if you are a foreign resident, except if you are a foreign resident in receipt of an Australian Government pension or allowance.

Yes ☐   No ☐

In what two situations would you tick 'YES'?

In what two situations would you tick 'NO'?

How Do Tax Returns Work?

Have you ever wondered how a tax return works? Do you end up with an extra pay check at tax time, or do you end up owing money to the tax office? We'll cover the basic logic behind a tax return in this chapter and clear the waters.

Tax Return?

or

Tax Bill?

During the year, you might be earning a solid stream of income from a single source, or you also might be earning money from lots of different income streams and paying a variety of taxes throughout the year. Whichever situation you're in, the end of the financial year is the chance to bring all of your income and tax information together. It's a chance to make sure you've paid the correct amount of tax.

What is a tax return?

Here's where we introduce our friend, the tax return. It doesn't sound very fun, but all it is really is.... is a chance to declare all of your taxable income and relevant expenses for the financial year. By doing this, you can then calculate the exact amount of tax you need to pay.

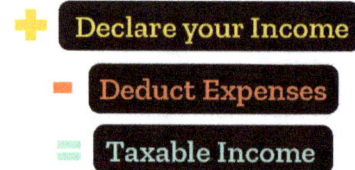

From here...
- If you've ended up paying too much, you'll get refunded.
- If you haven't paid enough, you'll end up with a tax bill.

+ Declare your Income
− Deduct Expenses
= Taxable Income

Tax Return **Tax Bill**

Do you have to do a tax return?

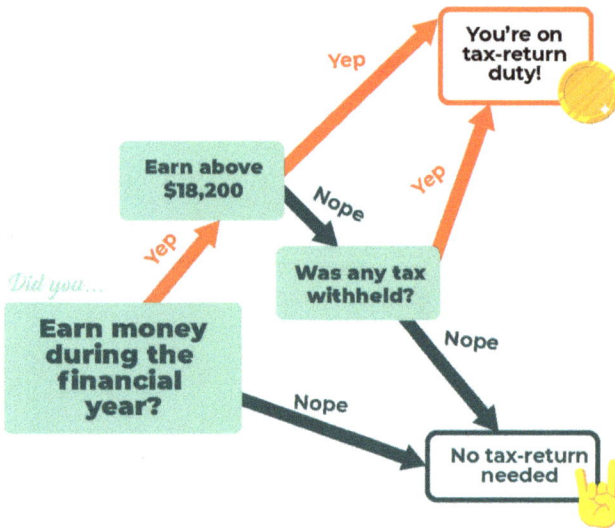

Did you...
Earn money during the financial year?

→ Yep → **Earn above $18,200** → Yep → **You're on tax-return duty!**

Earn above $18,200 → Nope → **Was any tax withheld?** → Yep → **You're on tax-return duty!**

Was any tax withheld? → Nope → **No tax-return needed**

Earn money during the financial year? → Nope → **No tax-return needed**

The simple answer is yes. If you've worked and received any income in Australia at any point during the financial year, you'll almost certainly need to complete a tax return.

There's only one realistic scenario where you won't need to do this. That's when you've earned less than the tax-free threshold of income AND you've had no tax withheld during the year. Perhaps you've done a few odd gardening or catering jobs here and there. While you don't need to do a tax return, you'll still need to let the ATO know you won't be completing a tax return. Alright, we know we need to do our tax returns. The next question is...

But you still need to let the ATO know that you won't be completing one!

When?

This happens at the end of the financial year during tax season. A personal income tax return needs to be completed between July 1st and October 31st immediately following the end of the financial year.

| July | Aug | Sept | Oct | Nov | Dec | Jan | Feb | Mar | Apr | May | Jun | July | Aug | Sept | Oct |

Financial Year ← → **Tax Season**

Time to complete your tax return for the financial year just ended

For example, your 2023/24 tax return will be completed between July 1st 2024 and October 31st 2024.

Thinking outside of the box...
Work through each of these four questions
& explore how they relate to tax returns!

What is the taxable income equation?
"Something" minus "Something" = Taxable Income

How could end up with a tax refund? How could you end up with a tax bill?

What kind of worker is more likely to end up with a tax bill.
Which kind of worker is more likely to end up with a tax return?

What is the latest date possible for you to get your tax return in on-time?

How Can I Lower My Tax Bill Through Deductions?

Have you ever heard the phrase, 'oh - don't worry, I'll claim that on tax'? In this chapter, we'll explore the concept of a tax deduction, and how this ends up in a lower tax bill. Let's start at the start. A tax deduction is an expense that lowers your taxable income (the amount of money that you end up paying tax on). This is a good thing for you, because it'll result in you paying less tax overall, and keeping more money in your pocket!

"Oh Don't Worry, I'll Claim That On Tax"

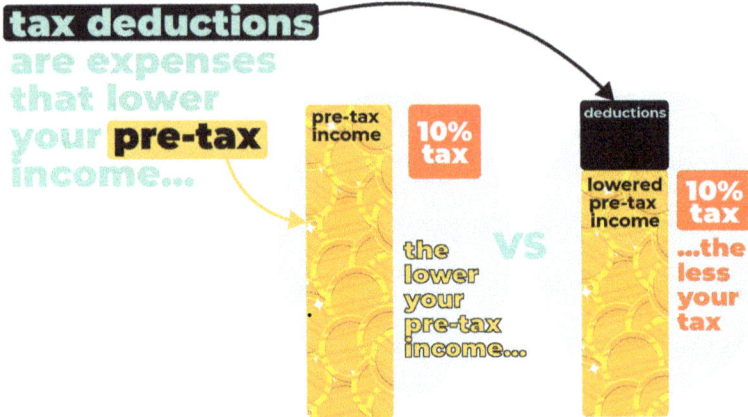

tax deductions are expenses that lower your **pre-tax** income...

pre-tax income | 10% tax

the lower your pre-tax income...

VS

deductions

lowered pre-tax income | 10% tax

...the less your tax

A deduction reduces your tax, but it does so indirectly. That means you can't just claim a $100 business lunch and expect to pay $100 less tax!

You'll need to take out the deduction amount from your total income before calculating your tax bill, rather than deducting it straight from your tax bill.

An Example...

Income: **$5000**
Work Expense: **$200**
Tax Rate: **20%**

Perhaps you've made $5000 dollars during the year, but you've also spent $200 in repair costs to the laptop you use for work. You want this expense to be a tax deduction.
- In scenario A, without deducting this expense from pre-tax income, you'd calculate your tax based on your $5,000 income.
- However, if you want to deduct the expense, in Scenario B, you deduct it from your $5,000 pre-tax income. Now you have a taxable income of $4,800, and you can go ahead and calculate your tax bill based on this. $40 saved!

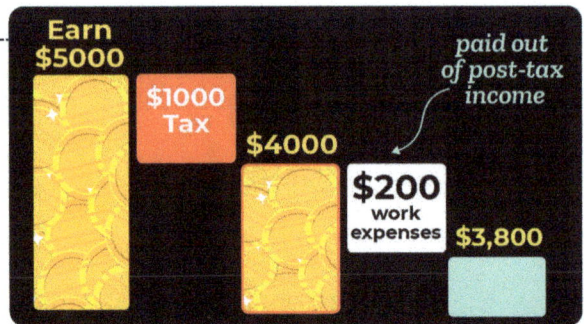

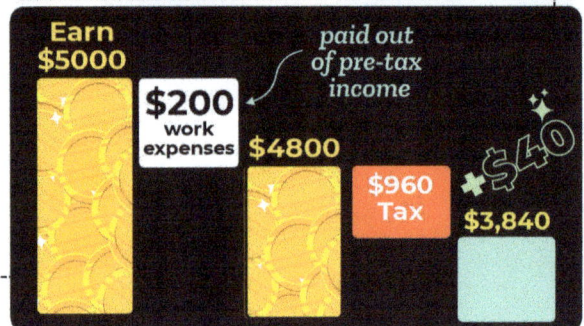

A

Earn $5000 | $1000 Tax | $4000

paid out of post-tax income

$200 work expenses | $3,800

B

Earn $5000 | $200 work expenses | $4800

paid out of pre-tax income

$960 Tax | $40 | $3,840

What can you claim?

there are limits to what can and can't be claimed as a tax deduction. The main thing is that tax deductions are for business-related expenses. For example, if you're a lifeguard, you might be able to claim your sunscreen and sunnies, because you need them for work. Or, if you're a pizza delivery driver, you might be able to claim petrol.

The three key criteria you need to meet are:
- You must have spent the money yourself and not have been reimbursed;
- It must directly relate to earning an income; and
- You must have a record to prove it (keep it for five years).

It's a tricky concept, but can be useful if you're paying a lot of expenses to help you with your job! To find out more about what you can and can't claim, the ATO website will be your best friend.

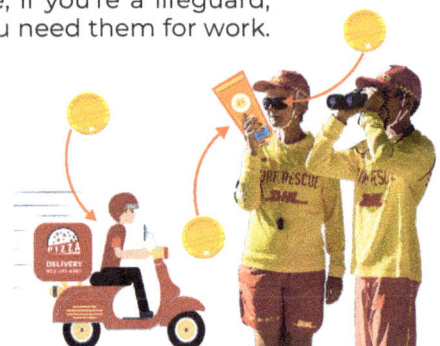

Real job tax deduction simulation
Link these "work expenses" to the different kinds of job for which you could possibly deduct them. Each can apply to more than one job!

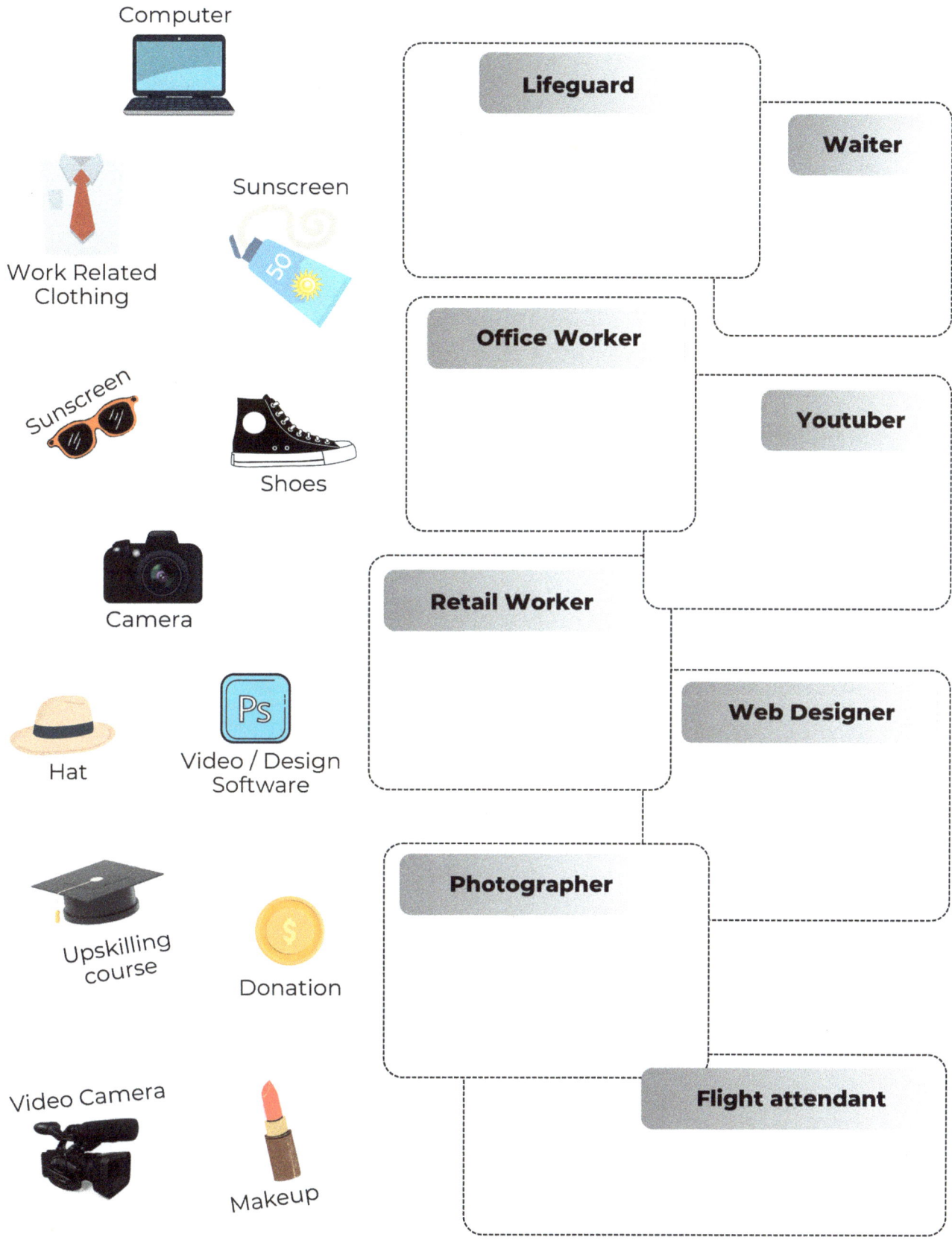

Computer

Work Related Clothing

Sunscreen

Sunscreen

Shoes

Camera

Hat

Ps
Video / Design Software

Upskilling course

Donation

Video Camera

Makeup

Lifeguard

Waiter

Office Worker

Youtuber

Retail Worker

Web Designer

Photographer

Flight attendant

Note, these are general examples, see a tax professional about your specific job and the specific item you are trying to deduct.

What's The Difference Between A Tax Bill & Return?

When you complete your tax return, there are two potential outcomes. First, you might be entitled to a tax refund, where the government refunds you tax that you've overpaid, or second, you might owe a tax bill, where you have to pay your outstanding tax. In this chapter, we'll cover why and how!

In the first scenario, a tax return...

Why on earth would you have you paid extra tax during the year? The main reason you might end up paying extra tax would be due to the way your employer estimates your tax on behalf of the ATO.

Every time your employer calculates your pay check, they work off the assumption that what you are earning this pay check, you will be earning every pay check. This is for simplicity and to be conservative. But! if you're paid by the hour, for example, and you work different shifts every week or month, this might not always be true.

For simplicity of tax calculation, your employer assumes that **what you get paid one paycheck** ...Is what you will earn every paycheck!

ie. $5000 one month

$5000 x 12 months =$60,000 → your employer assumes you get paid $60,000 a year... → calculating your annual tax to be $10,000 → **tax** for that month = **$833**

An Example

Let's imagine you work only a few shifts a month. By itself, these pay checks would likely have no tax deducted (falling under the tax-free threshold). Then, one month, you earn $5,000.

Pay **$5000** Taxed **$833**	Pay **$0** Taxed $0	Pay **$200** Taxed $0	Pay **$1000** Taxed $0
Pay **$1000** Taxed $0	Pay **$1100** Taxed $0	Pay **$1500** Taxed $0	Pay **$1500** Taxed $0
Pay **$0** Taxed $0	Pay **$500** Taxed $0	Pay **$200** Taxed $0	Pay **$0** Taxed $0

Total Pay Earned **$12,000**

Actual Tax Owed **$0**

Total Tax Paid **$833**

$833 - $0

▲ = **$833 Tax return**

For this $5000 payslip, your employer calculates this as if you're earning this every month. So, this payslip is taxed as if you're earning $60,000 for the year. That's a fair bit more tax than you'll probably end up owing.

Now, let's say at the end of the financial year, you add up all your income, and your total is under the tax-free threshold. However, you've paid a bunch of tax from that one big month. *Hello tax refund!*

Another reason which falls into the first scenario is slightly more abstract. Let's say you end up having a large number of tax deductions. You deduct these, which means your taxable income is reduced. If this reduces your tax owed BELOW what you've paid, you're in for a refund!

The second scenario, why a tax bill?

There are a few potential reasons...
- The biggest is if you're a contractor or sole trader. These are simply fancy words for when you run a solo business or do freelance-style work. As an employee, your employer takes care of tax. Yet when you're you're own boss, you don't have an employer taking care of your tax during the year. As a result, paying tax is your responsibility! If you haven't been contributing your tax during the year, when tax season rolls around... you'll have to settle up the amount you owe.
- Another potential reason you might end up with a bill could be if you've got extra income streams that aren't taxed during the year. This could be investments or side hustles or cash jobs.

Investment Profits

Cash Jobs

Business Income

Income not taxed during the year

You're a casual employee who gets paid monthly...
Complete the maths to figure to how much tax you'll be receiving back at the end of the financial year!

Pay **$4000**
Taxed **$586**

Pay **$0**
Taxed **$0**

Pay **$200**
Taxed **$0**

Pay **$1000**
Taxed **$0**

Pay **$1000**
Taxed **$0**

Pay **$1100**
Taxed **$0**

Pay **$3000**
Taxed **$334**

Pay **$1500**
Taxed **$0**

Pay **$0**
Taxed **$0**

Pay **$500**
Taxed **$0**

Pay **$200**
Taxed **$0**

Pay **$0**
Taxed **$0**

Use this working out space to fill in the blanks on the right hand side diagram

Total Pay Earned
$ _____

Actual Tax Owed
$ _____

Total Tax Paid
$ _____

$ _____ - $ _____

= $ _____
Tax return

How Do You Actually Submit A Tax Return?

How do you actually go about the process of submitting a tax return when tax season shows up? In this chapter we'll have a look at a couple of methods for doing this, as well as some key pieces of information you'll need.

1 Directly via MyGov

MyGov is a one-stop shop for a bunch of online services when it comes to everything Government and essential life admin - including your tax returns.

You can DIY your Tax Return via MyGov

Everything is pretty clearly signposted on the MyGov website, so all you need to do is read carefully through the online process and provide the information they ask for. There are also plenty of resources out there to help you work through your return!

2 Outsourcing to an accountant

If your tax situation is more complex than you'd like, the second method is to get the help of a professional. Accountants and tax agents can be useful if you've got a bigger investment portfolio, run your own business, or don't love the DIY method.

Or get a professional tax agent to manage it

Regardless of which method you choose, there are a couple of pieces of information you want to have ready to make the process super easy...

Traditional income

Payslip
Invoices
Income statement

Firstly, you want to know how much you earned during the financial year. To help with this, at the start of the year, figure out where to store all your earning information, like your payslips, invoices or welfare payments.

Investment Income

Bank Statement
Investment Summary

Secondly, you want to make sure that you know where to find all your end-of-year statements for your investments, if you have any. All investment income such as interest on savings need to be reported to the ATO.

Expense Receipts

And thirdly, you'll definitely want to note down your tax-deductible expenses during the year and keep the receipts for these in one place, to minimise your overall tax bill.

Having all this handy will put you in a good spot to work through each stage of your tax return. As you go, it's good to remember that the ATO takes your tax return at face value. In other words, it trusts that what you're saying on your form is true.

However, even if you don't get directly audited, the ATO will use third-party information to check that all your information adds up. This includes use banking information and other industry benchmarks. So while it can be tempting to use rough estimates or exaggerate your figures, don't forget that if the ATO comes knocking on your door, you'll have to be able to provide evidence for your numbers!

True or False?
Using what you have learned about Tax Returns, discuss these statements and figure out whether they are true or false!

Don't worry too much about tracking your invoices and paperwork, the ATO automatically has all of that.

True or False? Why?

The two methods through which you can submit your tax return are MyGov or through a verified tax agent.

True or False? Why?

The ATO takes your return at face value, so you are fine to estimate your numbers!

True or False? Why?

TAX

A space for your notes, questions, plans!

Congrats!

You've completed the...

ESSENTIAL SYSTEMS
micro-credential

Budgeting

Super

Tax

To collect your certificate and resume badge...

1 Complete this knowledge quiz

2 Email **microcredential@mandymoney.com.au** with your **quiz ID number** and a photo of this page!

Get a parent, teacher or librarian to complete this!

tinyurl.com/22wdb7cj

I,_____, can confirm that
(First and last name of teacher)

_____ has completed the activities for
(First and last name of student)

this micro credential, to the best of their ability.

Signed:_____ Date:_____ Email:_____
(In case we need to check that you're real!)

FUTURE FOCUSED
micro-credential

MINDSET

Learn about your money mindset, how money influences equality, and how to set money goals!

Lesson 1
Healthy Money Mindset

- ☐ 1 Money, Your Mind & Mental health
- ☐ 2 Building A Healthy Money Mindset
- ☐ 3 Building Financial Knowledge & Skills
- ☐ 4 Building An Entrepreneurial Mindset

Lesson 2
Money In An Equal Society

- ☐ 1 Money In An unequal world
- ☐ 2 Economic Policy And Social Equality
- ☐ 3 The Nuances Behind Social Inequalities
- ☐ 4 Solving Social Inequalities

Lesson 3
Goal Setting

- ☐ 1 Importance Of Goal Setting
- ☐ 2 Putting Purpose Behind Your Goals
- ☐ 3 Healthy Financial Goals
- ☐ 4 The Power Of Delayed Gratification

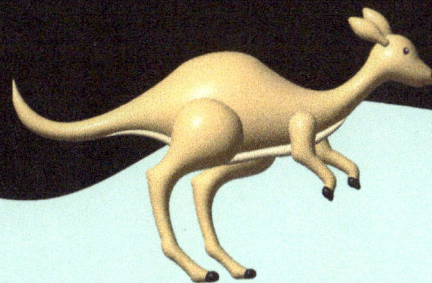

Money, Your Mind & Your Mental Health

Your mind is a powerful thing! It is constantly taking in information and interpreting these inputs. How your mind interacts with the 'input' of money is really personal for each of us. A mind can interpret money as a dangerous and terrifying topic. It can confuse money as being part of your identity (for example, having money means that you're a deserving person, and poverty; undeserving). Your mind can exaggerate how difficult a money task seems. It can convince you that money is a good replacement for true happiness and community. These interpretations are a shared human experience. They are experienced in one way, shape or form by every person on the planet. Let's explore the mind of money and how we can build healthier interpretations, behaviours, and attitudes.

Money can bring up unpleasant emotions...

Money can make you feel:

- Unhappy
- Overwhelmed
- Stressed
- Inadequate
- Anxious
- Scared
- Jealous
- Unworthy
- Shameful
- Greedy
- Guilty
- Defeated

Many people "sweep it under the rug" (in other words, they ignore their money situation). This only makes these negative feeling stronger, and their money situation, worse!

Did you know, the statistics say that money is the number one source of stress in most people's lives!

But it doesn't have to be this way!

There are two things (in your control) that you can work on to build a positive money experience...

1 Your Education & Skill Building

- Learning the theory behind how money works will help you understand and deal with it in a much calmer and logical way.
- Learning the skills to manage your money will help you deal with it much more easily and effectively.
- Learning the essential maths will make your money much less intimidating and help you make smarter financial decisions.
- Continuously up-skilling your work skills can help you experience less income stress.

2 Your Mindset & Money Story

- Understanding your "money story" will help you notice your money-related thoughts and behaviours more clearly. This will make unhealthy behaviours easier to identify and change.
- Building a healthy mindset will help you react to tricky money situations in a less stressed-out way. This can help you make more logical and empowered decisions.
- Developing a healthy money mindset will help you help your community embrace and face their tricky money situations.

Quick tips dealing with money stress.

- Remind yourself that **money is not your world, only a tool to help you get where you want to go in the world!**
- Speak to friends, family, school councillor, a teacher. Simply talking about your problem or feelings can make it all feel much lighter. Perhaps they could even help you find a solution!
- Look around you and list all the things you are grateful for. gratitude is the best tool to cut through negative feelings!
- Do an act of generosity. It doesn't have to involve money, but it will shrink your worried feelings (even just a little bit).
- Make an action-plan (or an education-plan) to tackle it head on!

Your behaviour and attitude is more impactful than your income! 61%

Your salary only accounts for 7% of the influence on overall financial wellbeing, whereas your behaviour and attitude account for up to 61%!

A 2018 study by an Australian bank

Your brain is a powerful tool... And it is yours to control! Reflect on your money story, your mindset and money behaviours. Which aspects do you like? Are there any you would like to change or improve on? Building a healthy relationship with money is slow, a bumpy road and takes work. By focusing on education and mindset to improve your behaviours and attitudes, you're heading in the right direction!

Your mind and money...
Think about your own situation when working
through these questions and prompts.

When you think about 'money', what are five
words or concepts that come to mind?

What is one belief you have about money, that you would like to
change? What is the new belief that you'll work towards?

What are three ways you could introduce positive
news or education about money into your life?

Who are three people in your life you could talk to
if you have questions or worries about money?

What are 3 things you are grateful for today (not money-related)?

What is one act of generosity you could do today?
It doesn't have to be related to money!

Building A Healthy Money Mindset

In this chapter, we're going to explore what a means to have a healthy money mindset. To start, your 'money mindset' is your personal set of beliefs and attitudes regarding money. It describes the way you think, feel, and talk about money. There are countless factors which impact these beliefs and attitudes, including your background, culture, experiences, money story and your own financial situation right now. Your money mindset is truly as unique as you are! However, there are two general categories we can use to talk about mindset: **'Scarcity'** or **'Abundance'**.

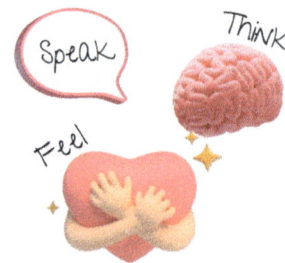

Scarcity

A **'scarcity mindset'** assumes that there isn't enough money to go round. You don't have enough, and - matter of fact - you'll never have enough! If others succeed, it's taking away from your own ability to succeed. When you do come into some money, you'd better spend it as quickly as you can, because money has a habit of disappearing.

Abundance

On the flip side of the coin, an **'abundance mindset'** is a sense that what you have is enough - it's gratitude for what you do have, rather than envy of what you don't. Even if you're not as financially secure as you'd like to be at the moment, you know you will find opportunities to get back on track, and that taking these opportunities is entirely within your control. An abundance mindset allows you to be genuinely happy for others when they achieve success, because there's more than enough to go round!

So why does it matter?

Believe it or not, your mindset is your most important financial asset. It influences decisions you make today about *saving*, *spending*, and *handling money*. Yet it doesn't just affect you - it also affects the wellbeing of those around you.

A **scarcity mindset** might lead you to regard money as a taboo discussion - one that you avoid having, particularly with close friends and family. You treat money as a very personal and private thing - your income or wages, as well as your expenses, should never be shared. If you're in debt, that's your business and nobody else's! Having money isn't something to talk about, and not having money is just shameful. The unfortunate case is that for most, this is the reality. But in the long run, it does more harm than good.

To flip this narrative, and tap into the power of an **abundance mindset**, it might start with you taking a step back, and seeing money as a system or a tool for both you and the people around you to improve your lives. Speaking openly and frankly about it, will help everybody interact with the system better, and you might bring to light injustices or struggles that your friends and family have been battling by themselves. A struggle shared is a struggle halved!

Healthy open discussions about things such as wages and financial troubles should focus on learning together, and helping each other work through problems together. Speaking openly with people you care about and trust is a great way to minimise judgement. Plus, it helps both you and them to find ways of improving your lives. Use this opportunity to ask those you care about any money worries they might be having!

The most important thing to remember is that you can grow and change and improve your mindset!

Two sides of the mindset coin...
Think about your own situation when working
through these questions and prompts.

What mindset do you currently resonate with most?
Can you give some examples of why?

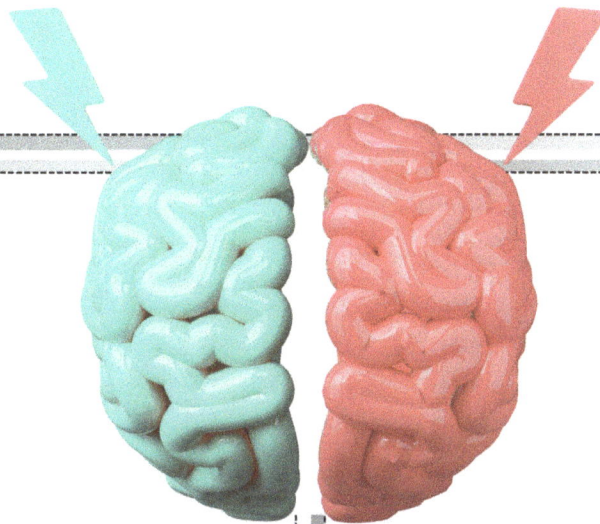

What could be
some issues with
having a scarcity
mindset?

What stands in the
way of someone
developing an
abundance
mindset?

What is one thing related to money you would like to be able to talk about
openly with your friends or family It could be a specific problem you are
facing, or a general topic!

Building Your Financial Knowledge And Skills

A big part of your financial wellbeing puzzle is accumulating the knowledge and skills to be able to earn money, plan ahead and manage your money. Don't stress if not a single one of these makes any sense to you yet... You have a long learning road ahead of you and that's exciting! These theories and skills are less complicated (and less maths-y) than you might think! Here's a checklist of the education you need in your life, plus why each one of these is important.

CoRe Money Theories to LeaRN

Why?

- [ ] The Australian **Tax** System and your tax obligations → To understand your legal tax obligations
- [ ] Australia's **Superannuation** system and super funds → To help you prepare for retirement
- [ ] Interest and the power of **Compound Interest** → To maximise wealth & avoid expensive debt
- [ ] Common **debt** types and how they work → To avoid dangerous debt situations
- [ ] Basic **Investment** principles, products and strategies → To maximise wealth building opportunities
- [ ] **Wealth Building** theories & methods → To help you achieve financial freedom
- [ ] **Employment** documents, obligations and processes → To secure income and know your legal rights
- [ ] **Budgeting** methods, tools and strategies → For future life planning & peace of mind
- [ ] **Saving** theories, methods and psychology behind it all → To achieve life goals and financial safety
- [ ] True costs of **essentials** (car, living, renting, property) → To make informed money choices & plans
- [ ] Different **insurance** types and contract purchases → To make better wellbeing & purchase choices
- [ ] HECS, your **entitlements** to opportunities and protection → To maximise your life quality & opportunities
- [ ] Centrelink, Government and other **support** avenues → To find help easily, and have peace of mind

CoRe Money Skills to Build

Why?

- [ ] **Curiosity** and courage to learn new money skills → To stay active in your up-skilling journey
- [ ] Completing a basic **tax return** → It's a legal obligation and helps you reflect
- [ ] Building a **basic budget** and reviewing it → To make accurate and up-to-date plans
- [ ] Designing a **savings goal** & building it into your budget → To achieve life goals and financial security
- [ ] Contributing to and **completing a savings goal** → To practice habits formation & achievement
- [ ] **Reviewing** your spending & saving activity critically → To reflect and improve your behaviours
- [ ] Keeping **paperwork organised** (e.g tax receipts) → To make money admin easier in the long-run
- [ ] **Researching** and comparing financial products → To make informed & financially clever choices
- [ ] Going through the **job application** process → To secure and improve income opportunities
- [ ] Basic **banking** tasks (accounts, transferring, statements) → To make essential banking tasks enjoyable
- [ ] Setting up banking **automations** & other tech → To level-up and streamline your money
- [ ] Making **investments** and building a portfolio → To maximise wealth building opportunities
- [ ] Designing & reviewing your **Super** investment strategy → To make your retirement the best it can be

The list of skills to learn is much longer in reality, but this is a great start and will take you a long way towards true financial wellbeing! Many of these skills and education topics only become relevant later in life. They aren't essential to master while you're still in high school. BUT! Learning as much as you can will give you the confidence to face the challenge when it does become relevant!

The Good News? All these theories and skills are taught in this textbook!

Reflecting on your own situation...
✓ Tick the theories/skills you're already comfortable with
♡ Heart the theories/skills you're interested in learning
✗ Cross in the theories/skills you're nervous to tackle

Core Money Theories to Learn

Use this space for any notes, comments or plans!

- [ ] The Australian **Tax** System and your tax obligations
- [ ] Australia's **Superannuation** system and super funds
- [ ] Interest and the power of **Compound Interest**
- [ ] Common **debt** types and how they work
- [ ] Basic **Investment** principles, products and strategies
- [ ] **Wealth Building** theories & methods
- [ ] **Employment** documents, obligations and processes
- [ ] **Budgeting** methods, tools and strategies
- [ ] **Saving** theories, methods and psychology behind it all
- [ ] True costs of **essentials** (car, living, renting, property)
- [ ] Different **insurance** types and contract purchases
- [ ] HECS, your **entitlements** to opportunities and protection
- [ ] Centrelink, Government and other **support** avenues

Core Money Skills to Build

Use this space for any notes, comments or plans!

- [ ] **Curiosity** and courage to learn new money skills
- [ ] Completing a basic **tax return**
- [ ] Building a **basic budget** and reviewing it
- [ ] Designing a **savings goal** & building it into your budget
- [ ] Contributing to and **completing a savings goal**
- [ ] **Reviewing** your spending & saving activity critically
- [ ] Keeping **paperwork organised** (e.g tax receipts)
- [ ] **Researching** and comparing financial products
- [ ] Going through the **job application** process
- [ ] Basic **banking** tasks (accounts, transferring, statements)
- [ ] Setting up banking **automations** & other tech
- [ ] Making **investments** and building a portfolio
- [ ] Designing & reviewing your **Super** investment strategy

For the topics you're a bit nervous about... how can you tackle these feelings to make sure you don't avoid learning them?

Building An Entrepreneurial Money Mindset

An '**Entrepreneurial mindset**' lives under the umbrella of an abundant, or positive money mindset, but is a little bit unique! It describes an abstract and big-picture way to think about earning money and building a life of financial freedom. Here it is in more detail...

What exactly is an entrepreneurial mindset?

"An entrepreneurial mindset is a set of skills that enable people to identify and make the most of opportunities, overcome and learn from setbacks, and succeed in a variety of settings".

When it comes to money, this mindset extends to the way you look at earning money and achieving financial freedom. An entrepreneurial money mindset takes a proactive look at income and believes that you can grow your income and earn money beyond simply a salary at a traditional job. This could look like buying or building assets (for example, investments... Or an online business selling shoes) and making these assets make money for you. An entrepreneurial mindset focuses less on how **MUCH** you get paid, but **HOW** you get paid. Are you trading your time and lifestyle for money? Or, are you making your assets work for you to earn you freedom of time and place? Start by reading "Rich Dad Poor Dad" By Robert Kiyosaki.

So why does it matter?

Looking back to many cultures in recent history, an entrepreneurial mindset was something largely reserved for the vagabonds and risk-takers. It wasn't an essential skill, as you could mostly just follow a clear pathway, tick the right education boxes, get a good job, buy a house and live a relatively financially secure life. Yet, in today's rapidly changing world of work, these pathways are less clear and the boxes to tick are unique for everyone. **This is not something to be afraid of, but something to embrace.** There is so much freedom in how you design your life, derive an income and spend your time. How exciting!

How to build an entrepreneurial mindset?

Building an entrepreneurial mindset is an act of constantly reframing the way you look at challenges & opportunities until it becomes an **in-built thinking pattern**. There are many books which focus on building entrepreneurial mindsets in general, and books that focus on building entrepreneurial 'money' mindsets. Study entrepreneurs that you admire and learn from the way they think & approach problems. Follow influencers who teach you about business and money. Most importantly, get amongst it! Start finding problems, creative solutions, failing and then trying again (and again!).

1 Build Resilience

Try, fail, and try again (and again)! Failing is the best thing that could happen to you for learning & growth. Develop "Grit".

2 Develop Creativity

Look at problems with a creative lens, think of creative solutions. Practice 'outside of the box' living.

3 Get Curious!

Be constantly curious about the world around you. Ask questions & look for ways to learn, grow, and expand!

What if I don't want to be an entrepreneur? That's ok! An entrepreneurial mindset will help you on whatever pathway you're on. It can help you find opportunities to get promoted, or get a really cool project to work on, find a better job, start a side-hustle, or make better investments!

Developing your mindset...
Reflect on your own situation when answering these questions!

Why is developing an entrepreneurial mindset import
for you, your life purpose and your goals?

How can an entrepreneurial mindset help you while you're at school?

Brainstorm things you can do start developing your entrepreneurial mindset!

What is one thing you could do to build resilience TODAY?	What is one thing you could do to develop creativity TODAY?	What is one thing you could do to show curiosity TODAY?
What are one thing you could build resilience generally?	What is one thing you could do to develop creativity generally?	What is one thing you could do to show curiosity generally?

How Does Money Contribute To An Unequal World?

It's no secret that we live in a world that isn't particularly fair or equal for everyone in it. A large part of this comes down to the way money has been used to create these inequalities. It is a really complex and heavily layered topic, but we'll do our best to explain how money fits into the inequality picture.

Let's look at three types of inequality...

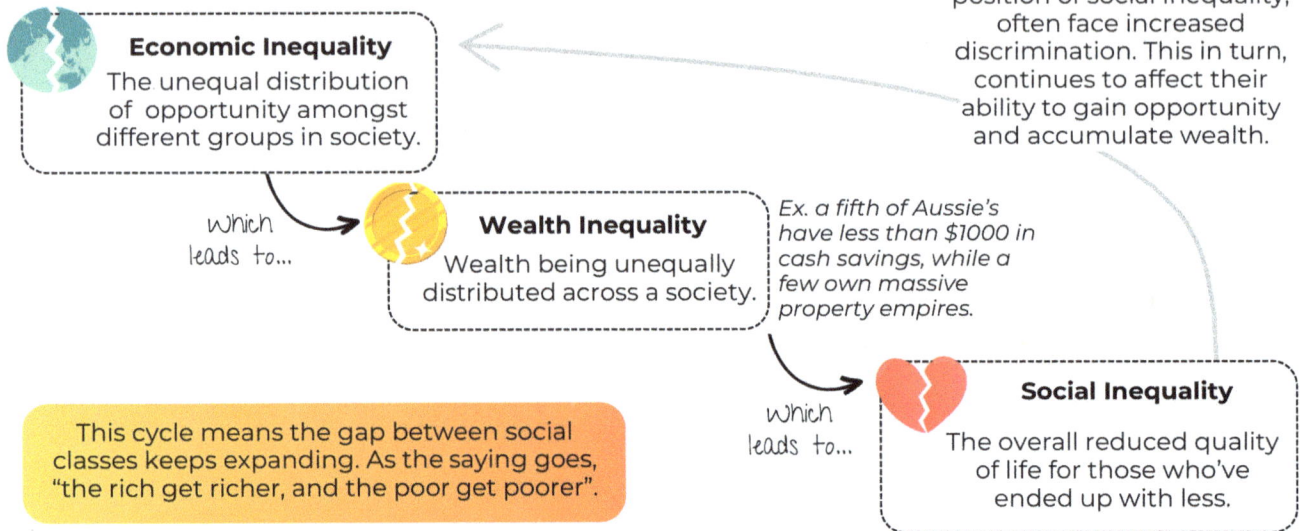

Economic Inequality
The unequal distribution of opportunity amongst different groups in society.

which leads to...

Wealth Inequality
Wealth being unequally distributed across a society.

Ex. a fifth of Aussie's have less than $1000 in cash savings, while a few own massive property empires.

It is a cycle! Those in a position of social inequality, often face increased discrimination. This in turn, continues to affect their ability to gain opportunity and accumulate wealth.

which leads to...

Social Inequality
The overall reduced quality of life for those who've ended up with less.

This cycle means the gap between social classes keeps expanding. As the saying goes, "the rich get richer, and the poor get poorer".

Example: Alex has moved to a new country with their family

Economic Inequality
Their education from their home country isn't relevant anymore, meaning Alex and settles into a low-income job.

Alex's children are now exposed to the same lack of opportunities and enter into the cycle

No Relevant Education
Low Income Job
Few Progress Options
Bad health

Alex is experiencing wealth, economic, and social inequality.

Wealth Inequality
They can't afford further training for advancing their career and are now also unable to purchase property or accumulate wealth.

Social Inequality
They now might not have access to great education for their children, and if they fall sick, their insurance might not cover their treatment.

Why should we care?

It's well-understood that anyone who faces these injustices can suffer long-term effects throughout their life. For example, a child brought up in poverty is unlikely to perform as well as others at school, and their health may suffer if they're unable to afford proper healthcare. On a wider level, economic stability and growth, including social services such as our health system will also suffer as a result of the inequality cycle. This dangerous cycle drives a wedge between the socio economic groups and leads to dangerous outcomes across the spectrum.

M4.5.1

Brainstorm and research...
Consider examples of Social, Wealth and
Economic inequalities in the world around you.

What's an example of **economic** inequality in your world around you?

What's an example of **wealth** inequality in your world around you?

What's an example of **social** inequality in your world around you?

How can Alex's children 'break the cycle' and why is it difficult for them to do so?

How Does Economic Policy Play A Role In Creating Equity?

The life around us is built upon the rules the government makes and enforces. We refer to 'economic policy' as a collection of a set of these specific rules. In this chapter, we'll explore how economic policy can contribute to the creation and continuation of social inequality.

Think of it like this: economic policy is an invisible machine. The machine's purpose is to influence or control the behaviour of the economy. This machine is made of lots of different components, or levers: taxes, subsidies, tariffs, laws and regulations are just some of the levers that can be affected.

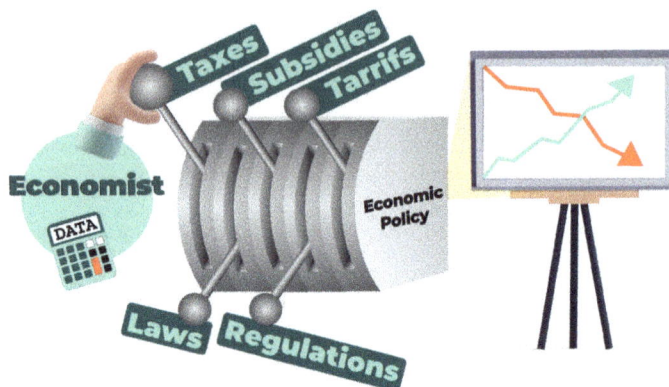

Each lever directly or indirectly influences different outcomes across society. When we refer to 'pulling a lever', we mean things like increasing or decreasing taxes, or changing the laws that affect businesses.

This begs the question: who knows which levers to pull?

That, is the job of an Economist. An Economist's main goal is to predict which levers to pull to create better social outcomes. They scientifically attempt to predict the future by using historical data. They consider immediate, short term and long term impacts, and a whole ecosystem of directly and indirectly related factors. Their predictions are then passed to law makers and government to decide which of these lever pulls to enact.

Example: Puling Specific Levers

Put yourself in the shoes of an Economist tasked with reducing income inequality and cutting the numbers of individuals who fall below the poverty line.

Economist | **Reduce income inequality & poverty numbers**

Government spending

How about stepping up investment in schools and colleges - train teachers, build better facilities, and level up education. This is an example of a long-term investment, which boosts the economy over time and will help alleviate poverty.

Long-term poverty alleviation

Tax Rates

Or, you might increase tax rates for more affluent people to adjust the distribution of resources to less wealthy parts of society.

Increase Wealth Distribution

Pension Rates

You could even adjust pension rates for retirees if you thought that generous pension rates for today's retirees might be at the expense of those for the next generation.

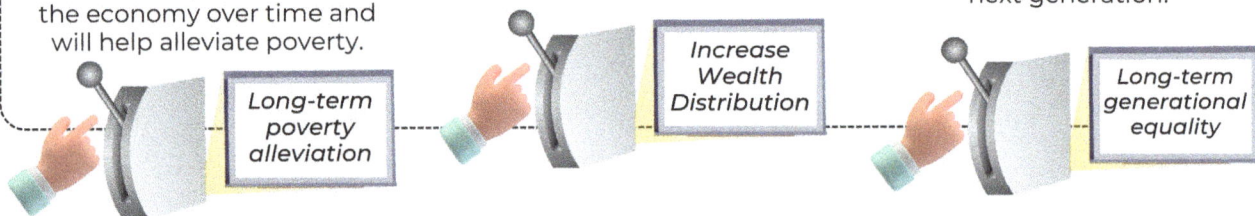

Long-term generational equality

By changing tack on policies such as these, economists can target various economic inequalities that are affecting our system. These are big, sticky problems, but with the right set of policies we can start to solve them.

You may not want to be an economist, so what should you do with all of this info?
A good start is to make sure you assess the financial world around you with a curious eye. Just because rules exist doesn't mean they're good ones! Some rules work for us; others have the ability to work against us. People have created laws, and people will be the ones to change them. Could you be the one who brings change?

Brainstorm and research...
Consider each of these economic levers. Find an example of how each of them work in making economic change.

Research or brainstorm an example of how adjusting 'Personal Tax Rates' could lead to greater levels of equality.

Research or brainstorm an example of how adjusting 'Subsidies and Tarrifs' could lead to greater levels of equality.

Research or brainstorm an example of how adjusting 'Laws and Regulations' could lead to greater levels of equality.

The Nuances Behind Social Inequalities

Social inequalities aren't black and white. Their causes and cures are infinitely complex. In this chapter, let's analyse why the answer is not as easy as simply changing one or two policies. While we'd love for Economic policies to be magic bullets that fix everything overnight, any policy change will have many different outcomes, some of which are expected and many which may be unexpected.

For Example...

We heavily increase investment in education while reducing spending on other services such as healthcare.

Here we might end up with population who's bad health gets in the way of their ability to work.

Unhealthy population equalling lower productivity rates

Invest in Education

More Skilled workers

We might decide to raise taxes, believing it will result in better wealth distribution. Instead, we are left with the unintended consequence of high-income earners becoming demotivated to work. Or they buy a first-class ticket to another country or state with lower tax rates.

High income earners stop working or leave the country (now there's less tax revenue to distribute)

Raise Taxes

Better wealth Distribution

Social Considerations before implementing a policy

Before pulling a lever on the economic policy machine, you might want to consider a few things first....

1 Cultural Factors
- Does a policy disturb the usual way of life?
- Is the timing right with current social trends and issues?
- Will everyone understand it in the same way?

2 Public Support
- Will people accept and adopt the new policy?
- Will authorities be able to enforce it?
- What is the policy's impact on formal institutions such as private companies, other political parties, and religious groups. If they're negatively affected by a policy, they might have the political weight to challenge or change the outcome.

3 Population Demographics politics, resources
- Is the policy compatible with population demographics & habits
- Is the policy inline with the political climate and trends?
- Are there available resources to implement the policy.

There may be unintended short- or long-term consequences stemming from any of these areas which makes policymaking a tricky task. When an economist addresses an issue, they form economic theories, trying to hypothesise exactly what these outcomes and effects might be. But, these are only theories. You can hypothesise until the cows come home, but you'll never understand the full set of results until long after the policy is implemented.

So the question is, if they're so complicated, are policy changes the only way to change things? Well, change can come from many different places. However, when it comes to formalising change and making impact on a large-scale, we're often reliant on policy changes from the top. So if you're ever in any position to change the world through economic policy, you know what to do!

Use your abstract thinking brain...
Consider each of these hypothetical scenarios and predict some of the unintended flow-on-effects! Think of short and long term impacts and everyone impacted by the change.

If the government were to lower personal income tax rates to try an encourage people to work more, can you predict **3 possible unintended flow on effects?**

Lower Personal Income Tax Rates

Greater workforce participation

If the government were to increase minimum wage to help everyone afford rising costs of living... Can you predict **3 possible unintended flow on effects?**

Increase Minimum Wage

Support people with the rising cost of living

Solving Social Inequalities Using The IEEJ Scale

How might you go about finding solutions to the crunchy problems in today's world? In this chapter, we'll explore one way to approach this using the IEEJ scale. When trying to solve a social issue, there are four distinct levels of solution to aim for, let's start at level 0 of the IEEJ scale, inequality.

I Inequality

What inequality means is that not everyone has equal access to the same resources. For example, inequality might look like a hiring manager not interviewing applicants of a specific ethnicity for a job. This is the ground level, not where we want to be on the scale.

E Equality

The first solution begins at level 1, with equality. This is when everyone has equal access to the same resources. However, it's important to remember that equal access to resources doesn't necessarily lead to equality of outcomes. Let's say this time, people of all races are interviewed for the job. This doesn't necessarily mean all of the applicants are being seriously considered.

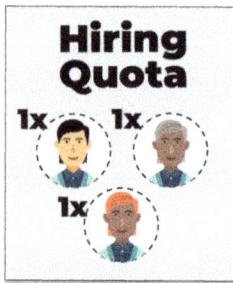

E Equity

Hiring Quota
1x 1x
1x

Levelling up from this to level 2, we have equity. It's a step up from equality which involves giving people different resources according to their needs, which therefore starts to become a better solution for addressing imbalanced social systems. For example, one person might need more support than their friend, so an equitable approach will see them receiving this support even though this isn't strictly 'equal'. Putting equity into the interviewing context might look like businesses having quotas to ensure equitable hiring practices.

J Justice

Finally, we have justice - and no, we're not talking about Batman! Justice is the final level on the scale; it fixes the system in a way that results in long-term, sustainable, equitable access to resources for generations to come. More simply, it will have a lasting positive effect. This might look like introducing strong leadership and company policies that ensure all races have an equal chance of the job, both now and in the future.

Inclusion & Diversity Policies

Leadership Meeting

Equality   Equity   Justice

You might have seen a picture of people standing on boxes to look over a fence at a game used to illustrate this concept. Equality means everyone stands on the same-sized box, even the children who still aren't tall enough to see over the fence. Equity would mean redistributing the boxes so shorter people can see just as well as taller people. However, justice might look like changing the fence so that everyone can see the game!

Hopefully, you can now start to see that a policy change here and there might create band-aid fixes for problems, but in order to create lasting social change, a strategic and coordinated series of changes and adjustments is needed. That's why big-picture thinking is so valuable in today's world!

Considering gender inequality at a sports club...
Describe what each of these levels could look like. If you prefer, you could choose an issue more relevant to your community.

How might **Inequality** look when it comes to gender inequality at a local sports club?

I **Inequality**

How might **Equality** look when it comes to gender inequality at a local sports club?

E **Equality**

How might **Equity** look when it comes to gender inequality at a local sports club?

E **Equity**

How might **Justice** look when it comes to gender inequality at a local sports club?

J **Justice**

Why It's Worth Taking The Time To Set Goals

Setting goals not only motivates us - it can also improve our mental health and our level of personal and professional success. In this chapter, we'll understand why goal setting is important as an exercise, but even more important as a tool to get you where you want to go!

You, going places

Your goals, getting you places

Picture this. You're a pirate, on a boat, all set to sail the seven seas, ready to adventure to new lands. Awesome! You hoist the anchor, excited and ready to go explore the unknown, you jump behind the wheel and then suddenly realise.... You don't know where you're going, all you see is the horizon and nothing but questions.

So what do you do, turn around and go back? Of course not! Just like all the movies, what you need is a map! It's got a desire - the treasure; and a method to get there - a direction. Now take the parrot off your shoulder for a second, and realise that in everyday life, we need this kind of a treasure map to get what we want too, whether that be buried treasure, a good grade, a big purchase or anything else. Goals help you **envision** where you want to get to, **plan** how you're going to get there, and most importantly help you **commit**, by remembering why you want to get there in the first place. A few key elements there:

The three elements of a goal...

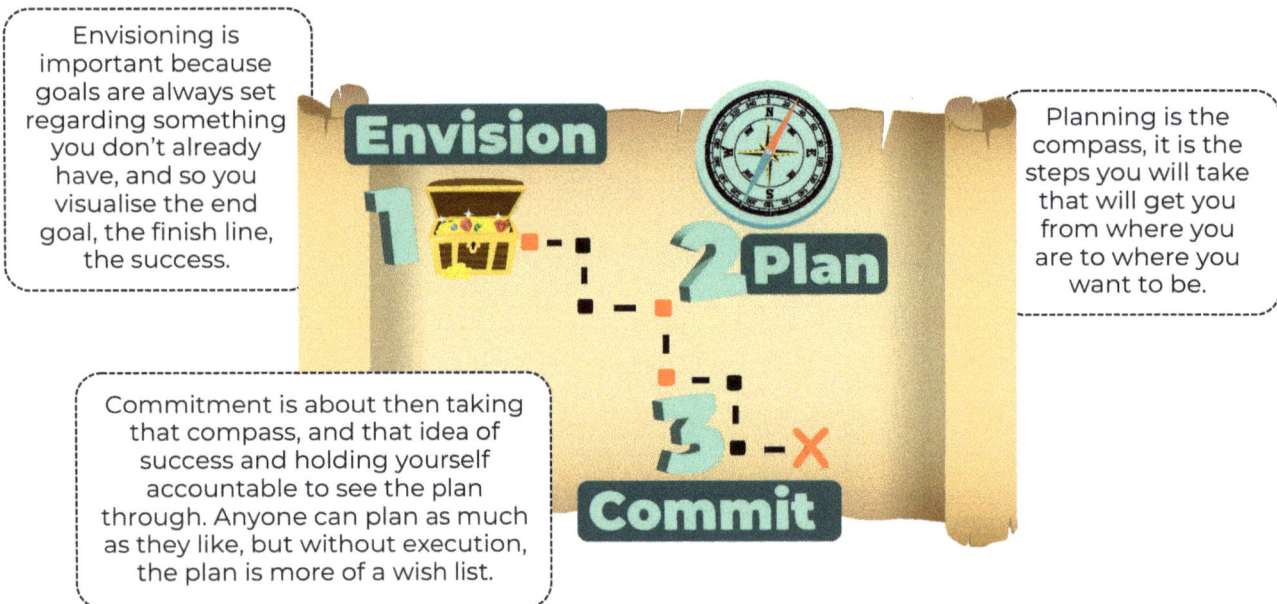

Envisioning is important because goals are always set regarding something you don't already have, and so you visualise the end goal, the finish line, the success.

Envision
Plan
Commit

Planning is the compass, it is the steps you will take that will get you from where you are to where you want to be.

Commitment is about then taking that compass, and that idea of success and holding yourself accountable to see the plan through. Anyone can plan as much as they like, but without execution, the plan is more of a wish list.

The power of goals

Hang on... you do things every day without a dedicated goal. You don't need to set a goal to eat lunch everyday! Well, goals are useful when you've got a task that requires lots of work to be put in over a longer period of time; when there are a few steps in between envisioning and achieving. Here are the key things that goals allow you to do:

1 Re-inforce new behaviours

Firstly, goals help to trigger and reinforce new behaviours. They pick you up on your bad days, give you momentum, and hold you accountable to the idea of achieving that goal in future.

2 Align your focus

Secondly, Goals also align your focus, and promote a sense of self mastery. By actively tracking progress towards a certain target, you can re-adjust the methods you use to move yourself towards that target, meaning it can be reached sooner.

3 Personal Success

Finally, personal success, whatever that may mean to you, is an important contributor to overall mental health. Achieving goals can create a snowball effect, giving you the confidence to set and achieve more and more ambitious goals in the future.

Reflecting to your situation...
Explore what each of these steps might look like in a practical sense! Is there a goal you have that you could apply it to?

Your Goal

Use the S.M.A.R.T goal framework covered later in the Mindset Topic!

Envision

Describe your goal 'end state' in vivid detail. How will you feel? How will it impact other areas of your life?

Plan

What is your plan to get there? This can change over time!

Commit

Write your commitment statement! What rewards or behaviour changes will you commit to? Who can hold. you accountable?

Putting Purpose Behind Your Goals

Goal setting in itself isn't inherently rewarding, much like Robin Hood doesn't become better at shooting a bow and arrow by simply setting up targets. In this chapter, we'll explore the power of goals in helping you find direction, and unlock your purpose.

Two Distinct Concepts

- **The purpose:** your purpose, or "why", is the north star, the guiding visualisation of things yet to be achieved - motivating you to keep moving forward in the right direction.
- **The goal:** Goals themselves, are your "how", the individual, actionable steps that move you closer to your destination.

Purpose + Goal

We like examples, so let's pretend you're on a ship sailing through life. You sail from island to island, enjoying the sights and adventures on the way. You work hard to get to each island, but! you find that you're only enjoying each island for a moment before you start thinking about what's next. The success of reaching new islands loses its meaning.

For example, Olympic athletes might spend their lives training for one event. Yet, many report that the saddest day of their lives is the day after they win Gold; their goal has just been completed and they find themselves asking, "Well now what?!"

Now What?

Meet your 'North Star'

This is a bigger purpose or vision that is the strong undercurrent guiding your journey. It puts the highs and lows of island hopping in perspective, and keeps the bigger picture in the front of your mind. The goal of each new island is just a stepping stone in the journey towards your north star.

Back to reality: we aren't buccaneers, we're just young people trying to get to where we want to go. So, what does it mean for your money life? In a financial sense, if you've got a higher sense of purpose then it releases you from being tied to a 'finish line'. You might have a goal to buy a house or a nice pair of shoes, which is great - but a bigger purpose will inform how you feel about achieving those goals.

For example, if your North Star is to live a relaxed and fulfilling lifestyle, buying your dream home is only the start of your journey - not the end of a savings goal.

Or, you might have a vision to wear clothes that make you feel good and help to strengthen your identity. This might mean that buying the shoes won't be an empty purchase, but instead will be part of fulfilling that purpose and vision.

Or, if your north star is to have freedom of time, you might realise that working tirelessly for an endless amount of money is not actually one of your goals.

Your purpose, or your "why", is the thing that gets you out of bed in the morning, with your eyes on the horizon. You move towards your purpose using goals as stepping stones, always asking yourself "how am I going to get closer to where I want to be".

Philosopher Friedrich Nietzsche

One who has a "why", can endure almost any "how"

M4.10.1

Your goals and your purpose...
Use this chance to really think about your personal goals and purpose. These can change over time, and many people don't figure it out properly until much later of life.

Step 1: Write down three goals you have. They could be short, medium or long term goals. They could be money related, or not at all.

Goal 1

Goal 2

Goal 3

Step 2: Now, looking at those goals... Can see a trend behind them? Can they allude to your 'Why' or 'Purpose'? It's ok if you haven't figured it out yet. Try your best.

How to Set Good (Smart) Money Goals

Ever heard the phrase "work smarter, not harder?" Well, this applies to goals as well. In this chapter, we'll break down a key techniques you can use to better implement and work towards your goals.

Meet the SMART system. The acronym SMART stands for Specific, Measurable, Achievable, Relevant and Timely. A goal that has all of these bases covered is one that is more likely to be achieved in the long run, by design. Let's run through these!

Specific

Specific relates to the objective of the goal, making sure you know exactly what you want. For this example, let's say you want to buy your first car.

Measurable

Measurable is a metric, or quantifiable way to track progress towards an end point. A process goal, such as saving each week may be measured by a habit tracker, whereas an exact goal may be needing to save a specific dollar value over time. Because you can stop at any time and see how you're going compared to these values, they give accountability and a source of motivation. To develop our example, you may want to make your end goal $12,000.

Achievable

Achievable means keeping perspective in goal setting, knowing that if your goal is too hard it'll be demotivating. In our example, let's remember to sense-check whether $12,000 is a realistic amount to try and save based on your income and lifestyle.

Relevance

Relevance relates back to how much your vision aligns with your goal. If you're setting goals to save for a car, but don't particularly want a car, the motivation to save $12,000 might not be there. Perhaps you really want a car because you enjoy the freedom to travel.

Timeliness

Timeliness is important when quantifying your goals. All assignments have due dates, because otherwise there is no sense of urgency around when they should be done. A short-term goal may be days-to-months, whereas long-term goals may be reassessed every one-to-five years. Let's say our car savings goal is 24 months from now.

Save $12,000 to buy a car in 24 months time to be able to travel

What's next?

Next, we need to put it into action. Keep it within sight... on your lock screen, desk or bathroom door. Simply by writing things down, you're 42% more likely to achieve your goal. That's cool.

Other strategies include taking away the barriers. If your goal is monetary, set up an automated transfer. If your goal is exercise in the mornings, get your clothes and breakfast ready the night before. Most things that stop a goal in the moment often relate to willpower, so make the first step effortless.

Now it's your turn to set your own SMART goals!

M4.11.1 **Choosing your favourite goal...**
Convert it into a "Smart" goal down below.

S **Specific**

M **Measurable**

A **Achievable**

R **Relevance**

T **Timeliness**

The Power of Delayed Gratification

There are a few logistical things behind achieving your goals. However, the secret sauce to staying on track your goals (especially saving or money-related goals) is to master the art of delayed gratification.

What is delayed gratification?

"resisting an impulse to take an immediately available reward in the hope of obtaining a more-valued reward in the future"

Examples include:
- Not spending your savings to invest for something bigger
- Not snacking because you want to have room for dessert
- Not eating a second dessert because you want to run a marathon
- Resisting social media before bed because you want to sleep longer and better
- Spending money and time on education to earn more money and time later in life

Resist Now

For a later (better) reward

Three steps to strengthen your delayed gratification muscle...

Step 1
Develop goggles into the future. To be able to say no now, you need to know what you're saying yes to in the future! What exactly is the **'later (better) reward'**?

Step 2
Paint that future picture as vividly as possible. Knowing exactly how good your future reward will feel, taste, look... Will help it be the obvious option to choose!

Step 3
Compare your current option to the future reward and make your decision. If your future reward is something you want badly enough, the choice will be easier!

and then...

Repeat! Delayed gratification is like a muscle that takes consistent building and exercising. Your muscle can grow and shrink over time, so keep at it!

Why is it important?

Developing a strong sense of impulse control and self-discipline will give you what you want MOST in life over what you simply want NOW. Most of the greatest achievements in a person's life happen over long stretches of time. 'Overnight success' is a story the newspapers invented (to sell newspapers)! Whether your goal is to build wealth, a beautiful family or an artistic career... These things typically take time. Over the course of that time, you must make (often challenging) decisions to choose the end goal instead of the immediate pleasure. Delayed gratification is key to achieve long-term goals.

Search online for the marshmallow experiment... An interesting example of delayed gratification in action!

The catch?

Delayed gratification is an awesome skill to help you achieve long term goals. However, life is fleeting and it's important to enjoy the moment. Find a good balance between looking out for future you, and making the most of the present moment.

M4.12.1

Strengthen your delayed gratification muscle...
Choosing your favourite goal, work through these three steps!

Your Goal: What is the goal you are trying to achieve (use the S.M.A.R.T System).

Step 1: Develop goggles into the future. To be able to say no now, you need to know what you're saying yes to in the future! What exactly is your 'later reward'?

Step 2: Paint your future picture as vividly as possible. Knowing exactly how good your future reward will feel, taste, look... Will help it be the obvious option to choose! Get creative here and sketch it out if that helps.

Step 3: Compare your immediate temptation option to the future reward. For this exercise, can you think of some example 'temptations' that you might face in this journey?

MINDSET

A space for your notes, questions, plans!

EMPLOYMENT

Learn the key steps to getting a job, preparing for your future of work, and dealing with Admin!

Lesson 1
Getting Your First Job

- [ ] **1** The Job Acquisition process
- [ ] **2** Resume Crafting
- [ ] **3** Cover Letter Writing
- [ ] **4** Acing Your Job Interview

Lesson 2
The World Of Work

- [ ] **1** The Modern World Of Work
- [ ] **2** Skills Preparation For The Future
- [ ] **3** Pathways Beyond Employment
- [ ] **4** Introduction To Wealth Building

Lesson 3
New Job Admin

- [ ] **1** Basic Employment Economics
- [ ] **2** New Job Admin Obligations
- [ ] **3** Interpreting The Payslip
- [ ] **4** Job Contract Under A Microscope

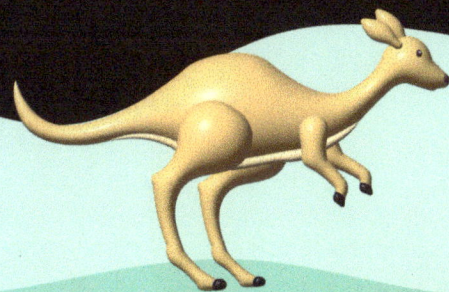

Navigating The Windy Road Of Getting A Job

The process of getting a job can be overwhelming! In this chapter, we'll give you a speedy, birds eye view of the process of how to go about getting a job you love.

Applying for a job can be anything from a single conversation to a year long process. The fine details will vary from place to place, but the key steps are similar. Here's what lies ahead for your job hunt.

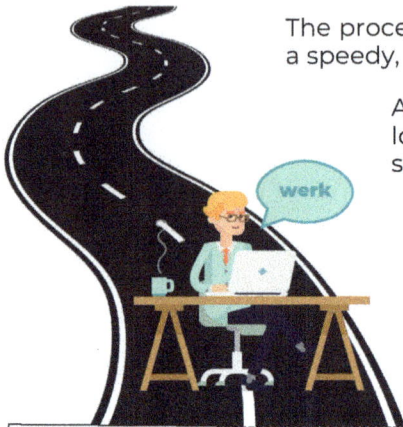

werk

Jobs

First up, think about what sort of job you want and who you want to work for. This requires a decent amount of thought, so don't rush it. Be organised: draw up a list of the places you'd like to apply to and start working through this.

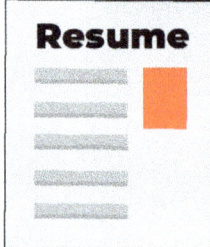

Resume

Once you have found where you want to apply: now, you have to frame yourself as the best candidate for the job. Start by writing a resume: this gives your potential employer a quick scan of your qualifications and skillset to prove you can handle the work.

Cover letter

You'll likely also need to write up a cover letter to add colour to your application and give insight as to whether you're a good cultural fit. Remember, the employer knows what they're looking for, and it will be up to you to put yourself in their shoes and pitch yourself as this ideal person. Don't change who are for the sake of a job, but it is worth highlighting the qualities they're looking for.

Call

Email

Carrier Pigeon

After constructing the perrrrfecttttt resume and cover letter, it's time to hand them in! There are many ways to do this: email, call, or drop in and talk to someone. The trick here is to find the 'richest' communication method available. In an ideal world, that would be a face-to-face conversation with the employer. This allows for direct personal contact, instant feedback, and immediate clarification, but sometimes a call or email is the next best thing.

Good news just in: you've been invited to an interview! Whether this is a phone call or an in-person chat, it's an opportunity to prove everything you've written in your resume. Most importantly, it gives you the ability to showcase your unique you! Interviews can be intimidating, but the employer needs a chance to see whether you'd be a good fit within their team, and to make sure your resume checks out. In any case, it's an excellent chance for you to ask any questions - employers love to see a genuine curiosity about the role.

Here's where things might change up a bit. Depending on the job you're going for, you might need to take tests, trials or multiple interviews, so be prepared. If you have no clue how to prepare, call the business and ask about their process, or reach out to someone in a similar industry.

Sometimes trying to get a job can end up harder than the actual job itself. So, whenever you don't quite make it, reach out and ask for some honest feedback. Be open to improvement because failure shows us what to work on. The more you can tailor your approach to each workplace, the more likely you are to succeed. It can be a tough job, haha, but remember... It's just a numbers game!

E5.1.1

Getting your first (or second) job...
Whether you already have a job or not, use this as a chance to plan your job application process, thinking about where exactly you would like to apply.

Step 1: List 3 (or more!) jobs you would like to apply for. Make sure they are real, specific ones in your local area, not simply generic job categories.

Step 2: Choose one of these jobs, writing down how you plan on applying and getting this job! Be as detailed as you can. Maybe even write down dates for each step.

How To Put Together An A-Class Resume

Talking about yourself and isn't something that comes naturally to most. So, in this chapter, we'll focus on developing A-class resume writing skills, to communicate what you're good at and why you're the right person to hire.

The main purpose of a resume is to give the employer a highlight reel of your skills. It's simply a quick snapshot of who you are, what you've done and what you can do. Keep it crisp, clean, and snappy - make sure it's easily understandable and not just big words thrown onto a piece of paper.

Who you are
What you've done
What you can do

The Key Elements

Begin by choosing a suitable resume format and layout. There are so many great templates you can find with a quick Google search! If you think the hiring manager will like it, get creative and make it stand out from the crowd. Just don't lose sight of what's important: make sure it's short and presents the information clearly, and you'll be good to go.

1 Next up, make sure to include your personal details and contact information, so the team can reach out to you - hopefully to organise an interview!

2 You might also want to describe yourself using a personal summary or resume objective. Keep in mind though, it's a quick snippet of who you are, not a love letter!

3 Now, the most important part: list out your work experience, achievements, and qualifications. This means giving a summary of where you've previously worked and anything you've achieved in these roles. It could also mAchievements ean including your educational background.

When you're applying for your first job, you're probably not going to have a long list of past jobs and qualifications. Here is where it's time to get creative, and show that the skills they're looking for... you either have, or have the attitude and capacity to learn. In one example, it could be talking about a sports team you've been a part of. This shows that you're a reliable team member. Or, it could be a market stall you've run to show that you're able to handle money and deal with customers. Look back over what you've been up to for the past few years, and chances are, you've got a long list of relevant experiences that you can draw parallels to.

Mandy Money
Freelance photographer

mandy@email.com
0412 345 678
Tolora, Aus
Linkedin.com/mandymoney

Student with experience in photography, specialising in portrait and landscape photography. Inspired by travel, and lover or unique and creative photographs.

WORK EXPERIENCE

Retail Assistant
Cotton on Pups
Jan 2024 – present
- Helped serve customers
- Updated store front windows to attract customers

Photography Assistant
Puppy pictures
June 2023 - Jan 2024
- Responsible for preparing camera equipment

Social media Assistant
Puppy Bowls
Jan 2023 - June 2023
- Took photos for their social channels

ACHIEVEMENTS
- Basic photography Cert
- Mandy Money Micro-Cred
- Year book photographer

EDUCATION
- Year 10 student
- Top subjects: **Art** (90%)and **maths** (80%)

GENERAL SKILLS
Teamwork Leadership
Time Management
Problem Solving

PHOTOGRAPHY SKILLS
- Portrait and Landscape photos and camera settings
- Using a DSLR camera (I own a Sony Riii)
- Using basic editing software to adjust colours, crop and minor photoshop

LANGUAGES
English
Chinese
French

INTERESTS
- Travelling
- Animals (dogs!)
- Cooking

---

4 Next, summarise your top soft and hard skills and clearly demonstrate what you can bring to the table. And if you're feeling good, it's not a bad idea to include additional sections to list your hobbies, interests, and even languages you speak. It helps to paint the picture of a well-rounded personality on paper, and makes for excellent interview conversation!

After all this, you'll likely end up with more than just one page of information for your resume, so put on your critical eyes, and cherry-pick the most relevant information for each job. A second pair of eyes also never hurts.

Have a go at developing your own resume!
Start by using this template version, or
download and fill out this online one.

WORK EXPERIENCE

SKILLS

OTHER SKILLS

ACHIEVEMENTS

LANGUAGES

EDUCATION

INTERESTS

How To Write An A-Class Cover Letter

Applying for a job is all about communicating who you are. In this chapter, you'll learn how to write an A-class cover letter. *First of all, what is a cover letter?* It's a one-page document that you'll need to submit alongside your resume. Its main goal is to introduce you, and introduce aspects of your professional personality that your resume didn't cover. For example, what motivates you or what you work like in a team.

Most cover letters should range from 250 to 400 words. The great ones will stand out to the hiring manager and get them to read your resume, which hopefully ends in them giving you an interview.

Here's a six-step process for making a great cover letter

Mandy Money
Freelance photographer

mandy@email.com
0412 345 678
Tolora, Aus
Linkedin.com/mandymoney

Sammy Sally
Sammy@legendsville.com
1st January 2024

Dear Sammy,

I hope this letter finds you well. I wanted to let you know how excited I am about the opportunity to work as a photographer at Legendsville. I'm a high school student who's really passionate about photography, and I'd love to be a part of your team.

I've been learning photography on my own and practicing a lot, and have even done a certificate in basic landscape and portrait photography. My most notable achievement is being selected as the yearbook photographer. Beyond this, I've also enjoyed helping a local business by taking photos for their social media.

What I like about Legendsville, is that you seem to care about taking unique and creative photos, just like I do. I think it would be awesome to learn from you and contribute my skills to your team.

I'm genuinely thrilled about the chance to work with you. Thanks for considering me, and I'm looking forward to talking more about how I can help out.

Sincerely, Mandy Money

1 The header needs to include your contact information so it's easy for the hiring manager to reach you.

2 Speaking of, you want to begin the actual letter by greeting the hiring manager. If you have a name, use it!

3 Next, focus your opening paragraph by grabbing their attention with why you're the perfect candidate they've been looking for

4 The second paragraph on the other hand, should explain two or three of your top achievements - the relevant ones, of course.

5 The last body paragraph is all about describing why you're a good fit for the company. Try researching their purpose and company values for this one.

6 Finally, a formal closing to round off - keep it polite and friendly.

Whether you want to follow this structure, or follow your own path, here are a few general pointers to keep in mind.

- **Firstly,** Don't just copy off your resume; this is the perfect chance to introduce some new information.
- **Secondly,** Get creative and steer clear of lazy sentences - employers can tell if it's a generic cover letter, so try and tailor it specifically for the job you are applying for. Google is your best friend here! Show them that you know the company and are passionate about working with them.
- **Thirdly,** Get a friend or an editing software to proofread it for you, so you avoid any shocker spelling errors!

It can be a bit of work to put together, but your cover letter should reflect parts of your personality, so be authentic and don't be scared to get creative with it.

Have a go at developing your own cover letter!
Start by using this template version, or download and fill out this online one.

How To Ace Your Job Interview

In this chapter, we're going to explore all the do's and don'ts of a job interview! Now, you might've heard the phrase "never judge a book by its cover". Well unfortunately, just like books, people make assumptions of you at a first glance, without even thinking about it. But it's not as straightforward as having a nice haircut and saying the right things.

Here's the breakdown:
- 55% of the impact of a spoken message is **visual**
- 7% of the impact of a spoken message is **verbal**
- 38% of the impact of a spoken message is **vocal**

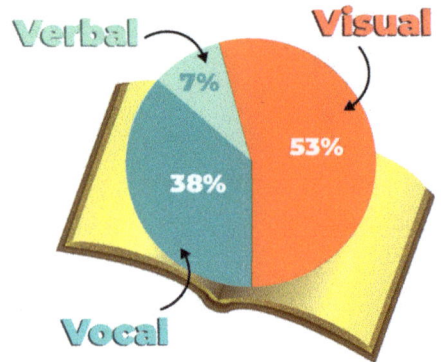

Verbal 7%
Visual 53%
Vocal 38%

That means 93% of a message is communicated without you even saying a word!

But hang on - What does good nonverbal communication even look like? One way to think of it is that an interview can be like a first date with a new job. The basics are the same - being clean, polite, and having good body language!

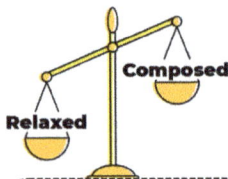

Cleanliness is a big one and covers everything from smelling nice to having clean clothes, hands, and hair. Clothes in particular are important here: dressing appropriately for a job's expectations means thinking about the right thing to wear. You wouldn't wear a suit and tie to a Hardware store interview, but at the same time, you wouldn't wear tracksuits to a hospitality job.

Friendly, kind, polite

Being polite and kind to everyone you meet isn't only good life advice, but important in interviews as well. You don't know who makes hiring decisions in a new job - anyone and everyone you meet may be a decision-maker. And if not, they may at the very least be a potential future coworker.

Composed
Relaxed

Cleanliness
Clothes, Hands, Hair

Body Language

X Clench Fists
X Fidget
X Cross Arms

✓ Sit up Straight
✓ Use hands
✓ Eye Contact

And finally, body language. The name of the game here is a balance between relaxation and composure.

Avoid clenching your fists, fidgeting, or crossing you arms. These all give off signals that you are nervous, bored, or unapproachable, which aren't what you want to communicate in an interview.

On the flip side, there are plenty of things you SHOULD try do.
- Make sure you're sitting up straight, but with a posture that is still and relaxed.
- Keep your hands in a comfortable resting position when not talking, and use them to help support you when you are talking.
- One of the biggest things to remember, is to make good eye contact, as this is a big sign of confidence, but also helps you connect better with the interviewer.

"Um" "Ah" "Like"

Lots to think about, but as they say, practice makes perfect! By far the best way to practice these techniques we've been talking about today is to record yourself talking. This can be very confronting, especially listening to yourself say filler words such as "Um", "Ah", or "like". It's worth it though - the awareness of these is the first step to improving your weaknesses, and making an impact in the interview room!

E5.4.1

Find a partner, or video yourself!
Here's an assessment chart to help you figure out how you can improve your interview skills. Being aware of what you're doing (or not doing) is the first step to improving.

Scoring your communication strengths & weaknesses, respond to these three questions (30 seconds roughly per response)...

- What is your favourite fish?
- What is your favourite dish?
- What is your biggest wish?

This activity is not about what is being said, but HOW it is being said (non-verbal)

Interviewer:_____ **Interviewee:**_____

Question 1	-1	**Question 2**	-1	**Question 3**	-1
Clenching Fists		Clenching Fists		Clenching Fists	
Fidgeting		Fidgeting		Fidgeting	
Crossed Arms		Crossed Arms		Crossed Arms	
Filler Words		Filler Words		Filler Words	
Nervous Laughing		Nervous Laughing		Nervous Laughing	
Talking too fast		Talking too fast		Talking too fast	
	+1		**+1**		**+1**
Good Posture		Good Posture		Good Posture	
Politeness		Politeness		Politeness	
Eye Contact		Eye Contact		Eye Contact	
Expressive Hands		Expressive Hands		Expressive Hands	
Smiling		Smiling		Smiling	
Good Talking Pace		Good Talking Pace		Good Talking Pace	
Total		**Total**		**Total**	

What did you do well?

What can you work on?

Meet The Modern World Of Work

The world of work in Australia looks very different in 2024 compared to when your parents were entering the workforce. Key differences include: The kinds of jobs available, the education and experience you need to get those jobs, and how you work within those jobs. Here's a quick introduction to where post-school education and careers meet.

Industry future predictions

Quick Stats

This is a tiny snapshot of predictions made by the Australian National Skills Commission for what the world of work will be like in the coming years. Keep in mind that these are just predictions!

Jobs projected to have biggest **growth** in demand are aged & disabled carers, software and applications programmers, and registered nurses. Secretaries, bookkeepers and bank workers are on a **downwards** trend.

By **2026**, more than nine out of 10 jobs will require further study after school. In fact, by 2040, Australians are predicted to spend 33% more time on education and training across their lifetime.

Automation is predicted to boost workforce participation and create opportunities particularly for women with children, workers over the age of 65 and people with a disability.

It's important to look at the future of your prospective career!

Undertaking further training or education will become more and more important.

Flexible work will change who can work and how they can work! How good.

University Pathway
These professions *typically* need a relevant university Degree

- Teacher
- Lawyer
- Nurse / Mid-Wife
- Paramedic
- Physio / Chiro / Osteo
- Accountant
- Architect
- Professional
- Psychologist
- Engineer
- Social worker
- Librarian
- Doctor
- Veterinarian
- Archaeologist
- Marine Biologist
- Meteorologist
- Occupational Therapist

Either!
These careers can be achieved through multiple education pathways

- Musician
- Actor
- Nutritionist
- Marketer
- Project Manager
- Bookkeeper
- Programmer
- Fashion Designer
- Agriculture
- Media Presenter
- Interior designer
- Real-Estate Agent
- Wine-Maker
- Designer

Non-Uni Pathway
These professions *typically* have (non-university) education pathways

- Police-Force
- Defence-Force
- Emergency Services
- Beauty services
- Barista
- Chef / Cook
- Tradie / Technician
- Aged Care Worker
- Admin / Secretary
- Disability Care Worker
- IT Specialist
- Flight Attendant
- Vet Nurse
- Dog-Trainer
- Pilot
- Lifeguard

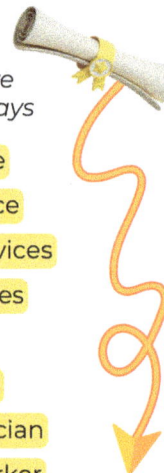

Neither!
These careers *typically* don't require formal education (but often, it helps!)

- Entrepreneur
- Author
- Delivery Driver
- Nanny
- Artist
- Content Creator
- Photographer
- Illustrator
- Cleaner
- Jeweller
- Farm Hand
- Florist
- Receptionist
- Videographer
- Hospitality

E5.5.1

What is your future of work?

Think of 3 potential career pathways and explore what exactly attracts you to that career, and how you could approach it.

Career Choice 1:_____

What exactly do you like about this career?

What are the different pathways you could take to achieve it?

Career Choice 2:_____

What exactly do you like about this career?

What are the different pathways you could take to achieve it?

Career Choice 3:_____

What exactly do you like about this career?

What are the different pathways you could take to achieve it?

Imagine your ABSOLUTE dream career (it doesn't have to be realistic). What would your job description be?

Hint: there are weird jobs out there... Something like it might actually exist!

Skills Preparation For The Future Of Work

Technology is an exciting, intimidating and unpredictable factor in all of our working futures. There are no two experts that predict the same thing. While we wait to see and experience how it all unfolds, there is one thing you can do to help future-proof yourself...

Developing "Non-Technical" Skills

"Non-technical skills are skills you have that do not relate to your specific job. They relate more to your personal qualities and habits than your technical abilities" - *Indeed*

It is predicted by **2030**, workers will spend 43% more time on work interactions that require well developed social and emotional skills (McKinsey & Company).

Also called "Soft Skills"

Which Skills are important?

Digital Literacy — The ability to work with digital tools such as apps, softwares and devices. For example, being able to send emails, make presentations and use a chatbot.

Data Literacy — Being able to collect, understand and analyse data. For example, creating a survey, understanding the numbers & making a conclusion from the results.

Critical Thinking — Being able to critically consider and question information, situations and problems. For example, seeing a news article and questioning its validity.

Emotional Intelligence — The ability to control & express our own emotions, and work collaboratively with the emotions of others. This forms part of broader social intelligence.

Creativity — Finding imaginative and abstract responses to questions, and solutions to problems. Thinking outside of the box!

Collaboration — Being able to work with others to achieve an outcome. Teamwork is becoming more dynamic as the internet changes the way we work.

Flexibility — Roll with the punches as they say! Being able to adapt and react quickly and positively to change is becoming more and more important.

Leadership Skills — Leadership is more than just a title. Being able to best out of other people and making sure they can thrive is a superpower across the board.

Time Management — Being able to manage your time to meet deadlines and complete tasks is key for work, but also to achieve a healthy work/life balance!

Curiosity & Continuous Learning — Having the attitude and habits in place to keep learning and building your skills is important for your career and a vibrant life!

How do I learn this Soft Skill?

- Embrace and explore the different features of tech at your disposal.
- Reading the news, Proactively creating and analysing surveys.
- Pausing to reflect, question & fact check news and social media.
- Get to know your emotional world through research & self-reflection.
- Put away your phone and start creating! Paint, build, dance, write...
- Practise team activities. Sport, debating, dance, board games, scouts.
- Identify changes as they happen in your day and list all the positives.
- You don't need a badge! Practise leading through small daily behaviours.
- Practise creating and sticking to a schedule to build time discipline.
- Ask questions, find what you're passionate about be curious to learn!

E5.6.1

What is your future of work?
Think of 3 potential career pathways and explore what exactly attracts you to that career, and how you could approach it.

Thinking about all your different career preferences, what skills do they all have in common? While your career pathway might change, having a set of skills that are transferable will be invaluable.

Challenge: Think of 15 or more skills!

On top of technology influences, it's predicted that Aussie's are likely to change jobs and careers more times than ever before in the decades to come. This doubles the importance of focusing on skills that will be relevant across your working life. These skills will help you engage in the world of work regardless of how your career changes.

This resource is great to se which skills are required for different jobs

What are the **three** top skills you're most excited to work on? What's one thing every week that you can do to begin this learning journey.

Skill 1

Skill 2

Skill 3

Pathways Beyond Being "Employed"

Being an employee has many pros and cons. It's worth considering the other options available to you in this modern world of work! This chapter is about general awareness... Don't sweat the details just yet.

Traditional Employment

Traditional employment is often the first thing that comes to mind when considering your future. This is where you're employed by an employer, are paid a salary, earn Superannuation, and have the general rights of being an employee.

You can be a Full-time, Part-time or Casual employee

Pros
- Less personal admin
- Stable income
- Paid Leave
- Employee Benefits
- Super guarantee
- Support of Employer
- Less responsibility (sometimes).

Cons
- Potential Boredom
- Limited income Potential
- Limited job security
- Limited input in what you do in your job
- Limited control over who you work with

"Working for yourself"

Working for yourself" is a broad way to describe a number of different working structures, including...

Independent Contractor

This is when you work for another person or company to complete contract-based jobs. You work via your own **ABN** (Australian Business Number) and invoice the 'employer' for your time. A few key features:
- The working relationship is very much an employee / employer dynamic
- The employer is able to dictate how and when you complete the job
- You can choose to accept or decline contracts
- You have to organise your own tax and admin
- You don't get paid super or any other employee benefits.

Self-Employed Owner

This is where you run a business selling products or services to customers under your own **ABN**. This is very much your own business where you:
- Decide what to sell, to who and how
- Have control over every aspect of your work
- Have to organise your own tax and admin obligations
- Don't get paid super or any other employee benefits
- Are legally responsible for all aspects of the business including debts and losses
- Can keep all the profits

Company Owner

This is a formal step-up from being a Self-Employed owner, where you formalise the business into a company, register for an ACN (Australian Company Number) and become an 'Equity Owner'. This is quite an involved topic, but a few key features include:
- The company's way of work is completely within the owner(s)' control.
- As an owner of the company, you can choose to take a salary or be paid profit dividends.
- You have to organise company tax & admin obligations AND your personal tax & admin obligations

Pros
- Greater freedom of how & when you work
- Larger earning potential
- More scope for creativity & control
- Personal growth

Cons
- Less certainty
- Source your own clients & income
- More responsibility
- Much more admin
- Mentally challenging
- Requires proactivity
- work/life blended

As the saying goes, "All roads lead to Rome". Your dream career can be approached through multiple, if not *all* of these avenues. For example, if you wanted to work as a Vet... You can be employed at a Vet Clinic, you could 'freelance' your services to different clinics as an independent contractor, or you could run your own Vet clinic!

The "gig-economy" is steadily growing, where individuals have various skills which they learn and then leverage to create multiple different income streams. It's worth being aware of how a side-hustle works!

E5.7.1 **What is your preferred pathway?**
Consider each pathway, what are your thoughts on each?

Employee

I like...	I don't like...

Independent Contractor

I like...	I don't like...

Self-Employed Owner

I like...	I don't like...

Company Owner

I like...	I don't like...

Do you have any side-hustle or business ideas that you would like to explore over the next few years? Would it work best as a contractor / self-employed owner or company model?

How Does Wealth Building Work?

"Building Wealth" is a term that you'll hear many times over your financial journey... But it's more than just getting a good job or having a side-hustle. Let's explore what it actually means and how you can begin to lay down the right foundations. There are four big parts to the equation...

Why is '**growing your savings**' first in the process? Because wealth building has very little to do with simply making more money. Wealth is the result of good saving, budgeting and investing habits... These key behaviours don't magically appear once you have more money!

4 Increasing your Earnings

The final part of wealth building is increasing your earnings. This could include strategies such as...
- Focusing on career progression to increase your salary
- Starting a side-hustle or business for extra cash
- Building freelance skills in a particular domain to be able to increase your income as you need to!
- Working as a contractor to be able to charge higher project rates
- Starting a business or company to attempt to take charge of removing your income ceiling.

1 Mastering your Savings

Building good budgeting and savings habits is a key part of wealth building. To break this down, you need to master the art of:
- Setting Savings Goals
- Creating a budgeting plan to strategise how to meet these goals
- Sticking to these plans and goals (tapping into delayed gratification!)
- Making your savings 'untouchable' to be able to accumulate and grow your savings

This is the foundational piece to be able to pool together the money you need to pursue further wealth building activities.

3 Tax minimising strategies

A key part of wealth building, (which is applicable across earning, saving and investing), is finding ways to make the most of financial rules and regulations, having them work in your favour. It can be as simple as making strategic tax deductions with the help of an accountant, all the way to more complex activities such as purchasing investment properties for tax benefits, or creating a 'trust' for your assets and investments. If none of this made *any* sense to you... Don't worry one bit. This is the more complex component of wealth building and isn't particularly relevant for the average person until much later in your journey.

2 Investing your Savings

Once you have mastered the art of saving, now is when you find investment opportunities to allow these savings to grow! Check out the investment chapter to learn more.

The key takeaway here, is that you don't need thousands or even hundreds of dollars to begin this investment journey. There are investment options that allow you to invest a few dollars at a time. Once you begin working with larger quantities of money or have larger investment goals, this is when you might consider talking to a professional (such as a financial advisor), or, investing in more investment education.

What can you start doing today?

Building wealth may seem like a daunting or far-away concept. It's simply about taking tiny steps that eventually amount to big progress. The two most important steps you can take today are:
- Building good savings habits
- Learn about investing, the options available to you, and how to get started

Think about your situation!
What are some steps you can take today to begin working towards up-skilling in each area. It can be the tiniest of steps!

4 Increasing your Earnings

Write 3 actionable steps you can take in each are!

1 Mastering your Savings

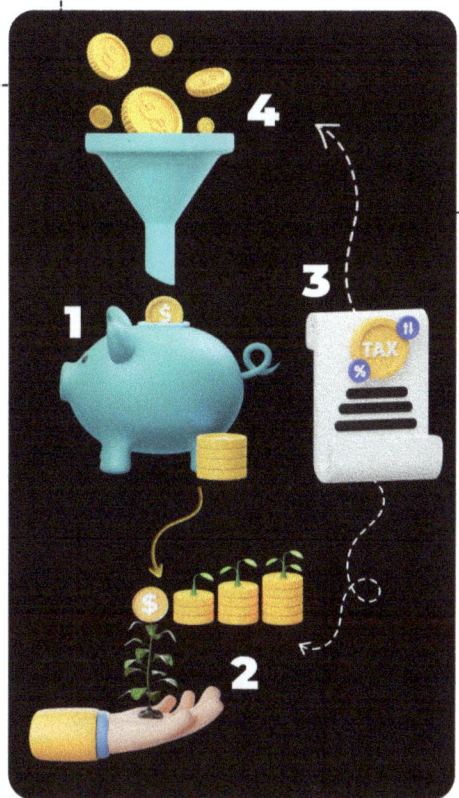

3 Tax minimising strategies

2 Investing your Savings

Why is important for you to build wealth?
Think about your purpose, goals and values.

Key Money Pieces Of The Employment Puzzle

Landing a new job is great, but did you know the dollar amount you agree to when you sign the dotted line is NOT what shows up in your bank account? Crazy right? Not to fear - this is completely normal. In this chapter, we'll explain why that is, and where all the rest goes.

Think of 3 different buckets that collect money every time you get paid. These three buckets are superannuation, tax, and your bank account. To illustrate how the buckets work, we'll track a single dollar of your earnings as we go.

% on top of $ → **Super**

% of $ → **Tax**

$ the rest → **Bank**

Super

Let's start with superannuation (or 'Super', for short). There's a bit to the whole concept, but in short, it's your own personal retirement fund - money will find its way here more or less from when you start working all the way up until you retire. The cool part is that your employer is obligated by the super guarantee to contribute to your Super ON TOP OF your agreed earnings. This means if your employer guarantees 10%, they will be putting 10c into your Super, and you get to keep all of your $1!

Tax

The second bucket is tax. This is the not-so-fun news: tax is the amount of your pay that goes to the Government, and is used to pay for things such as schools and roads. How much goes into this bucket? That depends on how much you earn each pay-check. Income tax, HECS repayment, Medicare Levy all fall in this general 'tax' bucket.

Bank

This leads us into the final and most exciting bucket; your bank account. This is the amount left over after the other buckets have received their portion. The great thing about this one, is you're free to spend or invest this money however you please! We call this 'post-tax income'.

Careful! Sometimes your 'advertised' rate can include super (to make the salary appear more attractive). More on this in the super chapter!

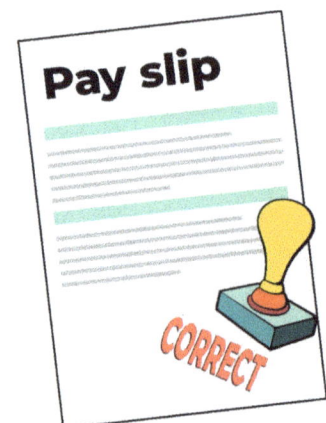

Pay slip

CORRECT

In summary, it's important to be aware of these buckets as this will help you understand where your money is going, and how much of it you'll end up with. This will help you keep track of your money, be able to accurately plan and make sure you're being paid fairly by your employer!

Consider this hypothetical scenario:
- *You work 8 hours a week*
- *You earn $20 an hour*
- *You are paid monthly*
- *The Super rate is 10%*
- *The Tax rate is 20%*

How much goes into each bucket of Super, Tax and bank Account this month?

% on top of $

% of $

$ the rest

Super

Tax

Bank

Nailing Your Admin Obligations When Starting A New Job

Landed a new job? Mintos! But wait a second - before you don the Bunnings green apron and talk about their low prices on TV, you'll first need to fill out some paperwork. In this chapter, we'll cover the three main forms you'll need to complete. These are:

- Tax Form
- Super Form
- Bank details Form

1 Your TFN is a bit like your tax passport

Firstly, tax. To fill in your tax form, you'll need your TFN, or Tax File Number. This number is similar to a passport, being your personal reference number in the tax and superannuation systems. The good news is that getting one is super easy. Simply hop on to the Australian Tax Office's website and follow the instructions. It can take a few days or weeks to get processed, but once you have one, your TFN is yours for life. Make sure to keep it super private!

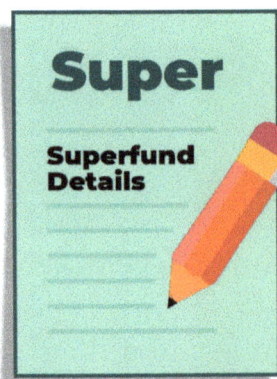

Tax

Tax File Number

TFN: 123 456 789

2 A super fund looks after your retirement savings

Secondly, Superannuation. To fill in your Super form, you'll need the name and details of your 'Superfund'. What's that, you ask? In simple terms, a Superfund is the business you pick to look after your retirement savings that your employer pays you. Providing your details to your employer will allow them to pay that money straight to your super fund account. You can choose the fund you like best, but if you've never had Super before, not to worry! Your employer can set up your Super with a fund of their choosing.

Super

Superfund Details

3 Your bank account details are how you get paid!

Lastly, your bank details. On your contract, there will be a section to fill out your personal details - including your bank account details so your employer knows where to send money to. These details include your BSB and bank account number, which you can find by logging onto your banking portal, or looking at any bank statements you have lying around. And this might seem silly to say, but it's pretty important to note that your bank account details, are not the same as your bank card details - The former is how you get paid, the latter is how you do the paying. It's worth not getting the two mixed up!

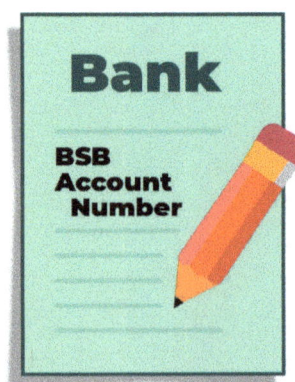

Bank

BSB Account Number

Your bank account details are how you get paid

BSB: 123456
ACC: 12345678   vs

Your bank card details are how you pay

Beyond these key three details, certain jobs may need additional information, such as a responsible service of alcohol licence, forklift licence, or a driver's licence. It's not the end of the world if you don't have all these details accessible on day one, but you likely won't get paid until you get these forms filled out.

When you start a new job...
What are the key details you need to provide when you start a new job?

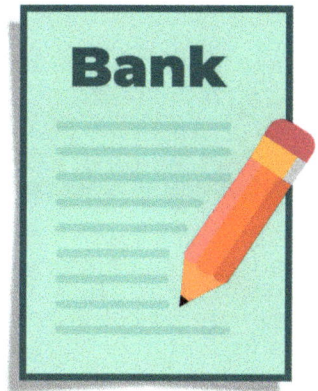

Super

Tax

Bank

Which key details do you need to provide your employer in each of these categories?

Super

Tax

Bank

Where can you find each of these details when you need them? (No, the answer is not "ask my parents"!)

Extra Q: Where will you store these key (private) details?

How To Interpret Your PaySlip

Picture this - you've just finished your first week at work and received your first payslip. However, you're a little confused as to how you managed to go from your agreed pay rate... To what's been paid to your bank account. Not to worry, in this chapter we'll break down a standard payslip from top to bottom.

The 5 Key Elements...

Firstly, your payslip should list particulars such as your personal details, to ensure they're paying the right person the right amount, and the 'pay period'. This is the period of time you've worked to earn the pay packet. For some, this may be just a week; for others, a month. This will be agreed and discussed with your employer when you first sign your contract.

Next up is the breakdown of your "gross pay". This sounds dramatic, but your gross pay is simply the amount you've earnt in the period, before any fancy maths is applied or anything is deducted. Unfortunately, it's not the amount that actually makes it to your bank account! It's important to check that this number is accurate, though, as it's the basis for the rest of the information on the payslip.

After gross pay is your employer's Super contribution, which tells you how much money was sent to your Superfund. In unfortunate situations, employers can take advantage of their young workers and not pay their Super correctly, so it's always a good idea to check that you're getting what you're owed. Make sure you're aware of the super rate and the eligibility criteria to qualify for this super.

After Super comes tax. If you're an employee, this is known as PAYG or pay-as-you-go tax, and it tells you how much of your gross pay, has been paid by your employer, to the tax office. This amount will depend on how much you've earned and other information you would have provided when filling out your tax form when starting your job.

Payslip

Pay Period: June 2022
Pay Date: July 1st

Employer: Mandy Money
ABN: 123 456 789
Employee name: Alex Simon
Employee status: Part-Time

Earnings:

	Unit	Rate	Total
Hours Worked Week 1	40	$20	$800
Hours Worked Week 2	20	$20	$400
Hours Worked Week 3	40	$20	$800
Hours Worked Week 4	20	$20	$400
Gross Monthly Payment			$2400

Super Contribution:

Superannuation <10%>	$240

Deductions:

Taxation (PAYG)	$168

Net Payment — $2232

Many payslips stop here. However, depending on the kind of job you have, there may be reimbursements, bonuses, benefits, or other uncommon payments mentioned here. If you believe your role entitles you to any additional payments, it's important to check here to ensure these have been included in your payslip.

And finally, we arrive at net pay. Net pay is your gross pay minus tax and other deductions (and plus any reimbursements). This is the amount that will end up finding its way to your bank account. Delish.

Fill in the blanks...
The best way to figure out how to understand a payslip, is to build one! Give it a go by figuring out each of the key line items.

Payslip

Pay Period: June 2022
Pay Date: July 1st

Employer: Mandy Money
ABN: 123 456 789
Employee name: Alex Simon
Employee status: Part-Time

Gross Monthly Payment (Before Tax & Super)

Earnings:

	Unit	Rate	Total
Hours Worked Week 1	40	$18	$?
Hours Worked Week 2	20	$18	$?
Hours Worked Week 3	40	$18	$?
Hours Worked Week 4	20	$18	$?
Gross Monthly Payment			**?**

Super Contribution:

Superannuation <10%>	**?**

Super (10%)

Deductions:

Taxation (PAYG) <20%>	**?**

Tax (20%)

Super

Tax

Net Payment	**?**

Bank

Net Payment

Why do you calculate super before you calculate the PAYG tax amount?

Red Flags to Spot Before Signing Your Job Contract

Job contracts come in all shapes and sizes, so it's a good idea to know what you're signing up for. In this c, we'll dive into three key things to check before you sign your contract and how they'll impact you and your financial situation.

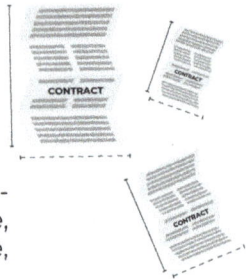

1 Legal employment structure

Firstly, you should be aware of whether your position is casual, contract, part-time, or full-time. The actual work can be similar regardless of the structure, but your rights are slightly different, and you'll be paid differently in each case, so there are some quick differences that you should remember:

- If you're a part-time or full-time worker, pay is usually based on an hourly or annual salary outlined in your Employment Agreement, your employer takes care of your super and tax, and you're entitled to annual leave.
- If you're a casual worker, you're paid what is typically a slightly higher hourly, to compensate for what are likely irregular hours, and the fact that you're not entitled to paid leave.
- In the case of a contractor (or sole trader or self-employed) your employer is not obligated to provide Super, paid leave, nor pay tax on your behalf. This leaves you with a lot of responsibility (like paying your own tax)! However, it can allow you a bit more flexibility... You set your own price and working terms, given you're not technically an employee.

Part / Full time	Casual	Contract
✓ Salary	✓ Hourly wage (+casual loading)	✓ Set fee or hourly
✓ Super	✓ Super	✗ Super
✓ PAYG Tax	✓ PAYG Tax	✗ PAYG Tax
✓ Paid Leave	✗ Paid leave	✗ Paid Leave

There are a few more nuances to each structure, so it's worth researching which one is right for you.

2 Award Rate

The second concept to be aware of is the 'award rate'. This tells you what category of worker you fall into, and hence what your minimum wage will be. It's important to ensure you're in the right category - and, if you don't fit into any award category, be aware that the national minimum wage will apply to you.

3 Super inclusivity

Thirdly, it's always important to be aware of the rate of pay, especially when it comes to being inclusive or exclusive of Super. While - technically - Super is calculated on top of your wage, some employers will advertise a pay rate with Super included to make it seem more attractive. This isn't illegal, but it's important to be aware of this before you get a shock looking at your first payslip.

exclusive

$30 + $3 = $33 total

$30 hourly (10% Super)

$27.27 + $2.72 = $30 total

inclusive

A few other things to be aware of are the other main entitlements and constraints of your contract such as your leave entitlements, probation period, and any special terms around resigning or leaving a contract early. If you're unsure, just ask: your employer should always be happy to keep things above board. As you progress in your career, checking your contract will become more and more important. For a part-time or casual job, there may not even be a formal contract. If this is the case, make sure you understand the terms of your employment clearly!

E5.12.1

Apply your knowledge:
Read these job descriptions and match them up to the right type of employment style!

The project I've been assigned to is really cool. Even though the last one wasn't as fun, I like that my hours are regular and I have a certain number of days each year to go on holiday while getting paid. It's also super easy because my boss pays my tax on my behalf and puts money into my super.

I enjoy the company I work with because I'm working on a project where I have total creative control, and am charging a price that I chose. It's good that I am able to set a high price for my work because I have to save up for my super, any leave I take, and tax I'll have to pay at the end of the year.

I really like my job, as my work is quite flexible and every week has different hours. I get to spend all my spare time relaxing as my employer takes care of paying my tax on my behalf, and contributing to my super. I can't take too much time off though because I don't get paid if I don't work.

What kind of employment structure do I work under?

What kind of employment structure do I work under?

What kind of employment structure do I work under?

Which of these is most compatible with your current life stage and work objectives?

EMPLOYMENT

A space for your notes, questions, plans!

INVESTING

Learn about investing as a concept, the details of investing in shares, and how you can get involved!

Lesson 1
Introduction to Investing

- [ ] **1** What Actually Is Investing?
- [ ] **2** Calculating Investment Returns
- [ ] **3** Risk Versus Return
- [ ] **4** Active & Passive Investing Styles

Lesson 2
Share Investing Basics

- [ ] **1** Share Basics
- [ ] **2** Share Income Mechanisms
- [ ] **3** How And Where to Buy Shares
- [ ] **4** Investment Research

Lesson 3
Investing Application

- [ ] **1** Understanding Diversification
- [ ] **2** Actively And Passively Managed Funds
- [ ] **3** Ethical Investment
- [ ] **4** Investing For Your Future

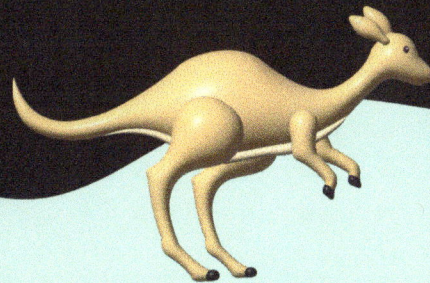

What Actually Is Investing?

Investing is a SUPER broad term. There are so many different types of investments with different purposes and different income mechanisms. In this chapter, we'll explore the underlying fundamentals. To begin, investing refers broadly to placing your money in what we call 'assets' (in other words, buying an investment). The hope is, that the value of these assets, and hence your money, will grow over time!

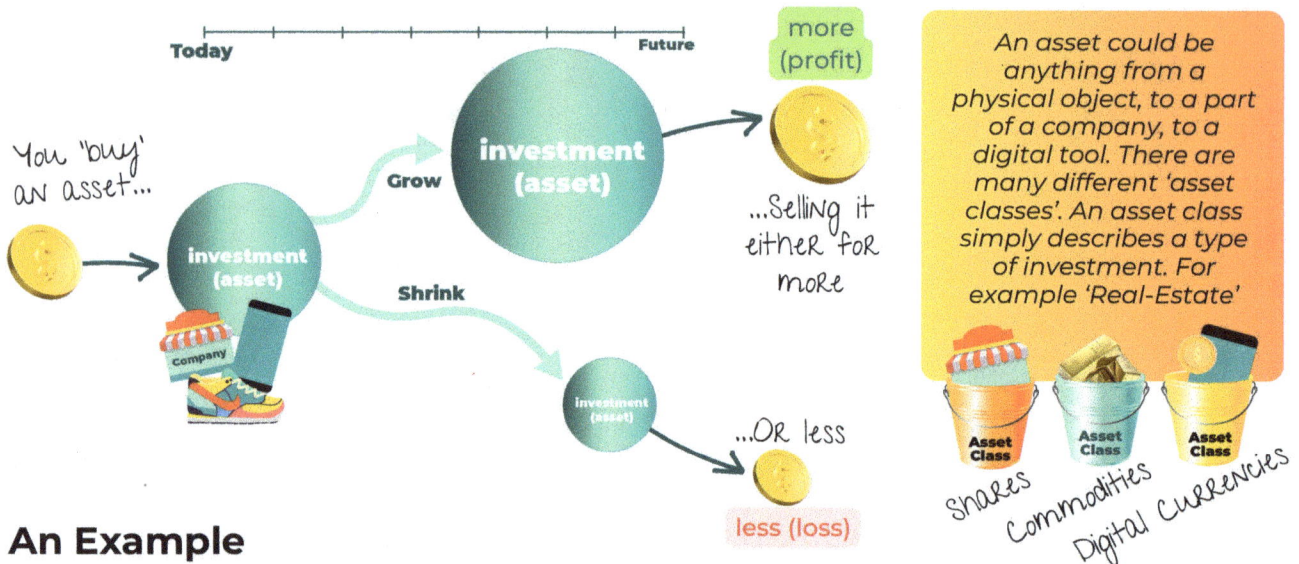

Today ———————— Future

You 'buy' an asset...

investment (asset)

Grow

investment (asset)

Shrink

investment (asset)

more (profit)

...Selling it either for more

...Or less

less (loss)

An asset could be anything from a physical object, to a part of a company, to a digital tool. There are many different 'asset classes'. An asset class simply describes a type of investment. For example 'Real-Estate'

Asset Class — Shares
Asset Class — Commodities
Asset Class — Digital Currencies

An Example

Let's say you've bought a bar of gold which is considered an investment. While you own the bar, more wonderful properties of gold might be discovered by scientists, so gold might become more valuable. This means you'll be able to sell it for more than you paid; a profit. Or maybe, they've discovered how to manufacture gold artificially, so it becomes more accessible and hence gold decreases in value. Now when you sell, you would have lost money. The art of investing is very much being able to understand what makes an asset grow or shrink in value.

Is this how all investments work?

The above example explains 'Capital Gains', which is a very common method by which investments work. You also have investments that work by earning interest. Interest is basically a 'thank you' gift that gets given to you when you lend your money to someone.
In a real life context; you put your money in a savings account or term deposit, and you're technically 'lending' your money to the bank. They then return interest to you.

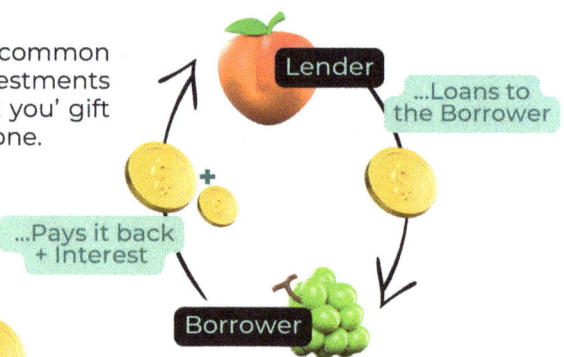

Lender

...Loans to the Borrower

...Pays it back + Interest

Borrower

Capital Gains

- Shares
- Real Estate
- Digital Currencies
- Currencies
- Exchange Traded Fund
- Commodities
- Funds (Active & Passive)

Interest Earning

- Term Deposits
- Saving Accounts
- Bonds

Most common investments tap into either (or sometimes both) of these mechanisms. There are also more creative mechanisms for some investments which you'll run into. For example, real estate can earn you money through renters living in your house and paying rent. Or, shares can earn you money by paying you dividends (covered later in this topic). You don't need to know all of these investments in detail... In fact, most people only ever invest in one or two different types. It's just good to be aware of what's out there!

16.1.1 Research each of these common types of investments...

Match the definitions to the correct investment type, and then match the example investment to the correct type!

Definitions

A. This is a type of investment that you typically need a large amount of money upfront, and involves the purchase, management and sale or rental of this asset.

B. This type of investment involves buying a part of a company, and as the value of the company changes, the value of your investment changes.

C. This is typically a raw product that is mined and used to build or create things. Its value is influenced by how much of it is available and how many people are buying it.

D. These are investments that can easily be converted back to cash that you can spend. They call them 'liquid' investments.

E. You buy this investment from a foreign country in hopes that it will strengthen disproportionately to your country's version of it. There are also digital versions!

F. This is a group of investments managed by a third party.

Examples	Type	Definition + Examples
Environmental **Exchange Traded Fund**	**Currencies**	Definition + Examples
A Savings **Account**	**Commodities**	Definition + Examples
A Crypto **Coin**	**'Cash' Investments**	Definition + Examples
Oil		
Diamonds		
Tech Company **Stock**	**Funds**	Definition + Examples
Gold		
An Actively Managed **Fund**	**Real Estate**	Definition + Examples
A Swiss **Franc**		
A Term **Deposit**	**Shares (stocks)**	Definition + Examples
An Investment **property**		

How To Tell Whether An Investment Is Successful

Understanding how well an asset is performing will help you determine which investments are worth buying, keeping or selling. In this chapter, let's figure out how to calculate investment returns.

First, what do we mean by a return? Put simply, a 'return' is the profit or loss you get back from an investment. It's a really important metric you'll hear whenever people talk about investing.

"A metric used to understand the profitability of an investment"

An Example

Let's say you made an $100 initial investment a year ago, and that investment has increased in value to $110 now that you've sold it. The difference between $110 and $100 is $10; thus, you have just made a positive return of $10.

But there's a flip side to this coin. There's almost always a chance you could make a loss on an investment. This happens when the money you get back from an investment is lower than the money you put in. For example, if you put in $100 and only get back $90, you have a $10 loss on your hands: in other words, a negative return.

Final Number	−	Initial Investment	=	Profit or Loss	Return

$110 − $100 = $10 (profit) **+10%**

$90 − $100 = $10 (loss) **−10%**

While you get full $110 back, you don't count the $100 you initially put in as 'return', since that was money you already had. You only count the extra $10 gained.

To calculate the percentage return, follow this simple formula:
- Take the return dollar amount...
- Divide it by your initial investment...
- Multiply x 100.

When we talk about returns, we get mathematical: we use percentages to describe them. Why's that? It's because it puts everything on a level playing field, which makes it easier to compare your investments...

An Example

Consider you made two investments, A & B. If A gave you a $50 return and B gave you a $90 return, which investment is more profitable? Surely it has to be B, right?

In dollar terms, perhaps... but what if investment A costs $100 and investment B cost $1000? Well, then we'd argue that A had the more profitable investment... You doubled your money.

	Profit	Initial Investment	Return
A	$50	$100	50% 👑
vs			vs
B	$90 👑	$1000	9%

Not quite convinced? Let's level the playing field and put $1000 into each of A and B. By these numbers, A would return you a groovy $500 profit, whereas B is still stuck at $90.

The bottom line... If we were to look at the dollar return exclusively, the result can be misleading. To solve this issue, we use percentages.

Compare the pair!
Using percentages, which of the following
investments provide a better return?

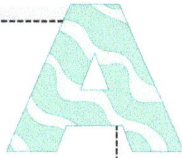
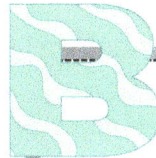

A $500 return on a
$10,000 investment

A $200 return on a
$2,000 investment

If you invested $1000 at the start of the year, and at the end of the year sold
your investment for $800... What was your percentage return on investment?

$1000

$800

If you then, the next year, invested that $800 and sold your investment for $1000 at
the end of that year... What was your percentage return on investment?

$800

$1000

Figuring Out The Risk Of An Investment

If you were to step foot in an Investing 101 class, you probably wouldn't last more than a couple of minutes without hearing about both 'risk' and 'return'. The two concepts have a super tight relationship, let's dive right in, taking a closer look at risk first.

Risk refers both to the potential size of a loss, and the potential likelihood of making a loss on your investment. Obviously, you're hoping for a profit whenever you're investing, but we know that doesn't always happen. So this is where knowing the risk is vital through answering questions like:

Size of risk

+

Likelihood of risk

> "If this investment goes sideways, **how much** money could I lose? **How likely** is it that to occur?"

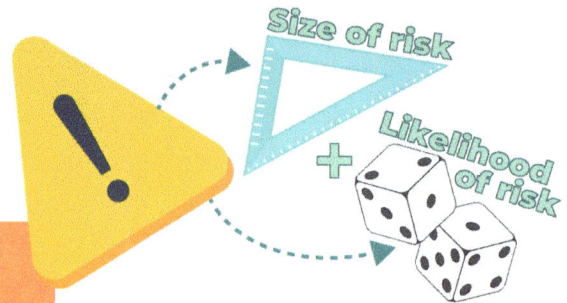

Risk by itself doesn't sound so fun. So, where does return come into the picture? In the world of investing and finance, the concepts of risk and return go inseparably hand-in-hand. The greater return you expect or are targeting on an investment, the greater the risk is. This relationship almost always holds true, and there is a tonne of science to explore here, but we'll try and explain it intuitively with a couple of examples.

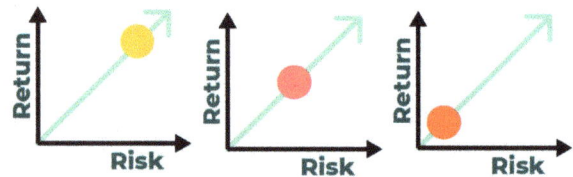

An Example

Let's take, for example, we can imagine an early-stage startup with an idea that could potentially revolutionise its industry. If you could invest in it by buying shares, its success could land you a jackpot.

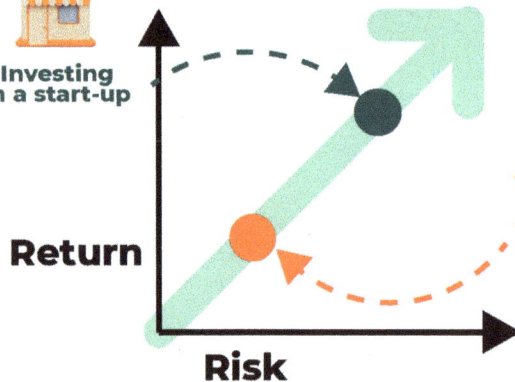

STORE

Investing in a start-up

Return

Risk

A savings account at a bank

THE BIG IF

But, that is a very big IF; there are many hurdles and barriers to cross before success, and it might fail at any one of them. So, we say it's high risk because success isn't guaranteed at all (and, the likelihood exists that that you'll end up losing everything!). But, in the event that it does go stratospheric, there are some healthy returns in store for you. Generally speaking, the higher the risk, the higher the expected return.

On the other end of the spectrum, money sitting in your savings account. Over time, it maybe grows a bit when the bank pays you interest. There is very little chance you will lose that money while it's sitting there, (unless the bank goes belly-up). There is also virtually no chance for it hitting a home run on the profit front. It's low risk, but it's also low return.

Since we apply the logic that increased return is linked with increased risk across all potential investments, we are left with a diagram that looks something like this:

Your Investment

Return

Risk

Assess the risk...
The following stocks have different returns and different risks to consider... Place them on the risk vs return graph!

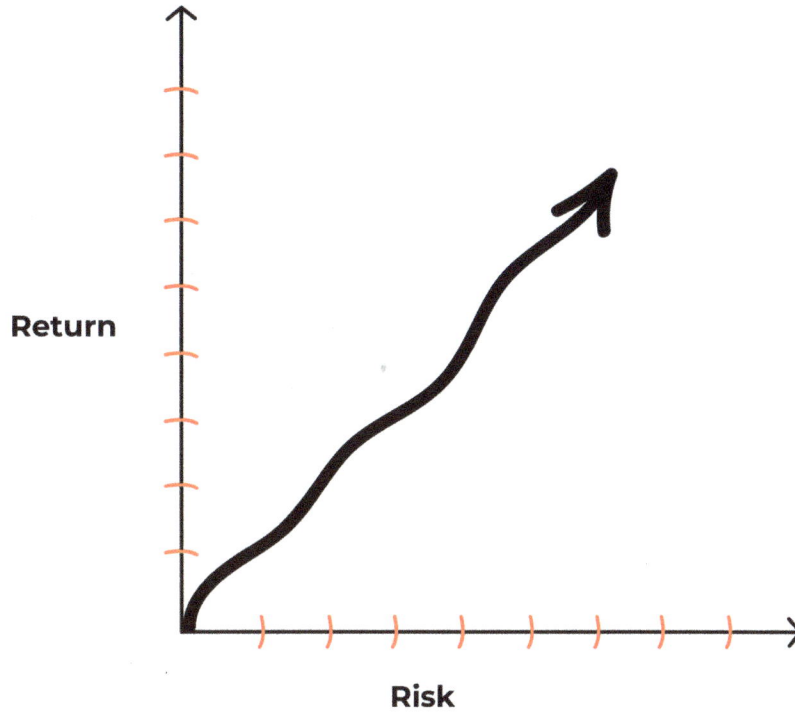

Return

Risk

A

5 year old business which returned 15% last year

B

Crypto Currency which returned 200% last year

C

Savings account which returned 1% last year

D

Large Bluechip Stock which returned 5% last year

Explain why you placed each of them in their chosen spot!

A	B	C	D

Types Of 'Investor' Styles

Investing is bit like baking a cake... you can make it as complex or simple as you like, so before you turn on the oven, it's worth considering what sort of investment style you want to take. In this chapter, we'll explore two of the main umbrella terms for investment styles: active and passive.

✦ Active investing

First up, we have active investing. This is all about a hands-on approach - constantly researching, buying, and selling. Active investors intention is to 'beat the market' by identifying new stocks and locking in their profits as soon as possible - sometimes trading up to multiple times a day. This can be a full-on job, and in many cases, a full-time job. It's not for the faint-of-heart: it requires lots of time, attention, and technical knowledge, as well as a love of reading the news and keeping up with markets.

✦ Passive investing

For a change of pace, the second approach is passive investing. This is a much more hands-off approach: it may look like picking a share market, industry, or group of stocks you like, then sitting back and letting the market do its thing.

The Theory...

You might hear a passive investor saying that "time 'in' the market" is much more important than "'timing' the market". They believe in the theory that economies and share markets cycle through their expansion, peak, recession, and recovery stages over a number of years, but will (hopefully) go up in the long run.

A passive investor's portfolio will still fluctuate in value – sometimes pretty wildly – on a day-to-day basis, but they try to think long-term rather than become phased by daily movements.

"Timing" the Market
Active investing

Time "in" the Market
Passive investing

It's critical to remember that as with all investments, past performance is not an indicator of future success. There is always an element of risk when relying on theories such as this - although it's a widely accepted theory, always expect the unexpected!

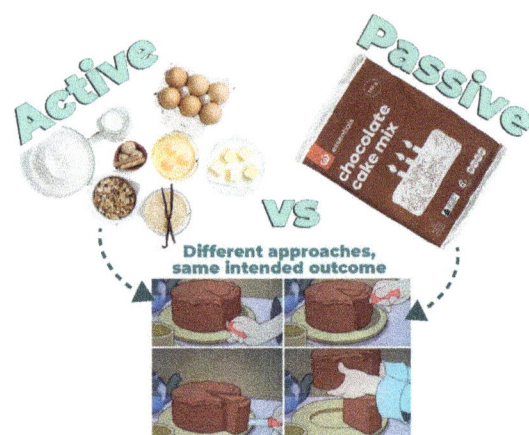

Different approaches, same intended outcome

Which investing style to pick?

Well, if you were making a cake and were picking between finding your own recipe or just going with the packet mix option, your choice might depend on how much you like baking, how much time you have for it, and whether you're any good at it!

If you're not much of a baker, the packet mix might be a friendlier learning curve. Or, if you're really keen to hang out in the kitchen, there's nothing stopping you from trying your hand at baking both kinds of cakes! Try one or both styles of investing and make a decision based on your results plus what you enjoyed the most!

Match these thought bubbles to the right investor!
What kind of investing thoughts might someone with an active investing style have, compared to someone with a passive style?

A
"I want to beat the market"

B
"I want to time the market"

C
"I'm more concerned with time *in* the market"

E
"I check finance news often"

D
"I want to buy low and sell high"

F
"I care more about long term market cycles"

G
"I anticipate and react to stock price changes"

H
"I don't pay too much attention to small movements in the market"

Active

Passive

Both

What Are Shares And The Share Market?

One of the most common investment types you'll run into are shares, or stocks. In this chapter, we'll give you the 101 on shares and the share-market.

To begin, all companies have owners. Being an owner means having a 'share' in the business. That's all shares really are: they're a certain amount of ownership stake in a company. If you own a share, you are typically a tiny-part owner of that company. the more shares you have, the larger the amount of the company you own.

Being part-owner gives you a claim to the assets and profits made by the company. Essentially, whatever the company owns or makes, you get to have a bit of that. Not bad, hey? Let's say the company owns a building; you own a small part of that building. If the company makes a profit, you might get a bit of that too. It's a strange concept to get your head around, as you don't really buy or own anything physical, but bear with us!

Multiple Owners

a Share

The "Share-Market"

Here's where we introduce the share-market. The share-market refers to a few different concepts. At a basic level, it's where buyers and sellers of shares transact; a marketplace of sorts, but for publicly listed shares.

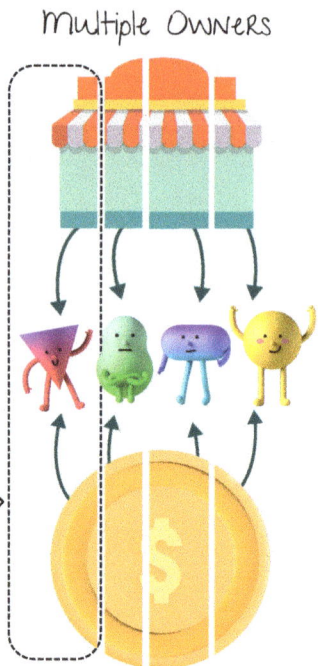

Australian Stock Exchange

Sellers → **Buyers**

Imagine sellers listing their goods and buyers going shopping for what they need, (except instead of old shoes or watches, it's shares).
- A seller looking to 'exit' or sell their investment will list their shares on the market for a specific price.
- A buyer will browse the market looking for shares at a certain price.
- When there's a match, the transaction is automatic!

Not just a place...

Confusingly, the term "share-market" is also synonymous for all the shares being traded on that market. Whenever you here, "the share-market fell 1% today", they're referring to the value of all the companies on that market (or all markets) dropping in price by 1% on average. It's like saying "BeeBay fell 1%" after seeing that on average, items on the BeeBay market are being sold for 1% less than yesterday.

It's an abstract concept, but it does help to think of the share-market as not only the marketplace where shares are bought and sold, but also the value of all the shares traded in that market.

Australian Stock Exchange market performance

+1%

Marketplace for listed shares

Reference to the value of all those shares

Tying it together

There are many different share-markets around the world. A company can only list their shares on a single share-market. If you want to buy a particular share, you need to use a stock-broking platform that gives you access to that share-market. Here's a visual that describes the relationship between each different component.

Share Market

A B C D E   F G H I J   K L M N O   P Q R S T

Shares listed on the Share market

Access to certain share market

Stock Broking Platform

"The Market"

16.5.1 So many names!

Stock exchange, stock market, equity market, share-markets, shares, stocks, share trading platform... Confusing! Label the diagram and answer the questions that refer to it.

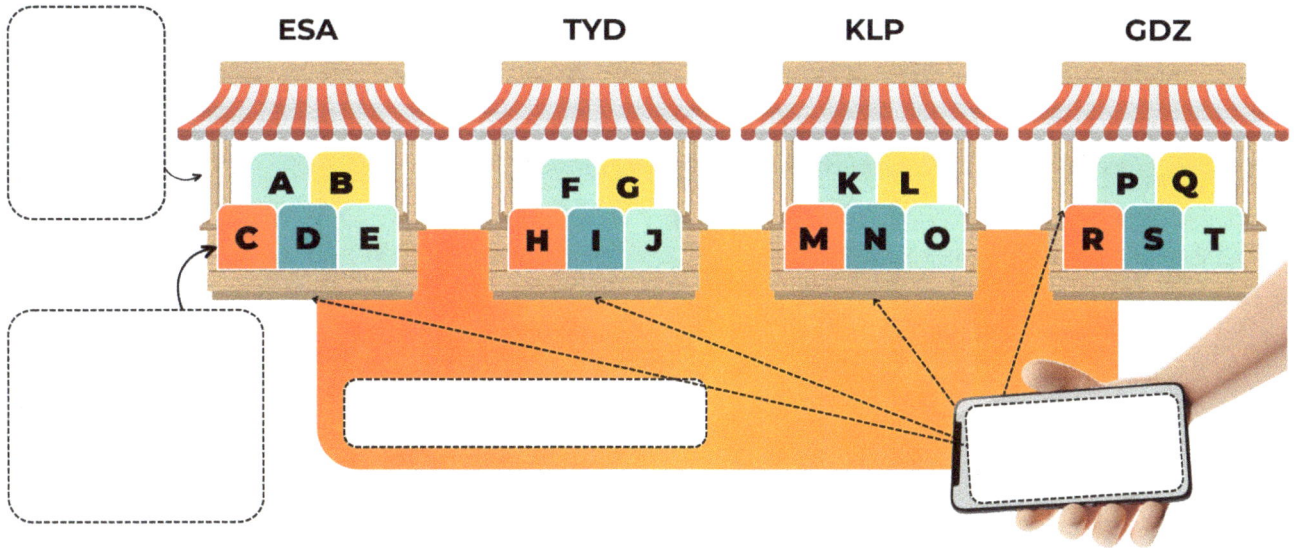

ESA   **TYD**   **KLP**   **GDZ**

A B   F G   K L   P Q
C D E   H I J   M N O   R S T

I want to buy a single share of company "M". Which share-market is it listed on?

After I bought it, company M's sales profits suddenly increased and the value of company M went up by 10%. By how many percent did the price of my share change?

I heard on the news that the KLP market has risen by 1%, what does this mean?

I heard on the news that markets have fallen by 1%, what does this mean?

What shares can I buy on the share-market called "TYD"?

Using which tool can I buy these shares?

How Can Shares Earn You Money?

You own a share to earn a return and eventually make a profit, right? So the question is, how do you actually make money? There are two distinct ways to make money off shares.

- Number one is capital gains
- Number two is dividends

Buy $1
Sell $5

1 Capital Gains

Capital gains simply refers to the profit you make by selling shares for a higher price than what you initially bought them for. Of course, the opposite can also happen, where the share price drops and you have to sell below your purchase price - that's a capital loss.

2 Dividends

Let's dive into the second type of earnings, dividends. Dividends are what we call a company's profit paid out to shareholders. What does this actually mean? Over the course of doing business, a company will hopefully make a profit. Some of this money will go back into the business to help it grow, while the rest is paid out to the shareholders.

As an example, let's say a company just made a a $100m profit. Instead of re-investing into the business, they choose to pay it out as dividends to shareholders (share owners)...

If the company has 100 million shares, each share will be entitled to a $1 dividend.

$100 million profit

$100 million profit / 100 million shares

= *dividend amount of* **$1**

So if you own one share, you will receive $1. And if you own 100 shares, you will receive $100; And the cool part, that's cash right into your bank account!

1 share
$1 *dividend*

100 shares
$100 *in dividends*

Why might a company they want to do this?

Unless you're a fast-growing tech business with serious capital gain potential, you're going to need to convince investors that buying your shares is worth their while!, Routinely giving shareholders dividends can be a way to incentivise them to invest their money in your business.

Invest in us!
Fast growing tech business with **Capital Gain** potential!

VS

Invest in us!
Stable bluechip **dividend paying company!**

Which to choose?

That's entirely up to you, your investing style and objectives. If you're looking for some serious growth and are happy to wait to cash in potential gains in several years... you might prefer companies that re-invest all their profits into growth and don't give out dividends as frequently. If you're after a regular income source through shares, though, you might look for companies that pay out regular dividends.

Regardless of what shares you end up with, you have to keep the tax man in mind. Any profit you make from your shares must be declared as taxable income. Make sure you know what tax will be waiting for you when you earn dividends or sell your investments!

Growth Investing

Income Investing

A little bit of maths!
Referring back to the chapter on investment
returns if you need, answer these three questions!

- The $20 stock (A) you bought for capital gains has gone up 10%
- The $20 bluechip stock (B) you bought has gone up 0% after paying you a $2 dividend...

Which share has gained you a bigger return?

- You own 10 shares in Company A.
- They have decided to pay their profits ($2,000,000) to their shareholders.
- There are 2,000,000 shares they need to distribute dividends to.

How much is each dividend worth, and how much are you getting paid in dividends?

Why might a person prefer dividends-paying shares of high growth shares? Can you think of a particular person in your life that likely owns some shares like this?

What type of investing are you more inclined towards? Why?

How And Where To Buy Shares

So you've done your research, and now want to purchase your shares! Exciting! In this chapter, we'll explore the ins and outs of choosing an online brokerage platform.

First up, What's a broker? Well, brokers act as 'middle person' to facilitate the dynamic market of buying and selling stocks - with thousands of trades being executed every second. Back in the day, if you said the word 'broker', you'd be referring to an actual person (think Wall Street, fancy suits) who would physically organise the exchange. Now, brokers are usually online platforms that allow you to trade by yourself. Here's a look at how a brokerage platform fits into the puzzle.

> Stock brokers still exist in modern day! Rather than perform the physical stock transaction, they focus on the strategy side of investing, and helping clients with more complicated investments.

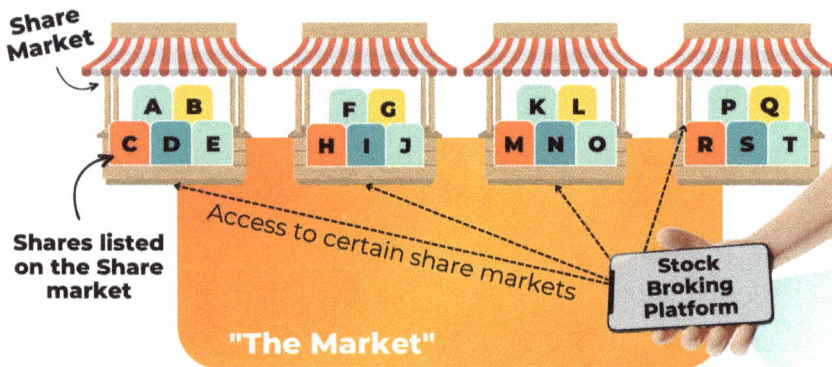

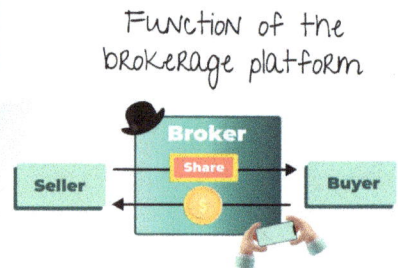

Share Market

A B C D E   F G H I J   K L M N O   P Q R S T

Shares listed on the Share market

Access to certain share markets

Stock Broking Platform

"The Market"

Function of the brokerage platform

Broker
Seller — Share — Buyer

Which Brokerage Platform To Choose?

So where do you find these online brokerage platforms? What do they look like? Well, there are a whole range of brokerage apps and websites out there, including those provided by the big banks. To make up your mind, here are a few things to look out for when you're picking a platform:

1 Fees

Firstly, fees. Each platform will have a different fee structure...
- Sometimes it will be a flat rate, like a subscription.
- Sometimes it will be a fixed or percentage-based fee for every trade.
- Sometimes you'll even find a platform that makes trading free after a certain number of trades.

It's important to think about how many trades you'll be making, how often, and which fee structure makes the most financial sense!

2 Market Access

Secondly, market access. A company decides to list their shares on a particular 'stock exchanges', like the Australian Stock Exchange or the New York Stock Exchange. Not all platforms will allow you access to every exchange. If you're interested in buying overseas tech companies, you'll want to make sure the platform lets you do this before signing up!

3 Consumer Service

Thirdly, customer service. You're trusting these platforms to handle a lot of your money, so it's worth researching whether the platform has a good reputation for helping customers when things go wrong!

There are plenty of other factors, but these are a good set to start off with. Weigh up your needs against the services each brokerage platform offers. Then, once you've picked a platform, it's simply a case of signing up and making your first investment!

16.7.1

Pros and Cons!
Consider the following three investment platforms and choose one that represents the factors that are important to you! Justify why you've chosen the one you have.

	Platform A	Platform B	Platform C
Fees	Low fees per trade	Monthly Subscription fees	High fees per trade
Market Access	Only has access to the Australian Stock Exchange	Access to the ASX & the New York Stock Exchange	Only has access to the New York Stock Exchange
Customer service	24/7, instant customer service	Slow customer service	OK customer service
Platform experience	Slow website and limited functionality	Easy to use website and app	Great to use, only available as an App

What's your choice? Why?

How To Research For Your Share Investments

It's time for the million-dollar question: which investments should you buy? Drumroll, please ...ah, unfortunately, if we could tell you what the future was going to hold, we'd be sailing around the Mediterranean on the mandy superyacht. All investments are uncertain, so there's no get-rich-quick secret sauce. That's not to say that you have to go in blind, though. Three words: research, research, and research. Conducting research is all about becoming an expert on the investment you're considering. In the case of share investments, this means really getting to know the company and its environment.

What to look for when researching?

Depending on your investing style and objectives, there are different research approaches you can take. However, there are areas of research which are key to consider in making your decision.

1 Company Performance

Taking a look at the numbers, are their financial results trending in a positive or negative direction? Are they outperforming their competitors? What does the news say about how they are doing?

2 Growth Prospects

What's happening in their industry? Can you see lots of potential for their products? Which factors in the wider environment might impact their growth?

3 Risk

Then, risk. If the company were to fail in the next few years, why would it be? Are there government regulations or other hurdles they'll struggle to get over?

Some good places to kick off your research might include...

- Company annual reports
- Financial news
- Professional reports
- Information provided by your brokerage platform

Factors you might also consider...

External Environment	Internal Environment	Personal Preferences
☐ Industry Trends	☐ Company leaders	☐ Your investment objectives
☐ Industry Predictions	☐ Vision & strategy	☐ Your ethical preferences
☐ Competitors	☐ Recent performance	☐ Your investor 'style'
☐ Regulations & Laws	☐ Innovation efforts	☐ Your budget
☐ Social Trends	☐ Customer reviews	☐ Your risk appetite

Both an art and a science!

Choosing investments largely involves learning how to interpret factors in and around an investment. This involves using creative thinking to predict how a factor will impact the company in the near and distant future. There are endless possible outcomes, which makes it such an interesting exercise.

For example, consider a company that owns a water reservoir.

As the country is heading into a drought period, you might expect the value of this company (and their shares) to go down... They'll have less water to sell, right? The opposite perspective is... Because there's less water, there's higher demand, and people are willing to pay more. Because the price of their water goes up, the company value might then also go up. But then! If the drought continued, and people could not longer afford to pay as much for water, so they started buying less and less... Then the value of the company might go down!

Please don't let the overwhelm of research keep you from investing!
- Explore pre-selected investment funds (up next!)
- Read the news to see what seasoned investors are investing in
- Start with companies that you know and interact with everyday

Meet FoodCo...
This is an independent analysis of the company. Looking at key categories, note down your findings, both good and bad!

FoodCo Analysis Report

This report takes a closer look at "FoodCo," a 10 year old food company operating in the food distribution industry. The industry is relatively stable due to demand, however faces risks of changing tax laws, environmental changes and unexpected events. Industry. is predicted to grow in line with population growth.

FoodCo's recent financial performance is impressive, with a 10% increase in share value last year (currently, $30 per share).

The company is led by CEO Bailey May, who is a young leader with little experience in the industry, but is well respected and liked by staff.

FoodCo aims to be a leader in providing healthy and eco-friendly food. Achieving this goal requires continuous investment in innovation, as many trends can be challenging to adapt to.

FoodCo's focus on innovation is praiseworthy, but the food industry is competitive. Other companies are also trying to be innovative, making it challenging to stand out.

The food industry has many big competitors. Despite FoodCo's strengths, they operate in a competitive industry with many new businesses starting each year. They currently have 30% marketshare.

FoodCo is committed to eco-friendly practices, but these sustainability efforts have increased operational costs, lowering profits. Balancing ethics with financial stability has been a challenge.

Despite this, customers have given FoodCo positive reviews for its delicious food and ethical practices.

Industry Trends

Industry Predictions

Competitors

Regulations & Laws

Social Trends

Company leaders

Vision & strategy

Recent performance

Innovation efforts

Customer reviews

Write is a single sentence summary of your findings and whether you would invest!

Building a Diverse Investment Portfolio

You've heard the cliche about not putting all your eggs in one basket, and it turns out the same idea is applied in the world of investing! Introducing, portfolio diversification...

"Diversification is an investing mechanism used to decrease risk. The aim is to make your overall investment portfolio resistant to the fluctuations of individual investments".

"A portfolio is a collection of financial investments"

'Diversifying your portfolio' simply means means buying and holding a variety of diverse investments."

An Example

For example, you buy shares in ten different companies. One day, one of the companies you've invested in suddenly goes bankrupt. You won't be happy when you see the news - but you have 9 other companies that are hopefully doing ok, so your entire portfolio isn't lost!

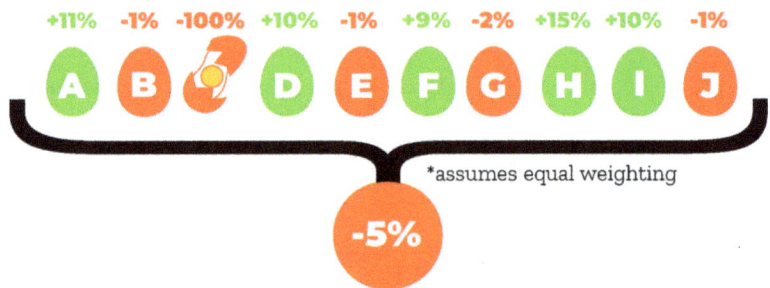

+11% -1% -100% +10% -1% +9% -2% +15% +10% -1%

A B ● D E F G H I J

*assumes equal weighting

-5%

But, buying different companies isn't the only way to diversify. You can diversify within an asset class, like our example with multiple different companies, or you can diversify across asset classes.

Let's say your investments include stocks, bonds, and cash; then, if the share-market crashed by 20%, you won't necessarily lose 20% of your total investment. Maybe the bonds rose 10% at the same time, steadying your overall portfolio return.

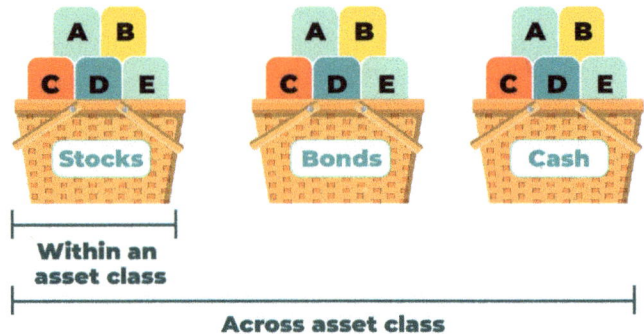

A B
C D E
Stocks

A B
C D E
Bonds

A B
C D E
Cash

Within an asset class

Across asset class

Continued...

The catch with diversification is that it limits your potential positive returns as well. For example, just because one of your investments went up by 20% doesn't mean your investment portfolio will skyrocket by 20%.

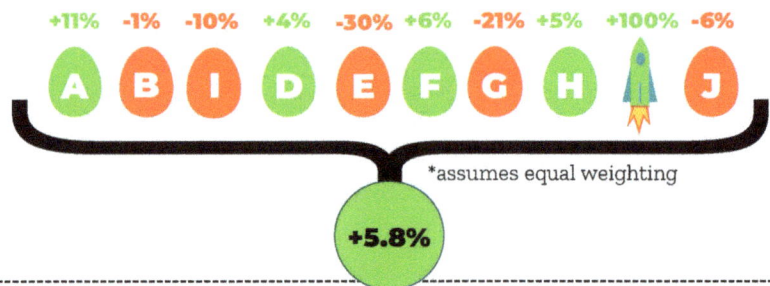

+11% -1% -10% +4% -30% +6% -21% +5% +100% -6%

A B I D E F G H 🚀 J

*assumes equal weighting

+5.8%

So how do you go about it? Let's look at two ways you can do this.

1 First is homemade diversity. It's basically where you select your own individual investments. Again, there is a tonne of science involved here, so it's worth consulting a professional.

2 The second option is to buy pre-diversified investment packages. These are broadly what we call 'funds'. There are many different kinds of funds, but the primary characteristic is that they host a number of different investments which are intended to achieve an element of diversity.

Diversifying your portfolio doesn't take away the risk, but when done correctly, can shield you from volatility. However you choose or don't choose to diversify your portfolio, it's worth talking to a professional to get their two cents.

16.9.1 **Diverse... Or not?**
Order the following investment portfolios from most to least diverse. Explain why you've placed them there!

| A | 3 different investment properties in Australia | C | ETF'S, gold, property |

| B | A mix of ETF's and shares. | D | 10 different shares of companies from different industries |

MOST DIVERSE

1 ●

● 2

3 ●

● 4

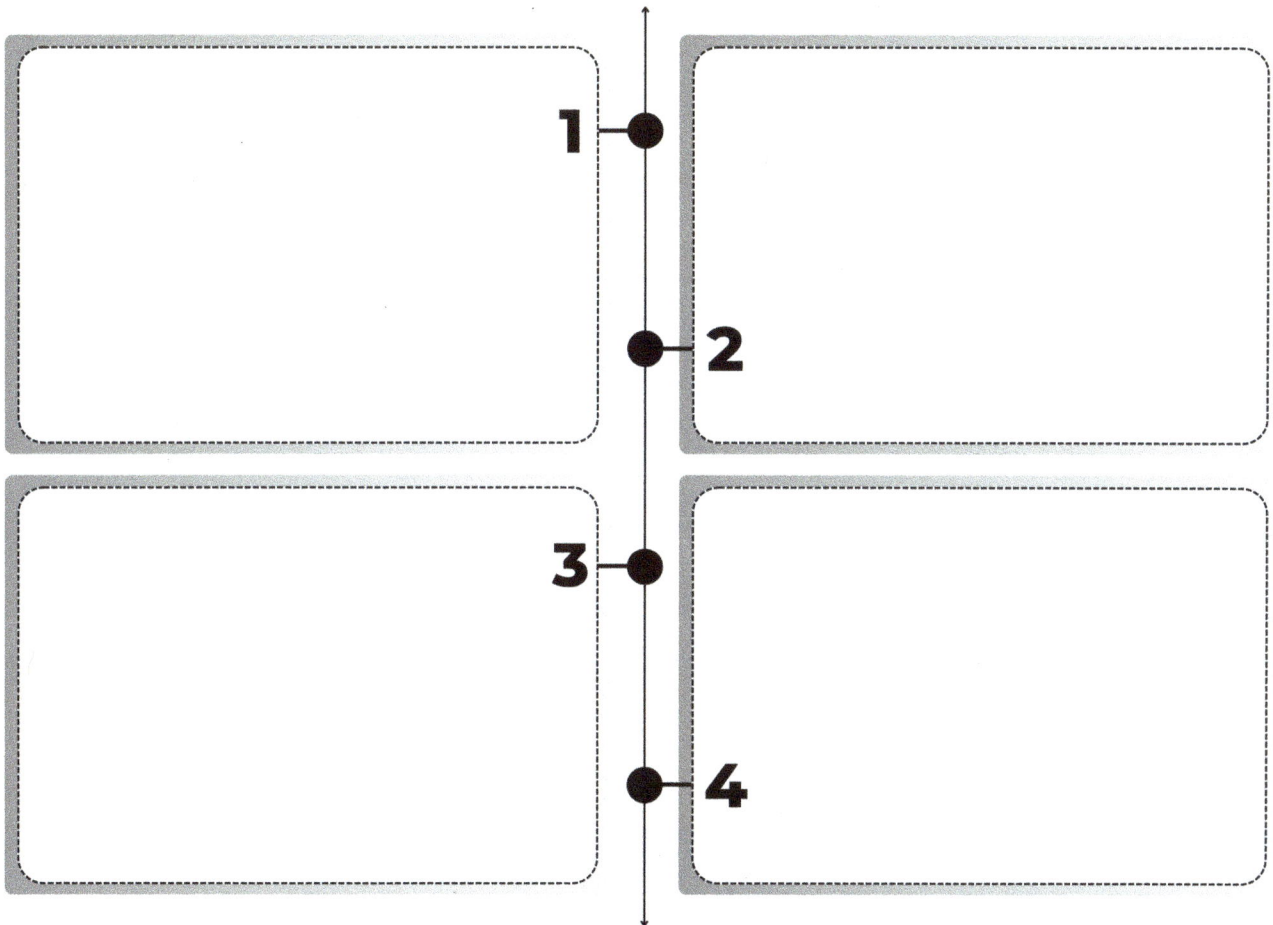

LEAST DIVERSE

Why do you think ETF's are considered as 'pre-made diversification'

Making The Most Of Investment Funds

Buying individual investments can be a great strategy to build out a portfolio. However, you can also buy into professionally selected investment packages called 'funds'. It's as if someone has designed a diverse portfolio for you! There are the two broad categories of funds: actively and passively managed funds.

1 Passive funds

Let's start with passive funds. These funds involve a bundle of shares (or other investments) selected according to a specific characteristic. *For example, the largest 200 companies in Australia. Or, 100 companies in the renewable energy sector.* Then you can buy that group of shares for a fraction of the price & admin! The buying process is similar to buying a single share on the share market, not 200 or 100 individual shares.

Individual Shares

$50 + $60 + $50 + $70 + $50 + $70

Total cost = $350

VS

You only get a fraction of each share, but you get exposure to all of them!

A B C D E F Fund

Total cost = $100

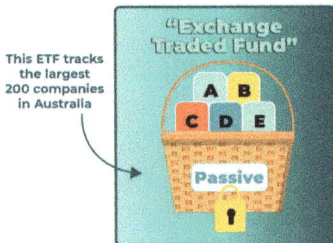

This ETF tracks the largest 200 companies in Australia

"Exchange Traded Fund"

A B C D E Passive

The key with passive funds is that they are passively managed, meaning that once the shares are grouped, they only change according to the "metric they track". In plain english: If the fund tracks the 200 largest companies in Australia... When that list changes, the list of companies captured within the fund changes.

An example is an "Exchange Traded Fund". Note that not all ETF's are passively managed, and not all Passive funds are ETF's!

2 Active Funds

For our second category, active funds. Taking the idea of a diversified fund a step further... Active funds often include a variety of asset classes. Yet, the key difference is that they are managed by fund managers who constantly research and change the investments within the fund, to make sure they're capturing the best performing investments available.

The intention here is to outperform passively managed funds. However, while they have the potential to outperform passively managed funds, their management fees are also typically higher.

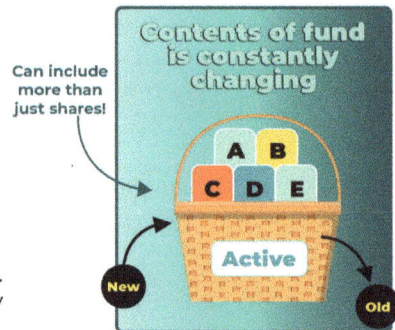

Can include more than just shares!

Contents of fund is constantly changing

A B C D E Active

New / Old

Passives simply "track" the market

A B C D E Passive

Actives try to "beat" the market

New / Active / Old

Higher fees

When you compare net returns **after fees**, actively managed funds aren't always better.

Buying actively managed funds is also a bit less straightforward. Because each fund is managed by an independent party, they are often not available to buy on the share market. You need to research to find individual funds and purchase via their individual buying processes and rules that they have in place.

Which is better?

It's your call! Consider your investing preferences and objectives to make a decision. Now that you have information on both fund options, go explore what's out there and figure out what could be right for you!

Passive Funds	Active Funds
Typically Lower returns	Typically Higher Returns
Typically Higher Fees	Typically Lower Fees
Simpler buying process	Less simple buying process

Comparing active and passive funds...
You need to compare their 'net return', which basically means returns after fees have been deducted. Which Investment has gained you a larger return? A or B?

Investment A: The **actively** managed fund.
- You have invested $100
- It has grown 10% the past year
- It charges $5 a year in fees

Investment B: The **passively** managed fund.
- You have invested $100
- It has grown 7% the past year
- It has $2 a year in fees

Investing With An Ethical Compass

Investing in a company by buying their shares is a way to support that company. Supporting their growth helps both what they do as a business, and the industry they operate in. But how do you know whether you're supporting the right businesses?

Now, traditionally speaking, investing has been typically focused purely on financial metrics, looking only at the profit potential of an investment. For example, if you were trying to buy into an ETF fund tracking the top 200 companies on the ASX, it's unlikely that you'd delve into each of those companies to understand whether their values align with yours or not.

Ethical Investing

However, there is a growing trend for investors to align investment choices with their values, which has led to the concept of ethical investment becoming a popular way to guide the modern investor's decisions.

a New factor in the investment selection process!

Invest → According to growth potential

But, how? *There are four typical ways by which you can approach ethical investing.*

1 Negative

Negative screening.
This involves excluding industries that you don't want to support from your portfolio. These could include weapons, tobacco, alcohol, gambling, or products which involve animal cruelty.

2 Positive

Positive screening.
This means actively seeking out companies that are trying to make a difference, and supporting their missions by investing in them. These could include companies in the renewable energy, education, and healthcare industries, amongst others.

3 ESG

ESG integration.
This involves considering different Environmental, Social and Governance factors. For example, when investing in a coal mining company, an ESG-centred approach would see them find an coal company with really good environmental standards, and one that treats its employees well.

4 Impact

Impact investing.
This refers to looking for companies whose business operations are focused on solving some of the world's biggest challenges. These are companies that have an impact at the core of their mission.

It's important to note that everyone's values are different, and that no single investment is black-and-white, ethical or non-ethical. This means it's up to you to figure out what 'ethical' means to you, and to make sure your investments align with this.

Consider your own ethical compass...
What's important to you ethically when making an investment? Is there a value that isn't on this wheel?

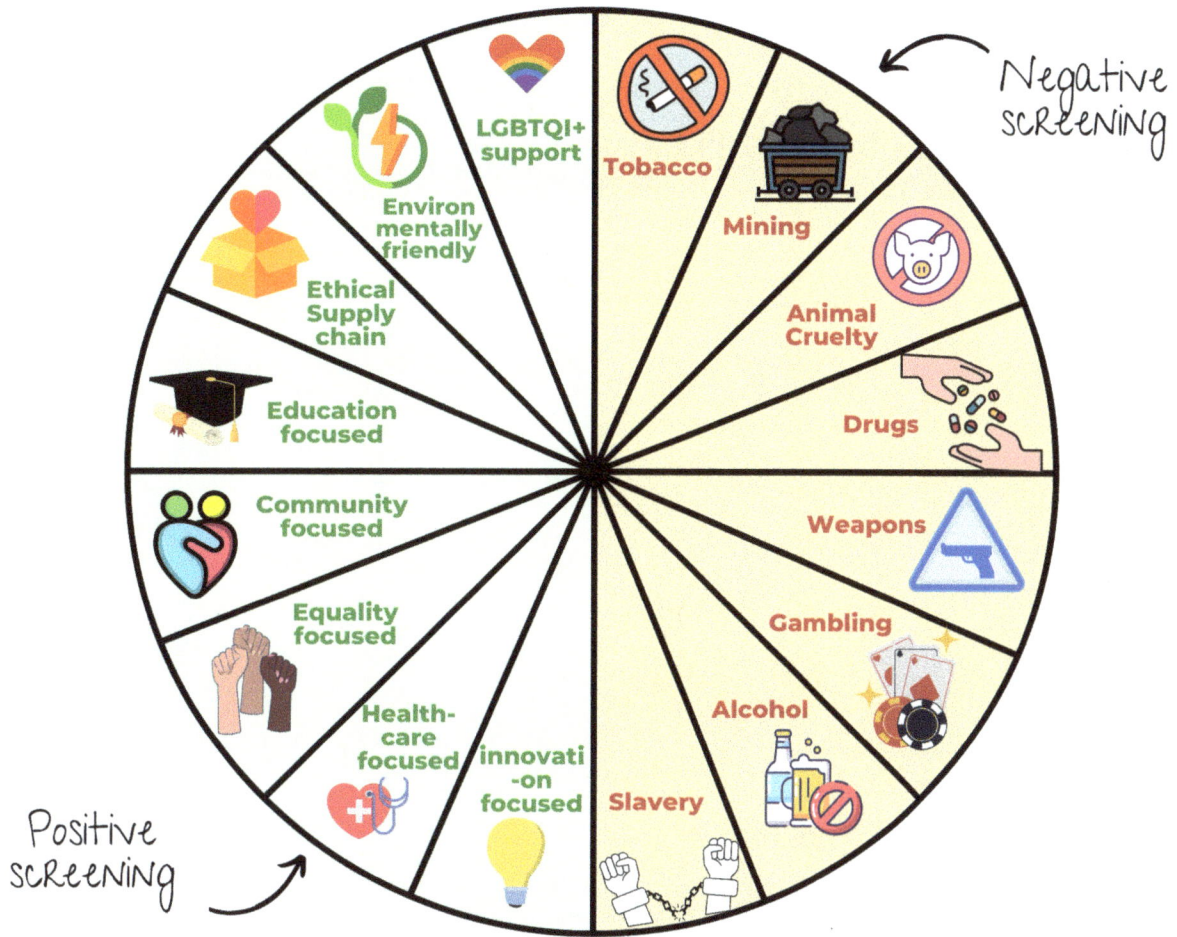

Negative screening

Positive screening

Pick your top 3 ethical values, and find examples of stocks (or other investments) that aligns with these values!

Value:

Example Investment:

Value:

Example Investment:

Value:

Example Investment:

Investing For Now And For Your Future

Investing is much more than meets the eye, and much more than just buying shares. It's a tool that is yours to use as you like, to achieve different objectives. Here is a wide-angled look at how investing plays a role in creating your dream future, both now as a high school student, and later in life.

Investing as a high school student

When you're at high school, there are limited investing options available to you... Partially because you have to be 18+ to purchase most investments, and partially because many investments require a larger amount of money to get started. This is ok! Before you turn 18, the goal is to simply learn as much as you can, learn how to talk about and interact with the concepts, and get comfortable. There are many steps you can take towards building skills as an under 18 investor...

Grow investment savings pool

Arguably the hardest part of investing is building the savings habits which enable it. Begin that savings journey today by...
- Building good savings habits
- Growing a dedicated savings pool to invest when you turn 18

Get your parents on board

Your parents are able to invest on your behalf in most cases. This includes buying shares, investing into funds and opening term deposits. If, you feel comfortable, this could be an option to explore.

Read the news & try simulation games

A big part of investing is being aware of the world around you and how your investment is likely to react to it. Start wrapping your head around the world (of investing!).

Invest in available options

At 14, you can open a savings account at most banks. Here, you can earn interest on your savings, a less risky option to begin with!

Investing once you're 18

Once you're 18, the (investing) world is your oyster. This is great but can also be overwhelming! **The only way about it, is to get started**. Find an investment option that you understand, feel comfortable with, and lets you invest with your budget. Then, take the leap! It could be an option towards the lower risk end (eg. a term deposit). Or it could be something where most of the decisions have been made for you (eg. an ETF or other fund). Or, it could be a share in your favourite company because you believe in their vision. Begin small, begin scrappy, begin intimidated... the key word here: **BEGIN!**

Investing for the long-run

As you progress through your life journey, investing becomes more than simply a savings tool. Once you hit certain milestones, having the right strategy will become more relevant. With the help of a professional or the right education, different investment strategies can help you...

Grow your savings

Whether short or long-term, investing can help you grow your savings and build wealth

Tax Benefits

Certain investments, can help optimise your tax situation and save on your tax bill. Eg. trusts & real estate

Protect against inflation

As inflation grows, the power of your money shrinks. Investing helps you keep up with inflation.

Earn an Income

Some investments can pay you an income while your money stays invested. Eg. Dividend paying shares & real estate.

Investing is a mental game

A tricky part about starting to invest is the mental hurdle. It can feel risky and intimidating (rightfully so!). We are lucky to live in 2024, where there are many options which allow you to invest, for free, with tiny amounts of money. For example, some banks or funds have a feature which round up a few cents or dollars from each of your card purchases, and invest that 'round up' money. We call it spare change investing! Explore options which allow you to start small and build confidence from there!

16.12.1 **Make an action plan!**
There are many things you can do today to start you on the
right investing track. Use this space to create a plan!

Would you like to set a savings goals to have
an amount of money ready to invest when
you are 18? Use the S.M.A.R.T framework!

What action will you take to begin working
towards that savings goal?

Are there any educational resources can you
work through to understand investing
better?

Are there any simulation games or tools you
can use to give investing a trial run?

Are there any news sources you can dip into
which introduce you to the world of
investing?

Are there any beliefs or mental hurdles you
have about investing that you would like
begin tackling?

Are there any other tasks you would like to add to this plan?

INVESTING

A space for your notes, questions, plans!

Congrats!

You've completed the...

FUTURE FOCUSED
micro-credential

Mindset

Employment

Investing

To collect your certificate and resume badge...

1 Complete this knowledge quiz

2 Email **microcredential@mandymoney.com.au** with your **quiz ID number** and a photo of this page!

Get a parent, teacher or librarian to complete this!

tinyurl.com/22wdb7cj

I, _____, can confirm that
(First and last name of teacher)

_____ has completed the activities for
(First and last name of student)

this micro credential, to the best of their ability.

Signed: _____ Date: _____ Email: _____
(In case we need to check that you're real!)

SMART FOUNDATIONS

micro-credential

INTEREST

Learn about the concept of interest, its powerful (and dangerous) sides, and how it impacts you!

Lesson 1
Interest And The Economy

- [ ] **1** Interest Definition
- [ ] **2** Functions Of A Bank
- [ ] **3** Interest As An Inflation Driver
- [ ] **4** Interest Rate Determinants

Lesson 2
Financial Products

- [ ] **1** Financial Product Basics
- [ ] **2** Positive Return Financial Products
- [ ] **3** Negative Return Financial Products
- [ ] **4** The Changing Financial Product Landscape

Lesson 3
Compound Interest

- [ ] **1** Simple vs Compound Interest
- [ ] **2** Calculating Compound Interest
- [ ] **3** Double Edged Compounding Sword
- [ ] **4** Debt vs Invest Decisions

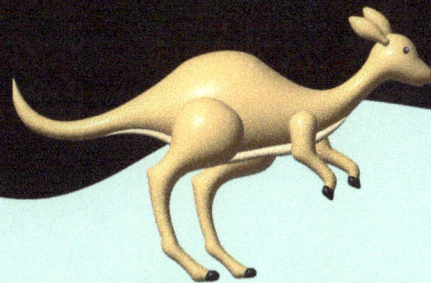

What Actually Is Interest?

Chances are you've come across the word "interest" in a number of different contexts. For example, "interest rate" or "interest free payments", but what does any of this actually mean? Interest manifests itself in many ways. It has the potential to have huge impacts to individuals like you and I, as well as the broader economy.

The word interest dates back to the early 16th century, to describe how much it costs to borrow money. Or, if you were the one lending the money, how much you would expect to earn when lending out your money.

IN other words →

> " the fee paid by a borrower to a lender "

You **Me**

The Broader Economy

An Example

Let's put ourselves in the shoes of a lender, as an example. You've signed up to a clothing hiring website, and you've listed a pair of shoes to lend out.

- Let's say the shoes are worth $100
- And the amount the users of this website pay you to borrow your shoes is $5.00

This $5.00 is effectively the interest you earned... by providing the shoes to a borrower. And it goes the other way: that same interest was paid by the borrower.

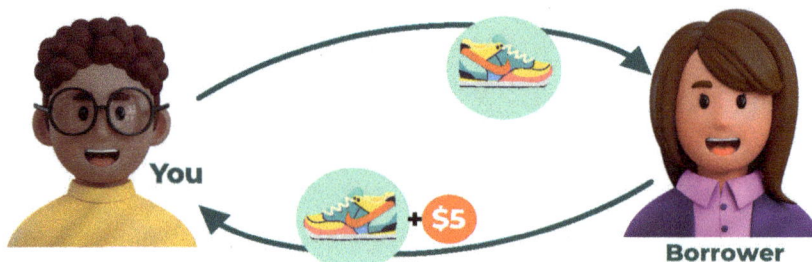

Clothing Hire

Shoes
RRP $100
Hire $5

You **Borrower**
+ $5

How to talk about Interest

Interest is generally referred to as percentages, being an **'interest rate'.** Interest rates are also typically referred to as an 'annual' interest rate, meaning the interest applies across one year.

An Example

- You borrow $100 from a lender
- They charge you $5.00 for the year.

This would be known as a **'5% per annum'** interest rate. You likely don't even need to specify annual, as it's usually assumed!

It's interesting to calculate the **'true cost'** of items when you add in the interest involved.

Going back to the shoe example, if you were to buy a $100 pair of shoes using your loan + 5% interest, the true cost of the shoes is actually $105... Then the question becomes, it might be worth $100, is it worth $105?

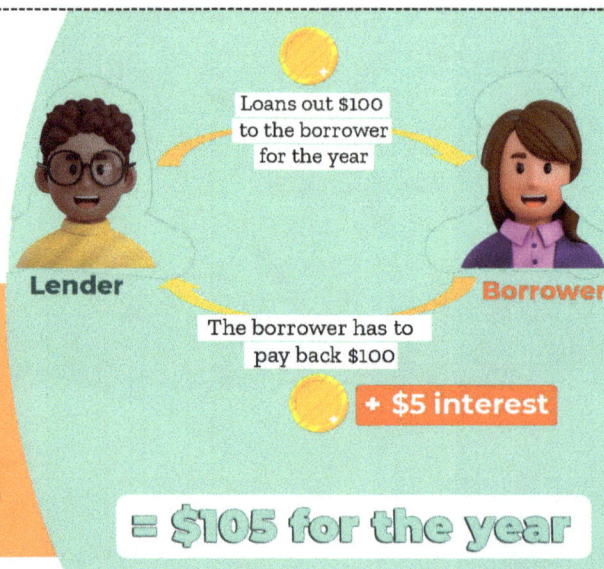

Lender **Borrower**

Loans out $100 to the borrower for the year

The borrower has to pay back $100

+ $5 interest

= $105 for the year

With this simple example, you can begin to see how interest has the potential to make purchases way more expensive than you might first think. However, you don't always have to be the one borrowing money - if you're lending, there's also an opportunity to make income.

Interesting...
Answer these quick questions about interest!

> If you borrow $90 and have to pay a total of $110 to the lender, how much interest are you paying?

> If you borrow $100 and have to pay 10% in interest for the year, how much will you be paying the lender in total?

> Why do you think a lender charges interest?
> Do you think it's an essential part of a loan?

> Can you think of any negative consequences or aspects of interest?

How Does A Bank Work?

The concept of paying interest is quite easy to understand in a real world context. You take out a loan, you pay interest. But when it comes to lending money and earning interest, that's a little bit more abstract. This is where we introduce the function of a bank.

Whether you're borrowing money to buy something new, starting a business or buying a house, you will, in many cases, be borrowing the money from a bank at a given interest rate. When you borrow this money, you will be repaying the loan plus interest.

One question might start to pop up - if everyone's borrowing from the bank, **where does the bank get its money?** Well there's a whole other side to the banking equation... and that's where *your* money comes into it.

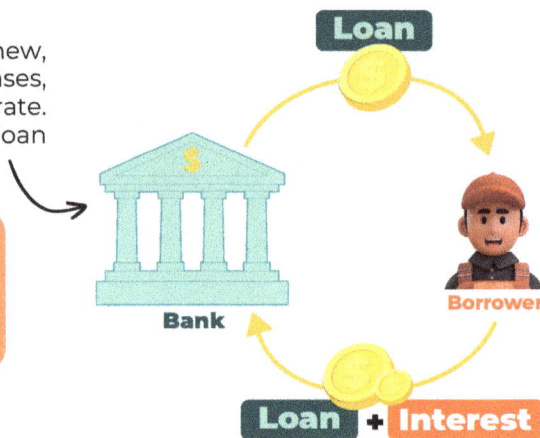

Loan

Bank

Borrower

Loan + **Interest**

The Two Sided Equation

When you deposit money in the bank, banks aren't just storing it for you! They're also using your money* to loan out to other banking customers. There's a little bit more complexity to this, but the core idea is that you have two sides...

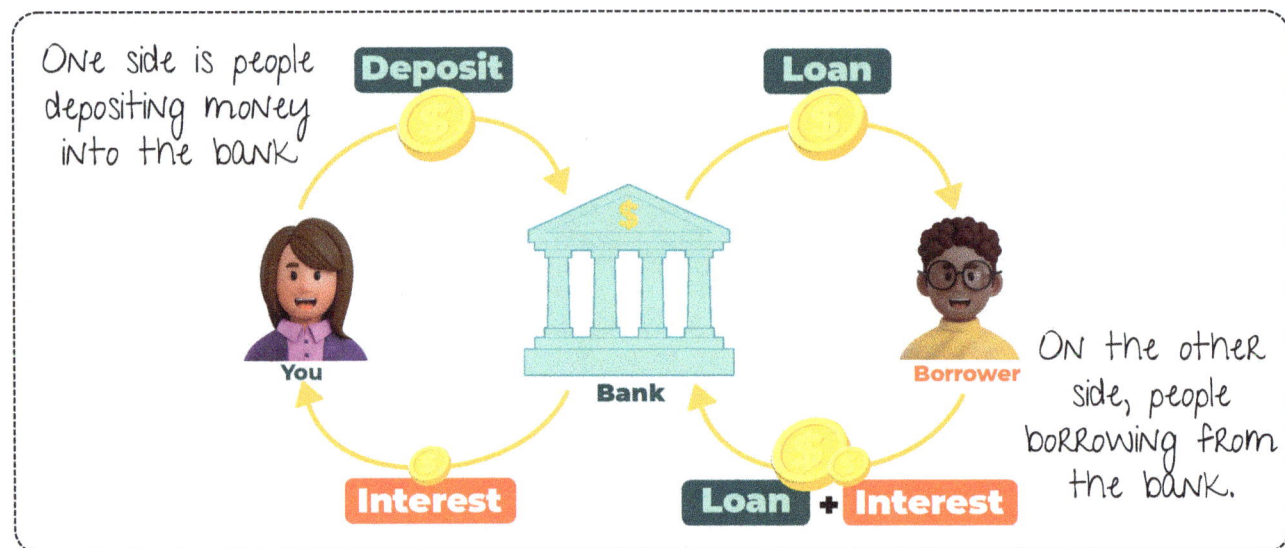

One side is people depositing money into the bank

Deposit

Loan

Bank

You

Borrower

On the other side, people borrowing from the bank.

Interest

Loan + **Interest**

How does the bank make money?

Where interest comes into this, is that those on the borrowing side, pay interest, and those on the lending or depositing side, get a little bit of that interest passed back onto them. Where the bank makes money from this model, is the difference between the interest they charge the borrower and the interest they pass back onto you*.
- If they're charging 5% for a lender...
- While offering you 1% on the money in your savings account...
- That's a 4% cut they're taking to keep the lights on (and keep doing what banks do).

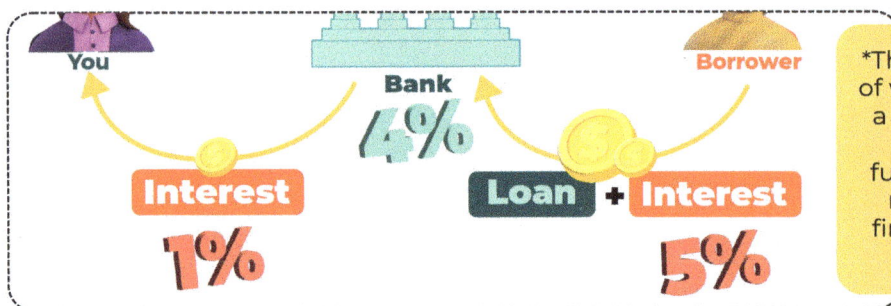

You

Bank
4%

Borrower

Interest
1%

Loan + **Interest**
5%

*This is an oversimplified version of what actually happens, but it's a good start! If you are curious, do some research into the function of a bank. If you find it really interesting, a career in finance or commerce could be an option to consider!

Which side of this diagram would you rather be on? Why?

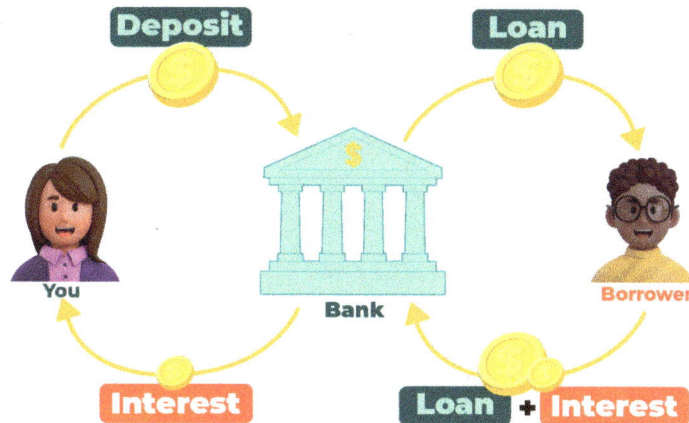

Can you think of any potential problems with this model? Is there potential for anything unfair or unethical to happen here?

How Do Interest Rates Impact Inflation?

Besides being a tool for personal finance, Interest plays a pivotal role in how an economy evolves and grows. Let's explore how different interest rates influence the economy.

1 High Interest Rates

First up... high interest rates. High interest rates make loans more expensive. People are likely to borrow less, and hence spend less. At the same time, it's worth saving more money because of the high interest you can earn. This all results in money being a bit more 'sticky' and doesn't move around the economy as fast. When borrowing slows, the economy also slows down.

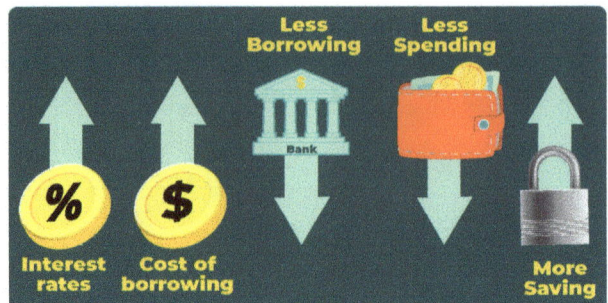

On the other side of the coin...

2 Low Interest Rates

When interest rates are low, borrowing becomes more affordable. This means more people are likely to be taking out more money, and spending more! Low interest rates also led to less saving, because they wouldn't typically earn much when putting it into a savings account.

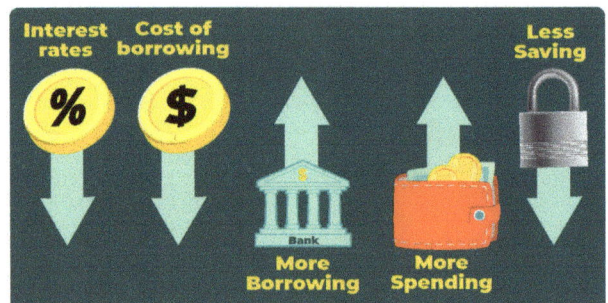

After seeing these two options, you may think low interest rates are the way to go. Make more people borrow and spend, boost the economy! BUT... this is where we introduce the concept of **inflation**.

Inflation

Inflation refers to the general price of everyday things increasing, and the power of your money decreasing. What do we mean by power? Well, there you are, going about your day as usual, and then BANG, you spot the canteen zooper dooper's have been marked up from 50c to 70c. Ouch. You now need 20 more cents to buy the exact same thing, and - would you look at that - 50c won't even buy you a lollipop these days!

So when interest rates are low, people will borrow more money. Because there is so much more money around in the economy, the demand on everyday items increases. In order for businesses to still be able to provide goods without always selling out, they need to raise their prices. This has a flow on effect to the price of everything in the economy, and causes almost all prices to rise too.

This might seem annoying, but it's important to remember inflation is a normal and healthy part of a growing economy, but as with all things in life, and - like zooper doopers - it's only healthy in moderation.

Inflation is driven by more than just interest rates, and the two don't always correlate. However, interest rates play a role in managing inflation, hence Governments need to walk a pretty thin tightrope... Encouraging Aussies to spend, but not over-inflating prices.

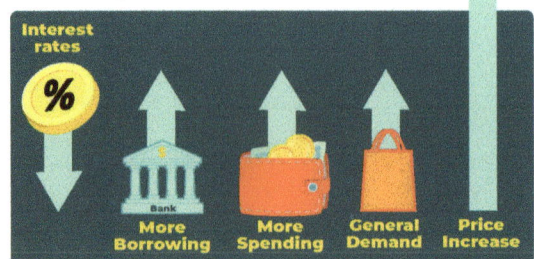

17.3.1 Sort into categories!

Consider the impact that high & low interest rates have on the economy. Sort each of the impacts caused, into high & low interest rate buckets.

A Loans are more expensive

E Encourages more spending in the economy

B Less spending in the economy

F People encouraged to save more

C Business activity increases

G Economy speeds up and grows

D Cheaper for more people & businesses to borrow

H Economy slows down & 'contracts' (shrinks)

Which are possible outcomes of Low Interest Rates?

Which are possible outcomes of High Interest Rates?

What is one way as an everyday Aussie can protect their money from inflation?

How Are Interest Rate Levels Decided?

First, setting the National Interest Rate

In Australia, the national interest rate is determined by a body called the Reserve Bank of Australia (RBA). While the RBA is considered separate from the Government, it has many roles to do with managing and issuing Australian Dollars. However, in this chapter, we'll focus purely on their role in managing interest rates.

RESERVE BANK OF AUSTRALIA

Once monthly, the reserve bank meet to take a look at the state of the economy. They figure out whether the interest rate, or the "cash rate" should be increased or decreased. To guide their decision making, they try to target annual inflation of 2-3% annually.

State of the economy

2-3% inflation

An economy is a giant concept, and a mammoth task to manage! There are so many factors to take into account and so many unpredictable variables that will influence the output. The easiest way to begin your learning journey about the economy and how it works is to find a trustworthy news source!

How does this impact personal interest rates?

Setting national interest rates for the country is step one... But how does this translate into the interest rate you receive when taking out a loan from the bank or earning interest from a savings account?

To explain this, it's key to understand that the banks that you bank with, also borrow and lend money from the RBA at the national interest rate (for a number of random reasons). Yet, when it comes to **YOU** borrowing from them or depositing savings... Rather than giving you that same interest rate, there are a few other factors they take into consideration. A key factor here is risk.

Higher risk, higher interest

The riskier you are as a borrower, the higher the interest rate you generally have to take on when borrowing. Banks don't want to lose their money... So if you have a bad track record of paying back money, the bank may consider you "risky" and give you a higher interest rate.

On the flip slide, if you've always paid your bills on time, the bank might offer you a friendlier, lower interest rate.

Jump to the chapter on Debt to find out more about what makes you a trustworthy borrower!

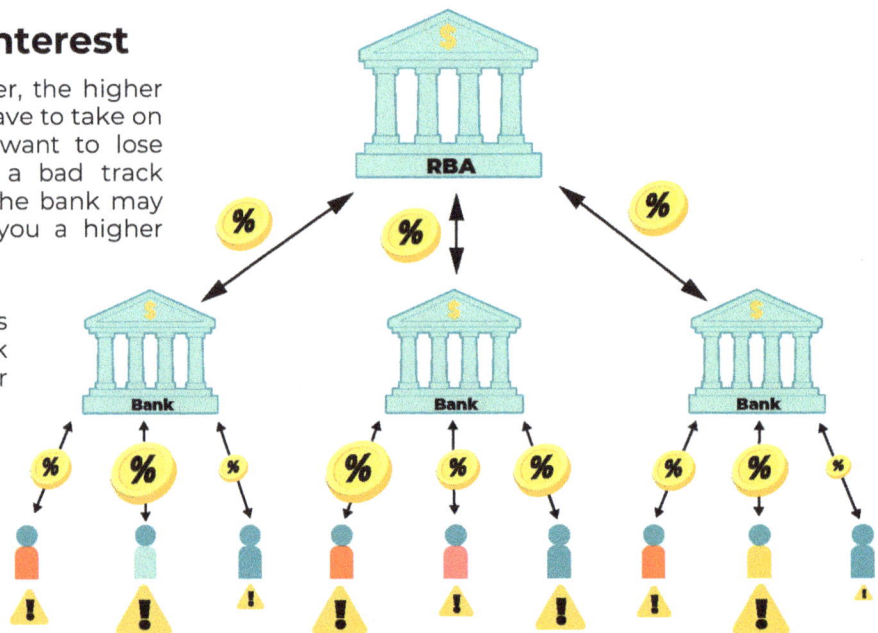

RBA

Bank   **Bank**   **Bank**

You can think of this whole process as the RBA setting the "trend" in interest rates, and banks adjusting this interest rate for each of their individual customers. Even though the RBA seems a bit like an abstract concept, you can see how decisions made at the top trickle down to affect your daily life.

True or False?
Explain why you've chosen your response!

The RBA determines the national interest rate every time the stock market opens.

True or False? Why?

You can bank with the RBA because they've got the best Interest rates for savings accounts.

True or False? Why?

The interest rate a bank may set for your loan is strictly dictated by the interest rate set by the RBA.

True or False? Why?

What Are Financial Products?

Did you know that it's possible for your money to both *earn* you money, and *cost* you money? In this chapter, we'll cover how different financial products give you access to these possibilities.

To start... What is a financial product? Broadly speaking, it's simply a tool which you can use to borrow money, save money or make a financial investment. While it sounds slightly complex, you're probably already interacting with a variety of financial products. For example, if you have a bank account, voila, you're dealing with a financial product.

To explore the categories of products, let's arrange these tools in our minds by thinking about whether they earn you money, cost you money, or are simply neutral.

"A facility that helps you to save, invest, get insurance or borrow money." – Money Smart

Invest — Save/Store — Borrow

Earn — Neutral — Cost

In the positive return category, your money is intended to grow in dollar value through interest or an investment return. You'll find products like term deposits, savings accounts, or shares. However, with investment products, it's important to remember they can be risky. While the intention is to earn a return, if they go south, they can also lose you money.

An example of a neutral product could be a simple bank account. Given there aren't any fees, the dollar amount you deposit, is the same dollar amount that will be there when you withdraw it Not taking account any value loss through inflation).

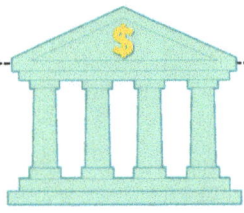

In the negative return category, we have money that costs money! These products include loans, credit cards, or buy now pay later borrowing. Because these tools charge interest or fees, it can cost you more money for something than if you had bought it with cash.

But! "**Negative**" doesn't necessarily mean "**bad**". Debt, when used correctly, can be incredible useful. In the context of starting a business, buying a house, or an emergency fridge, debt products can sometimes be the only option!

Intended Positive Return
via interest or capital gains
They can also have negative returns!

Deposit **Withdraw**

Loan

Lender — You

Loan + **Interest / fees**

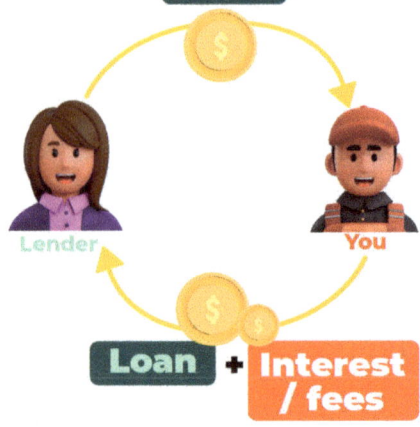

There are so many unique financial products which serve so many different purposes. This is simply one broad brush way of organising the types of products that exist! There will be many financial products available to you throughout your financial life. Wrapping your head around the different categories and general product landscape will make the space much easier to navigate.

17.5.1 **Think about real life!**
Financial products might seem a bit strange... Identify cases where you (or someone you know) might already be using products in each of these categories.

Invest	Save/Store	Borrow
Earn	**Neutral**	**Cost**
Real Life Examples?	Real Life Examples?	Real Life Examples?

Financial Products That Grow Your Money

"Earning a Return"

Having your money earn you more money sounds pretty good, right? That's what 'earning interest' or 'earning a return' means. In this chapter, we'll cover three types of financial products that tap into this magical concept.

When you consider your savings bucket for your budgeting plan... This is the area of products you might consider to help grow your savings!

1 Savings Account

Firstly, a savings account. This is an account typically held with a bank. The cool part, you get paid a percentage interest on the balance in the account. The not so cool part, there can be strict rules to be able to unlock this interest rate. For example, needing a minimum monthly deposit, or not withdrawing more than a certain amount each month. Sometimes there can be a base interest rate and a bonus interest rate, which can be harder to unlock. When choosing a savings account, you'll want to find one that balances a healthy interest rate with rules that work for you.

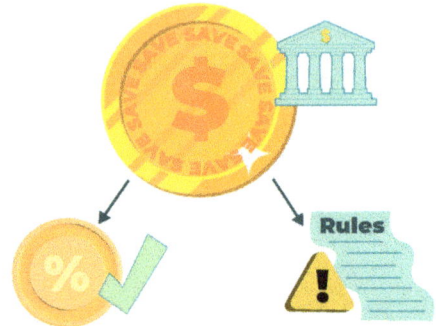

Rules

2 Term Deposit

Secondly, term deposits. While they are similar to savings... in that you earn a fixed amount of interest on your balance... There are some big differences. Your money is typically locked away in the term deposit for what we call the 'term'. The 'term' could be 3 months, 6 months, or three years. So, once you've put your money into the term deposit, you won't be able to access it, or the interest your money has earned, until the end of that term.

Term

Savings accounts and term deposits are offered by many different banks. There are constantly new and better offers emerging. Make sure to review your choices every so often.

3 Investment Products

Finally, we have the wide world of investment products. Shares, Property, Commodities, Currency, the list goes on. While many investment products don't technically earn interest, and grow your money using different mechanisms...

While the intention of investment products is to make positive returns...

...They can also make losses.

They are all products that have the ability to earn you a positive return. It's a huge topic on its own, but it's worth being aware of investment products' potential to grow your money.

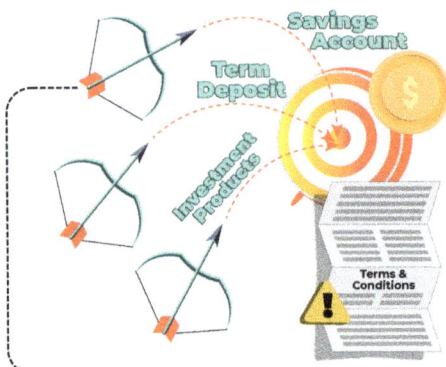

Savings Account

Term Deposit

Investment Products

Terms & Conditions

Check the fine print!

Whatever your financial goals may be, it's useful to know what different financial products can offer to help you achieve those goals. Yet with each product being so unique, it's essential to triple check the terms, conditions and risks involved with each product. Don't jump into a product until you understand and trust it fully!

17.6.1 **What's your take?**
Your friend is looking for somewhere to invest their savings...
Briefly explain to them how each of these products work and
list one pro and one con about each of these three options!

Savings Accounts Intro explanation

Pro	Con

Term Deposits Intro explanation

Pro	Con

Shares and other investment products Intro explanation

Pro	Con

Financial Products That Help You Borrow Money

Being able to borrow money is great, but it's important to remember that depending on where you borrow from, interest or fees could make it a very expensive exercise. Let's explore three types of debt products.

1 Personal Loan

Firstly, a personal loan. This is your classic sort where you A, borrow a certain amount of money and B, pay this sum, plus any interest and late fees. This could be through a formal or informal repayment structure. The complexity comes in if you can't stick to your repayments, where additional interest and late fees can push up the cost of the loan.

Some examples of loans are personal loans, pay day loans, car loans, and home loans (aka. mortgages). These all have the same core elements, but can differ hugely depending on how much you're borrowing, who you're borrowing from, and the terms of the loan.

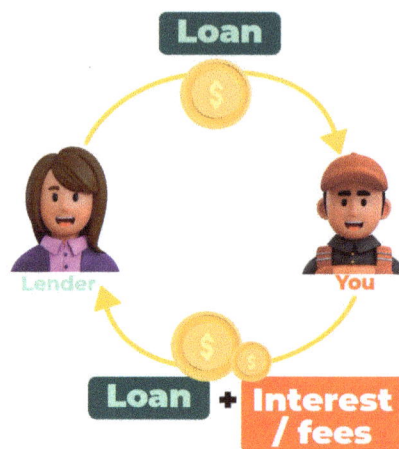

Loan

Lender   You

Loan + **Interest / fees**

2 Credit Card

The second debt product is the credit card. This is where you have instant access to a certain loan amount at any point in time. You can loan up to the pre-determined credit card limit, by tapping your way through coffee, couches, big items, small items.

You pay off the credit card debt as you *accrue* ("take on") the debt, typically with an interest-free borrowing period of a month. When the interest free period after your credit card purchase is up, the interest starts stacking up. Also, if you don't pay the minimum required amount off your debt balance each month, the late-fees begin. Your credit card can be a recipe for serious interest and late fee charges.

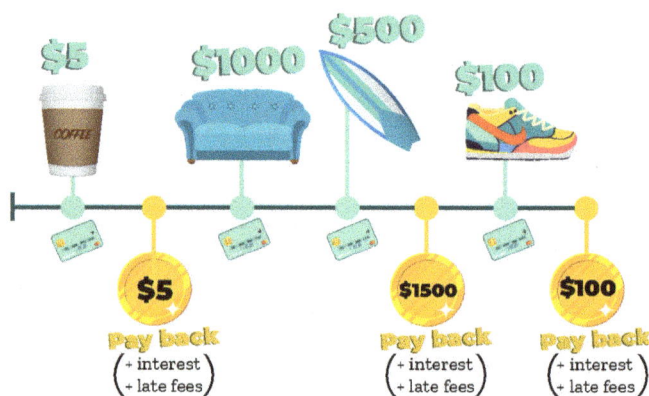

$5 $1000 $500 $100

$5 pay back (+ interest + late fees)   **$1500** pay back (+ interest + late fees)   **$100** pay back (+ interest + late fees)

Credit cards have lots of complexities to consider. Make sure you truly understand how credit cards work before signing up to one!

3 Buy Now Pay Later

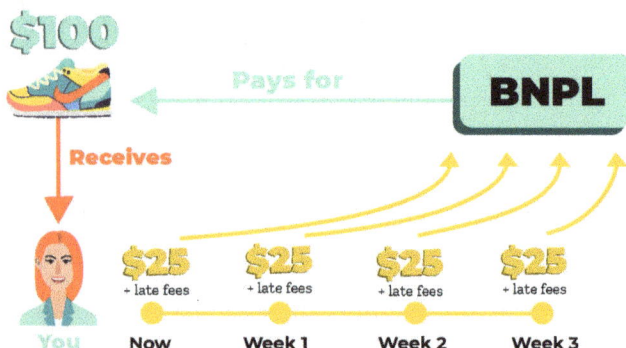

$100

Pays for → **BNPL**

Receives

You

$25 + late fees $25 + late fees $25 + late fees $25 + late fees

Now   Week 1   Week 2   Week 3

The last debt product we will explore is buy now pay later. This is when you purchase an item, paying for it across four "instalments". The idea is that you are spreading the cost over a period of time. When you buy something, the BNPL provider you are using, pays for the item. Then, you need to pay them back according to the terms you agreed to when taking out this mini-loan. However like all debt, if you don't stick to these terms, you're in for some serious late fees.

While there's no shortage of options available for borrowing money, it's so important to be aware of how they work. Think about how they fit in with your repayment abilities and the implications if they go wrong. Debt can land you in some seriously spicy water!

Different debt products for different use cases!
Your friends need advice about which debt products to use.
Match each of these needs with the most suitable debt product.

Alex is looking to fund an expensive car, to pay it back over the next three years.

Credit Card

Sam is wanting to buy an emergency microwave for $100, and will be able to pay it back over the next few months.

Loan

Bella is looking to pay for a few essential bills this week, and will be able to pay it all back by their next pay-check in a month's time.

Buy Now Pay Later

What safe-lending advice will you tell them before they take on the debt? Be specific!

"Careful! Before you take out a loan...

"Careful! Before you use Buy Now Pay Later...

"Careful! Before you use a Credit Card...

Figuring Out What Financial Products Actually Are

Tech is evolving super quickly, and with it, new financial products are popping up left right and centre. They have new names, colours, functionality, and promises. So, how do you know which products to use, and which to stay away from? We can't give you the answer, but we can help you ask the right questions.

There are four steps to follow when assessing a financial product...

Cool new product

Concept that's been around for years

1 Purpose

What is the purpose of this product? Does this product help you borrow money, store your money, or grow your money?

Borrow **Store** **Grow**

Let's use an example of a product offering to pay you your paycheck early. This might seem like a product that is growing your money, because you're getting your money earlier than you normally would, right? But in fact, you're taking money from what is essentially a loan provider and then paying them back when your actual paycheck comes through.

It can be really tricky to understand whether a new product is trustworthy and. a good choice for you. When making a big decision, consider reaching out to a professional. Spending a bit of money to get the right advice can save or make you much more money!

2 Comparison

How does the product compare with ones that you're maybe already familiar with? Is there an existing product that you've used before which you could use as a baseline comparison? So, now that you've determined the product is in fact a loan in sheep's clothing, what other types of debt are there?

Debt

- Are there safer options?
- Are there cheaper options?
- Are there options with better repayment terms?

3 True Cost

How much does it actually cost? You want to look at the structure of the cost and return, whether this is fees, interest, investment returns, or anything else. The key here is to figure out the dollar value for each comparison product, to compare apples with apples! As an example, let's say one option charges a flat 5% fee. How does this compare to a loan with a $5 fee?

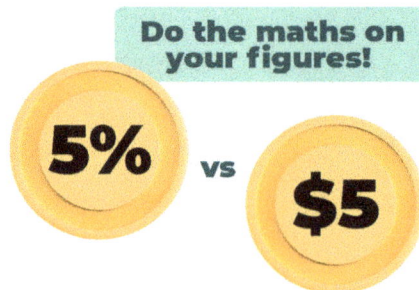

Do the maths on your figures!

5% VS **$5**

4 Ethics

How ethical does the product seem to be? As with anything, trust is key. Have you heard of them before? Do you know anyone else who has used them, and do they have good things to say? If it sounds too good to be true, follow that gut feeling and dig deeper!

From here, there are many further questions you should ask about whether the product is right for you. However, by using these four steps, you'll put yourself in a much better position to understand the new financial product that your friend's neighbour's cousin's aunty made millions from. Before hitting go on any product, pour over the fine print. You can even reach out to ASIC, the Australian Securities & Investments Commission. They are an independent commission of the Australian Government who regulate financial services and enforce laws to protect everyday Aussies.

Analyse this new product!
Put this example product, "Tiki" through the four analysis steps.
Or... Choose a real-life one that you're interested in!

Financial News

Tiki in legal battle with unhappy customers

Use New Payment method Tiki!

Pay for your $1000 product with a $10 monthly subscription over 4 years

Step 1: What is the purpose of the product? To help you Borrow, Store or Grow money?

Step 2: Are there any similar products that offer you the same purpose?

Step 3: How does the true cost of this product compare to the cost of these other products? *Hint: Figure out what the total 4 year cost of this will be.*

Step 4: Is this product ethical and trustworthy?

The Difference Between Compound & Simple Interest

Compound interest and simple interest, same same but very different. But first! A quick recap of what interest is. Interest is the cost to borrow money. Let's say you borrowed $100, that's the principal amount. If the loan has a 5% annual interest rate, after 1 year of having the loan, you would owe $5 of interest on top of the $100 you originally borrowed.

makes sense?
Let's get into simple interest.

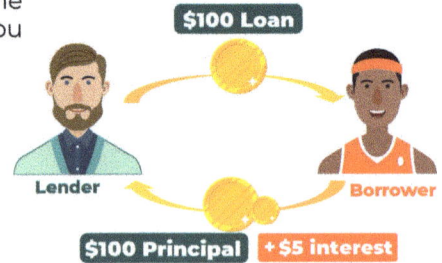

$100 Loan

5% annual interest

Lender   Borrower

$100 Principal   + $5 interest

Simple Interest

The 'simple' part means that interest is calculated based on the original principal amount. Continuing with our example, the interest after one year would be $5.00, calculated on the $100 principal. In year two, even though technically you now have $105, it would be $5.00 again, calculated based on the $100 principal.

$100 Principal + $5 Interest Year 1

$100 Principal + $5 Interest Year 2

$100 Principal + $5 Interest Year 3

Compound Interest

Compound interest is where the interest accrued (earned) is added to the principal (the primary amount) when calculating the next years' interest amount. This means the interest compounds - like a snowball. Going back to the same example... In year one of the loan, the principal is $100. The interest rate is 5%. This makes the interest amount $5, simple. In year two however, we add the interest from year 1 to the principal. This effectively makes the new principal $105, and the interest amount then becomes 5% of that... equalling $5.25. In year three, the principal is now considered to be $110.25. You get the idea!

$100 Principal + $5 Interest Year 1

$105 Principal + $5.25 Interest Year 2

$110.25 Principal + $5.51 Interest Year 3

Compare the pair

So you can start to see why compound interest might be much more common... Because the lender, (whether that's you, or a bank, or another provider) earns more money as time goes on. Compound interest is more math heavy than simple interest, but it's really important to wrap your head around.

Simple Interest   Total Interest earned by Lender $15
$5 + $5 + $5

Compound Interest   Total Interest earned by Lender $15.76
$5 + $5.25 + $5.51

Real life scenario!
Using your knowledge on compound interest, complete these two scenarios.

Charlie has $80,000 in a savings account that earns 7% interest per year. How much interest will they earn in 1 year?

Daisy has $1,000 in a term deposit that earns 5% interest per year (compounded). How much interest will they earn in 2 years?

Calculating Compound Interest

Compound interest describes the way that interest 'snowballs' over time. It can be painful to try and manually work this out, so let's tap into a formula. This formula gives the total balance after all the interest has been compounded.
- In the case of savings, this is the total amount of your savings balance.
- In the case of a loan, the total amount of the loan.

Here's the formula...
Let's break it down!

- **P** = the initial Principal of the loan or investment.
- **R** = the annual interest rate.
- **T** = number of years the loan or investment is held for.

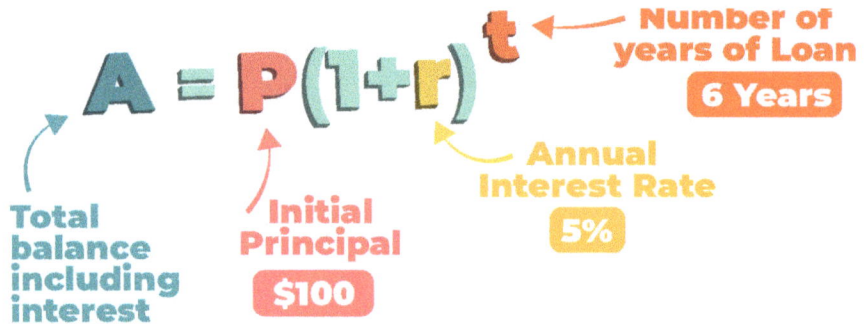

$$A = P(1+r)^t$$

Number of years of Loan — 6 Years

Annual Interest Rate — 5%

Total balance including interest

Initial Principal — $100

An Example:

Let's use an example with a $100 loan with a 5% annual interest rate, where the term of the loan is 6 years and you pay it back all the end of the 6 years.

We've got:
- P = $100
- R = 5% (or 0.05)
- T = 6 years

$\ggg$

Total Amount
$$= 100(1+0.05)^6$$
$$= \$134.01$$

$\ggg$

If you're taking out this loan, $134.01 is the total you'll owe at the end of the six year period. Or in the case of savings, the total you will have at the end of 6 years.

Compounding Frequency

One of the assumptions of this formula is that interest is calculated **annually**, where one a year the interest is compounded to create the new principal for the following year. This isn't always the case. For example, Credit card interest can be compounded and calculated daily. Here's an example...
- For a loan of $100, where you repay the full balance at the end of the year.
- Interest is calculated and applied **twice a year** (instead of once).
- In the first six months, you will earn 2.5% worth of this interest, and 2.5% in the second six months.

That makes the principal PLUS interest $102.50 after six months.

2.5% { Jan Feb Mar Apr May Jun }

Total amount (first 6 months)
$$= 100(1+0.025)$$
$$= 102.5$$

For the second half of the year, you will again have 2.5% interest applied, but this will be calculated on this new principal of $102.50. So, $102.50 times 2.5% = $2.56 interest for the second half of the year.

2.5% { Jul Aug Sep Oct Nov Dec }

Total amount (second 6 months)
$$= 102.5(1+0.025)$$
$$= 105.06$$

By calculating interest twice per year, instead of once per year, the interest for the entire year is $5.06 instead of just $5.00.

Annual Compounding $5

6 month Compounding $5.06

6c isn't a big difference when looking at such small numbers and only one year. But over many years and with bigger numbers, it's a different story.

The maths behind *compounding frequency* is a bit more complex, and definitely something to use an online calculator for. It's simply good to be aware how quickly it can snowball debt or investments.

Real life scenario!
Using your knowledge on compound interest,
complete these two scenarios.

If you invest $3,000 today in at term deposit at an interest rate of
5.5%. how much money will you have in your account in 3 years?

You invest $6,000 today in a term deposit with an interest rate of
6.5%. How much money will you have in your account in 5 years?

If I had an interest rate of 10%, and interest was compounded quarterly (every 3
months). How much interest would be applied in the first quarter of the year?

The Double Sided Interest Sword And How It Impacts Retirement

Compound interest is a very powerful tool. It has the ability to grow your savings or grow your loan. The magic factor here is time. Let's see why it's important to invest as early as possible, and repay debt as quickly as possible.

Investing Power

Let's illustrate this by sticking with the same principal amount and same interest rate but only changing the magic factor, time.

If we start with $10,000 an interest rate of 8%...

- After 10 years, you will have $21,589.
- After 50 years, you will have $469,016!

Despite not investing a single extra cent, you'll have ended up with almost half a million dollars after 50 years. Seems like a lot when compared to the small ~$22,000 after 10 years, right?

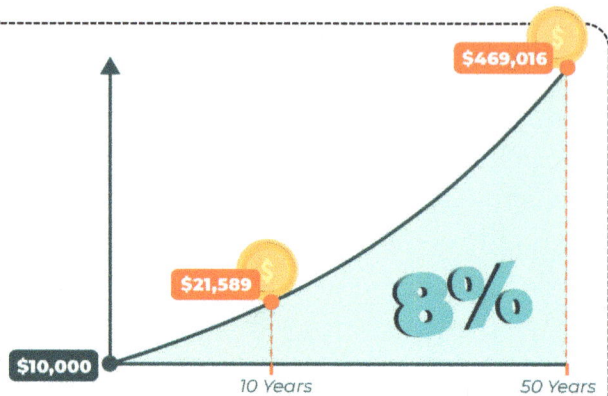

This is the power of compound interest. This concept should make the first principle clear: Invest as early as possible!

$469,016

$21,589

$10,000

10 Years

50 Years

8%

Don't have $10,000 to invest right now? Find a compound calculator online to figure out where you could be with simple $5 or $10 weekly contributions. Invest your spare change, or your birthday money or a few dollars of your pocket money. Start small, start imperfectly... Simply, start!

The best time to start investing was ten years ago, The second best time is Now!

Debt Danger

On the flip side of the coin, if you were borrowing this amount of money at the same interest rate, it's clear how compounding interest is your enemy. The math works in the exact same way - except it's working against you, given it's calculating what you owe.

Every loan is structured differently, however, generally, as you leave the loan accruing interest over a period of time, the more you will have to pay back.

Let's say you've taken out credit card debt to access $10,000 to fund a gap year. We'll use a more common credit card interest rate: 25% compounding daily.

You pick up a part time job and pay back the loan over the next two years. Given you paid it back within the year, you would have accrued a debt balance of $12,548, an extra $2,548 worth of interest on top of your $10,000.

But, if you decided to only make minimum repayments of 2.5%, your loan could take you as long as 52 years to pay off and end up costing you $51,821. That makes for an expensive holiday!

$10,000 Loan **25%** Interest Daily Compounding

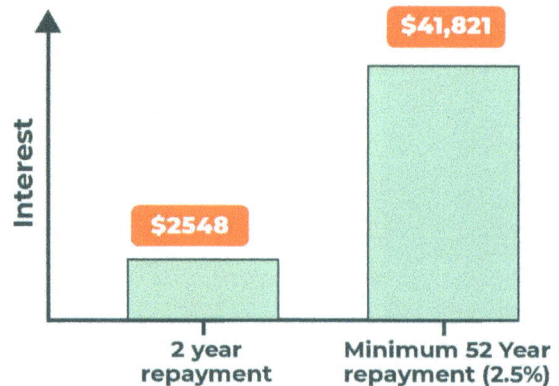

$41,821

$2548

Interest

2 year repayment

Minimum 52 Year repayment (2.5%)

This should make the second principle clear: the quicker you pay your debt, the less expensive it is.

To revisit the magic factor, the early bird gets the worm...

- The early investor earns more in interest.
- The early debt re-payer avoids the interest / fee snowball.

Referring to the relevant diagrams...
Why are these two statements incorrect?

"I'll wait to get my finances under control before I pay off my debt"

"I'll wait to start investing once I earn more money"

When To Invest And When To Pay Off Debt

So you've had a pretty smooth ride with your money situation, but now you're at crossroads. You have debt to pay off, but you've also heard through friends and family how good the returns are when investing money. Where to start?

The tradeoff between investing and debt repayment can be a difficult decision! It can be complex to figure out the best plan of attack when the amounts, interest rates, and compounding frequencies are all different. In this chapter, we're going to explore a few steps to walk through in order to determine the best decision.

To be able to make a decision, we need to figure out the individual cost of each financial product we are currently using and are impacted by.

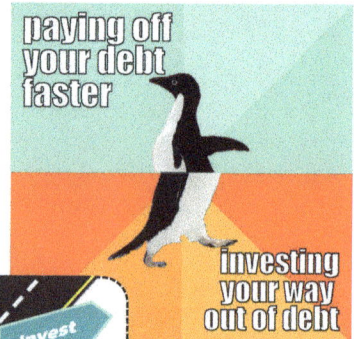

paying off your debt faster

investing your way out of debt

Debt Repayment — Invest

Fees
Interest rates
Compounding
+/- Returns
Risks

Example

Let's work through a broad example.
- You just received $1000 as a bonus in January for the hard work from the previous year.
- You also have $800 in credit card debt, which incurs 10% interest every year
- Your bank account has a savings account option, which currently pays 2% interest per year.

Do you think it's best to...

A Pay debt First, Save the leftover

$800 Debt — 10% Interest Annual Compounding

B Save it all first, Pay the Debt in a year

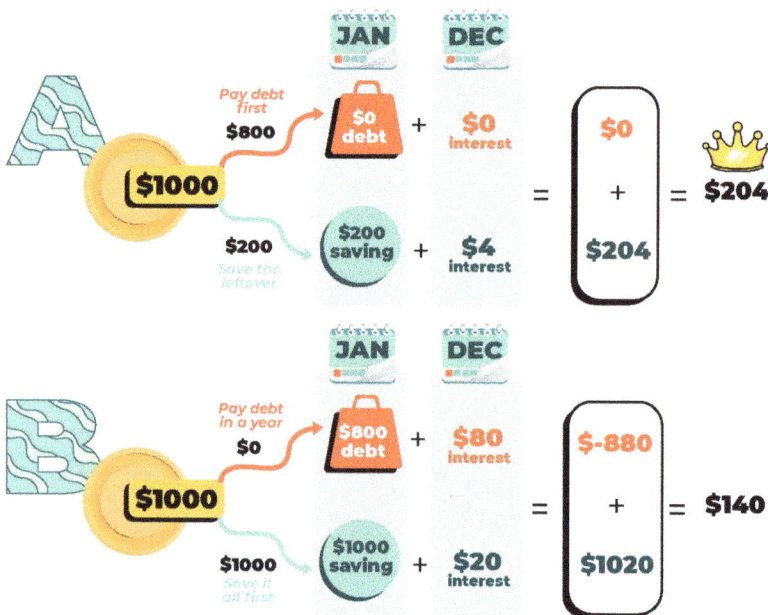

$0 Savings — 2% Interest Annual Compounding

A

$1000

Pay debt first $800 → JAN $0 debt + DEC $0 interest

$200 → $200 saving + $4 interest
Save the leftover

= $0 + $204 = $204 👑

The math for option A)
- You immediately pay your $800 debt with your $1000.
- This leaves you with $200 in cash.
- Investing this $200 in January will earn $4 in interest by December.
- Therefore, in December, you will now have $204.

B

$1000

Pay debt in a year $0 → JAN $800 debt + DEC $80 interest

$1000 → $1000 saving + $20 interest
Save it all first

= $-880 + $1020 = $140

The math for option B)
- The $1000 you saved in the bank at the start of the year will earn $20, leaving you with $1020.
- Meanwhile, your CC balance will grow from $800 to $880.
- If you then use your bank balance to pay the credit card in December, you will be left with $140 when all's said and done.

If we compare the two... Option A) leaves you $64 better off. It may seem counterintuitive at first to pay off debt, and *then* invest the rest of your money, but in this case the debt was more expensive than the savings account returns!

These decisions may have much more complexity in a real-life situation, but if you break them down and step through each option independently, you'll get a better idea of what the best decision is.

I7.12.1 Sammy the millionaire!

Use the following scenario information to answer questions about Sam's millionaire Journey.

- Sammy is 15.
- They want to be a millionaire by the time they retire at 65.
- Sammy saves $100 a week.
- Each month, Sammys put their savings into an 5% annual investment opportunity.

Do you think Sam's millionaire dream is possible? Why / Why not?

How much will Sam have saved by the time they retire? Assume they are not putting any money into investments!

Taking into account the 5% investment opportunity, How much money will Sam have for their retirement? Use an online compound Interest calculator.

- Sammy has just received $1000 for their birthday.
- Right now, Sammy has a credit card debt of $1000 with 20% annual interest.

Should Sammy pay off their credit card debt or invest their money into an investment opportunity with an 8% annual return?

INTEREST ✨

A space for your notes, questions, plans!

DEBT

Learn debt fundamentals, the products available to you, and how to make smart debt decisions!

Lesson 1
Recognising Debt

- [ ] **1** Real Life Debt
- [ ] **2** Debt Components
- [ ] **3** Credit Score Overview
- [ ] **4** Debt And Risk

Lesson 2
Staying Financially Safe

- [ ] **1** Dangers Of A Bank Loan
- [ ] **2** Dangers Of Credit Cards
- [ ] **3** Dangers Of Buy Now Pay Later
- [ ] **4** Dangers Of Pay Day Loans

Lesson 3
Debt Decision Making

- [ ] **1** Debt Use Case Scenarios
- [ ] **2** Debt Repayment Technicalities
- [ ] **3** Budgeting For Debt
- [ ] **4** Recovering From Debt

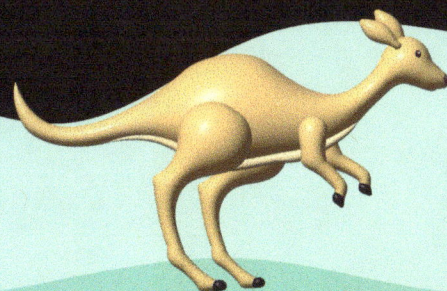

What Actually Is Debt?

Debt is a small word, but it stresses a lot of people out big-time! In this chapter, we'll walk through what debt is, and help you recognise it in a few real-life scenarios.

Is it Debt?

If you've ever had an 'IOU' with your friends or family, you're already familiar with the concept of debt. To be 'in debt' is quite plainly, to owe money to somebody. This could look like anything from owing your friend for the lunch they bought your earlier... To formal debt such as Credit card debt; personal bank loans; mortgages; buy-now-pay-later; business debts; tax bills; unpaid utility bills; the bills you now owe to debt collection agencies when your utility company decides they can't wait for you to pay your bills any longer; medical bills; and the list goes on!

"The state of owning money"

What's the key to spotting when you might be about to get into debt? The simple question to ask yourself whenever you're spending is:

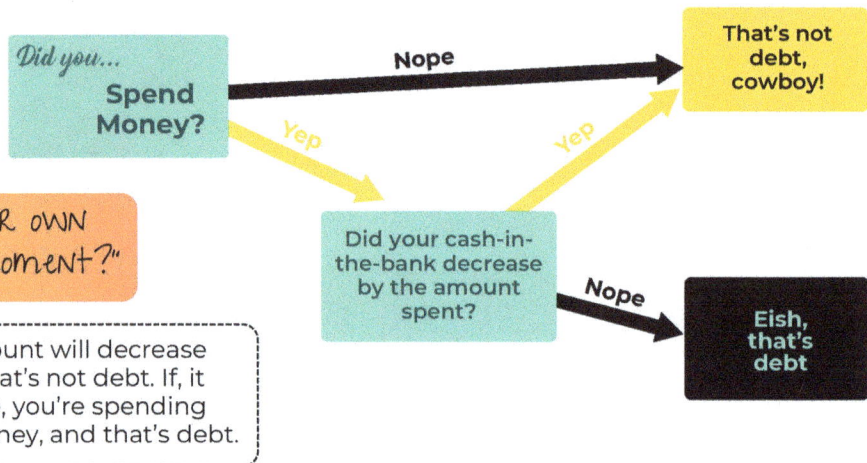

Did you... **Spend Money?**

Nope → That's not debt, cowboy!

Yep → Did your cash-in-the-bank decrease by the amount spent?

Yep → That's not debt, cowboy!

Nope → Eish, that's debt

"Are you spending your own money, right at that moment?"

If your bank account will decrease straight away, that's not debt. If, it doesn't decrease, you're spending someone else's money, and that's debt.

The Psychology of Debt

An interesting fact on the psychology of debt... Paying for something AFTER you've enjoyed the benefits of it, expresses itself as physical pain within your brain. For example, paying for a holiday after you've been on it, is not just unpleasant, but actually painful!

Purpose of Debt

When we consider all these things, debt doesn't sound so fun or straightforward. Why complicate things and hurt our brains by spending someone else's money? The reality is that sometimes debt can be unavoidable or even useful to help you 'buy today with tomorrow's money'.

Let's think of a home loan as an example. Unless you're a secret crypto millionaire, there's a chance you don't have the money to buy a house outright at this very minute. However, you could be on track to save for one in 20 years' time. Debt lets you access that future money today, so you can live in the house while you pay for it.

you, in the future

Gift of money

you, today

Today — **20 Years**

you, in the future

you, in the past

You used my money

you gave it to me

Do keep in mind the 'paying back' part here, though. Repaying debt is a legal obligation! By taking money from 'future you', you're making the assumption that 'future you' will be able to sustain your future lifestyle AND pay for past lifestyle decisions. It's a great question to ask yourself before taking on debt!

D8.1.1 **What do you think of when you think of debt?**
Put together a list of scenarios of when you may run into debt!

Brainstorm 10 different scenarios or reasons you might need to use debt in your life. Label each reason as a "Good", "Ok" or "Bad" reason to use debt (these are personal perspectives, there is no right or wrong!)

1.   **Good / Ok / Bad**

2.   **Good / Ok / Bad**

3.   **Good / Ok / Bad**

4.   **Good / Ok / Bad**

5.   **Good / Ok / Bad**

6.   **Good / Ok / Bad**

7.   **Good / Ok / Bad**

8.   **Good / Ok / Bad**

9.   **Good / Ok / Bad**

10.   **Good / Ok / Bad**

Select whether each of these is an example of 'Debt' or 'Not Debt'.
Some of these aren't as obvious as you think!

1. Buying clothes using Buy Now Pay Later.. **D / ND**

2. Buying Shoes using your Debit Card.. **D / ND**

3. Getting your salary paid in advance.. **D / ND**

4. Buying something using cash.. **D / ND**

5. Borrowing from Mum & Dad.. **D / ND**

6. Buying something on a credit card.. **D / ND**

7. Buying a phone on a plan.. **D / ND**

8. Getting a mortgage.. **D / ND**

9. Doing a degree using HECS.. **D / ND**

10. Paying 50% of your Holiday accom cost before and 50% after your stay.... **D / ND**

11. Pre-paying for a concert ticket.. **D / ND**

12. Owing your friend for yesterday's coffee.. **D / ND**

13. Buying something on Laybuy.. **D / ND**

Elements of Debt; Principle, Interest, Fees

When taking out a formal form of borrowing, the total 'debt' that you owe to a lender is made up of three distinct components. Principal, interest and fees. In this chapter we'll explore how each of these stack up.

1 Principal

The first component is principal. This simply refers to the core amount of the debt, excluding any of the extra costs. If you loaned $1000, the principal is $1000. If you paid back $100, regardless of what extra costs might have stacked up, your principal is now $900.

Core amount of Debt

Principal

2 Interest

Concept number two is interest. Lending can be risky business. Did you ever stop to think about what the lender gets out of the arrangement? For the borrower, the benefit is obvious: they get a lump sum of money they can spend today. What does the lender get? This is where interest comes in.

Essentially, it's the price a borrower pays in exchange for the privilege of accessing the lender's money for a period of time. So when a loan is paid back, the borrower will repay the principal, plus interest.

When a debt comes with a high interest rate attached, we consider it to be 'expensive', and when the interest rate is lower, we refer to it as being 'cheaper'.

Cheaper Debt

Interest % / **Principal**

More Expensive Debt

Interest % / **Principal**

3 True Cost

Fees are just another way to structure the cost of a debt! Fees can be a percentage, or a dollar figure. They can be an obligatory part of the debt, or conditional on certain terms not being met. They can be recurring, or once off. It's simply the term used for any cost of debt that isn't strictly 'interest'.

+ Fees

Debt Structure

There are many ways to peel an orange when it comes to "structure".

A debt's structure refers to the way the cost of the debt is set up, notably looking at how interest is charged, and which fees are added, when.

There are fixed interest rates, variable interest rates, borrowing fees, late fees, annual fees, or any combination of these! Different debt providers or different types of debt have different structures. This is nothing to be worried about, simply something to know about!

Low Interest %
Annual Fees

High Interest %
Late Fees

0% Interest
Monthly Fees

It's important to keep these different components of debt in mind as you navigate the waters of borrowing and lending. The structure debt structure can have a number of unique applications.

D8.2.1

Debt Components

To start, label the diagram below and define what each term means. Then, answer the questions that follow.

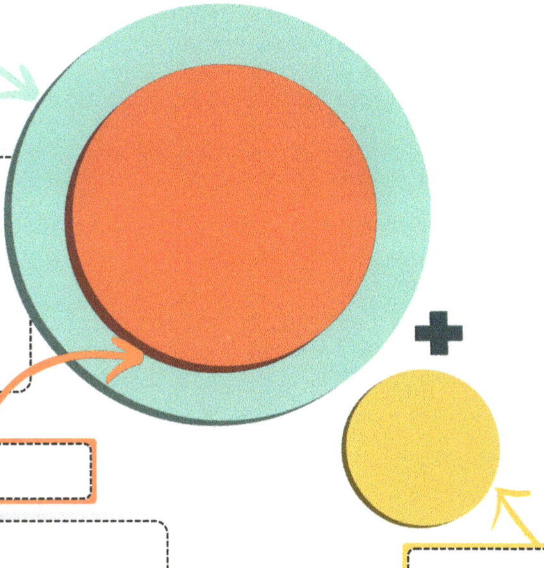

What are two things that could make your debt more "expensive"?

Which is better, when a debt product charges Interest or Fees? Why?

Why does it matter to know the 'structure' of your debt?

What Is A Credit Score And Why Does It Matter?

You might have seen futuristic TV shows where people walk around with a 'rating' above their head for everyone to see. The idea is a bit scary, but did you know you have a rating that tells lenders how well-behaved you are at managing debts? Introducing the credit score.

What is it?

0   1000

A credit score is a numerical rating of your credit performance, or - in other words - how good you've been at managing and repaying debt in the past. There are a few different ways of calculating credit score, but the most common way it's done in Australia is to rank everyone on a scale from 0 to 1000.

The higher, the better!

How is it calculated?

Credit scores are calculated by independent agencies based on information they receive from lenders about your ability to pay your loans on time.

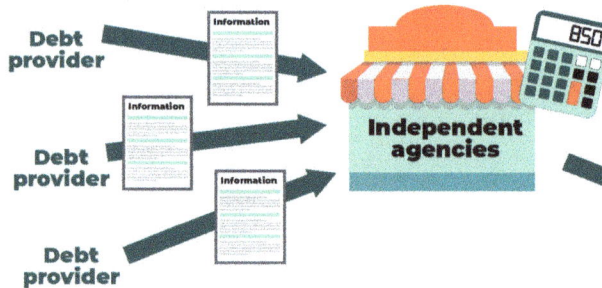

Then, it's used by future lenders to assess how reliable you are as a borrower, and therefore whether they should be trusting you with their money!

Debt provider
Information

Debt provider
Information

Debt provider
Information

Independent agencies

850

1000

Credit score

Your score effectively works as a running tally that tracks your credit behaviour - increasing your score for 'good behaviour', and decreasing it for 'bad behaviour'.

Good Behaviour
Conservative Debt Usage
On-Time Repayments
Not-so Good Behaviour
Over-Using Debt
Late or No Repayments

Good credit behaviour can look like only taking out credit where needed - don't go overboard! - and making all of your required repayments on time.

Bad credit behaviour, on the other hand, might look like taking out an excessive amount of debt, missing your repayments, or even completely defaulting on your debt.

This really is one party where you'll want to be on your best behaviour, because a good score actually pays off. A higher credit score might mean you're more likely to...
- Be approved to take out a loan
- Get a higher credit limit
- Get a cheaper interest rate

If you're curious about your score, the independent credit agencies that calculate your credit score in Australia are required to provide you with your latest score every three months for free, so it never hurts to be curious!

you, checking your credit score

realising that even if it's grim, you have the power to improve it

D8.3.1 **Credit score behaviour...**
Organise these into typically 'good' and 'bad' credit score behaviour categories.

1 Maintaining a long, positive history with the same accounts.

2 Missing repayments.

3 Making required debt payments on time.

7 Defaulting on debt.

5 Opening excess accounts.

6 Making Late Repayments

4 Only using credit when needed.

8 Switching and restructuring your debt often

Worse 0 1000 **Better**

Good	Bad

Why is it important to have a good credit score?

Why Does Risk Matter When It Comes To Debt?

How much debt are you able to take out, and how much will it cost you? The answer is almost entirely dependent on how likely the lender believes you are, to pay the debt back. In this chapter, we'll explore the relationship between debt and risk.

When a lender thinks about how 'risky' you are, they're not talking about your love for bungy jumping or longboarding - they want to calculate their own risk of not getting their money back. A loan provider will consider lots of factors when making this risk assessment, including...

- *Your credit score*
- *What kind of job you have*
- *Your income size, history, consistency and future outlook*
- *Your spending behaviour*
- *Your other existing loans and commitments*

Once a lender's made up their mind about how risky you are, there are four main ways they might adjust the terms of the loan they offer you:

1 Cost of debt

Firstly, the cost of your loan. If you're a risky individual, they're likely to charge you more in interest or fees to compensate for the possibility that they might never see their money again!

They might adjust your interest rate...

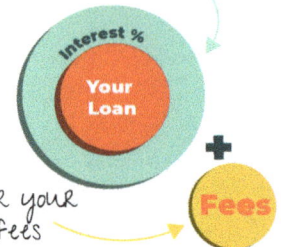

...Or your fees

2 Deposit Size

Secondly, the down payment, or deposit. Lenders will often need you to front up some of the cash for a large purchase.

An Example

If a provider required a 10% deposit on a $10,000 car purchase, you'll need to pay $1,000 towards the car before they'll consider loaning you the other $9,000. If you're a riskier individual, they'll want to see you pay more of your own way.

You need to pay a portion upfront

To show your commitment to paying the rest

3 Credit limit (size of loan)

Thirdly, your credit limit, or the amount they'll loan you. There are other factors at play here, but if a lender doesn't trust they'll get their money back, they'll keep their big loans close to their chest!

4 Loan security

Finally, the security on a loan. A loan can be secured or unsecured.

A secured loan means that you don't fully own an asset until you've paid it off - for example, a lender might give you money to pay off a car or a house, but they'll own the asset until you settle the score! You might hear the term 'collateral' used here to describe the asset.

An unsecured loan means that the lender doesn't have the right to recover anything if you can't cough up the loan balance. You'll need to be much more creditworthy to score one of these loans. Unsecured loans could also mean a more expensive interest or fee structure.

"I can offer you my house"

Secured Debt

Un-Secured Debt

"I can offer you trust"

It's pretty plain to see that there are plenty of ways a lender can reward you for being a trustworthy individual, or vice versa. Look after your lender by lowering their risk and you'll be rewarded!

Risk as a borrower...
What makes you a risky borrower, and what
can lenders do to account for this level of risk?

What are four of the key factors that influence how
likely the lender believes you are to pay the loan back?

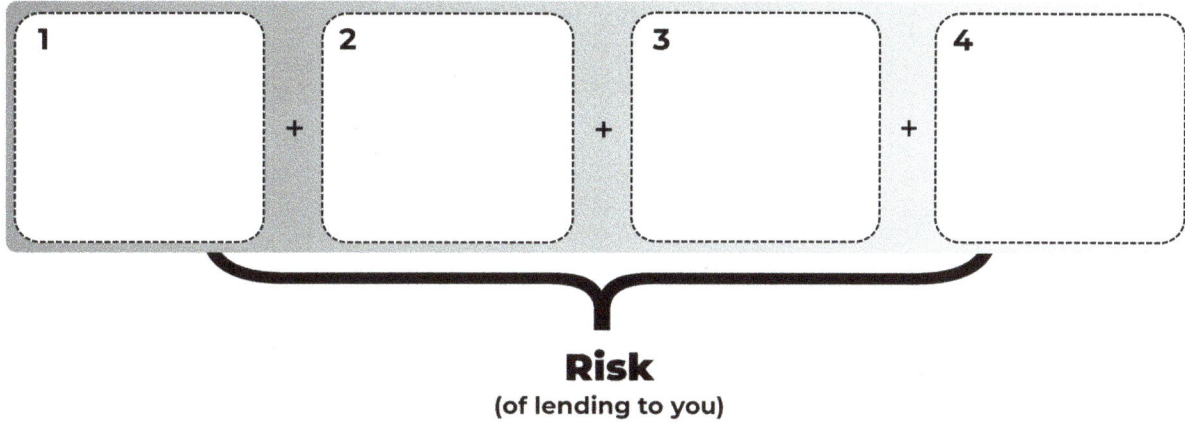

1		2		3		4
	+		+		+	

Risk
(of lending to you)

What components of a loan can a lender adjust to reflect your risk?	*As risk goes up, how might each factor be adjusted?*	*As risk goes down, how might each factor be adjusted?*
1		
2		
3		
4		

Red Flags When Taking Out A Bank Loan

So you're considering borrowing from a bank? In this chapter, let's explore the uses and dangers of personal bank loans. The word 'safe' doesn't always spring to mind as the best way to describe a loan. However, when comparing all the types of lenders out there, Australian banks can actually be more trustworthy than the typical private lender. Why's this?

Aussie banks have an ethical responsibility to look after their members. Particularly after the Royal commission, where banking ethics were given a huge overhaul, most banks aren't in the business of giving you loan-shark style debt that would knowingly put your quality of life at risk.

Banks are typically stable institutions, tightly regulated by the APRA, Australia's prudent regulator of banks.

Banks typically have a low risk appetite. They don't want to give money to someone who can't repay it, so they do their due diligence.

But let's not get too ahead of ourselves here. Not all banks tick these boxes, and even if they do, bank loans still do come with red flags.

1 Impact your credit score

Firstly, a loan from a bank can impact your credit score. Late payments can lower your credit score, making future loans harder to obtain. Paying back a loan is a serious legal obligation, and if you can't pay it back, you might find yourself in a fair bit of trouble!

2 Confusing & Expensive

Secondly, the interest rate you choose could leave you with unexpected loan costs.
- A **fixed** rate means that your rate is the same across the length of the loan. You risk missing out on cheaper interest rates later on.
- A **variable** interest rate adjusts according to the market interest rate. You could end up with a more expensive rate down the track!

Fixed Interest Rate

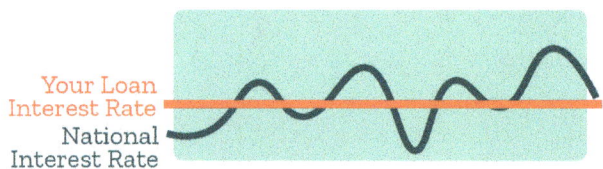

Your Loan Interest Rate
National Interest Rate

Variable Interest Rate

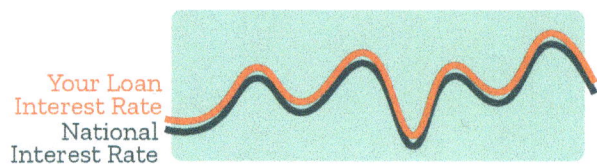

Your Loan Interest Rate
National Interest Rate

3 Collateral Loss

Lastly, if you end up choosing a secured loan, using your home or possessions as collateral, you could potentially lose more than just money.

If you can't pay back the loan

You could lose the collateral

Other red flags to look out for are in the fine print, including penalty fees for paying off your loan earlier than expected, any insurance attached to the loan, and their interest calculation methods. All in all, a bank loan can be a good call for the right reasons, but if you do end up considering one, it's useful to know what you're getting yourself into!

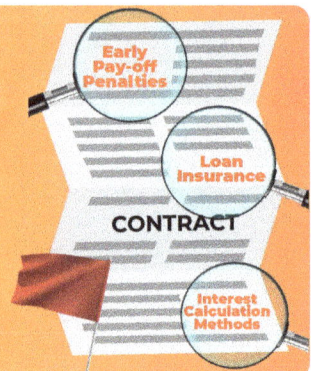

Early Pay-off Penalties

Loan Insurance

CONTRACT

Interest Calculation Methods

Bank Loan Safety...
What are three red flags to look
for in your bank loan contract?

CONTRACT

Red Flag Number 1

Red Flag Number 2

Red Flag Number 3

A friend wants advice about bank loans. Write a quick summary explaining what
a bank loan is, what they're useful for, and what to look out for!

Red Flags When Using A Credit Card

Credit cards are the most common form of debt in Australia, so it's pretty important to understand what the go is! In this chapter, we'll spend some time exploring the uses and dangers of credit cards.

These colourful rectangles work like a short-term debt facility, essentially giving you access to instant mini-loans up to your credit limit. Whenever a purchase is made with a credit card, the bank is the one paying for it at that point in time, leaving you to repay the bank later.

Credit checks and approvals are a natural part of any debt. In the case of a credit card, these will occur when you apply for the card, and if successful, you will receive your card with a credit limit. After this, you are free to spend up to your credit limit at any point in time.

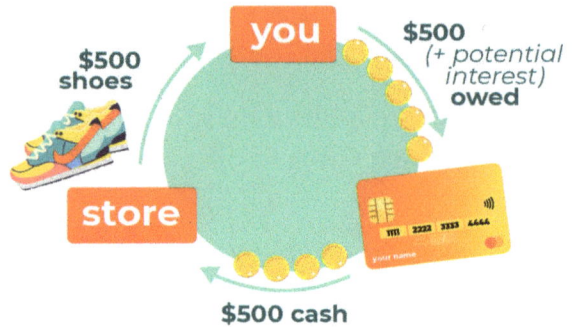

$500 shoes — you — $500 (+ potential interest) owed — store — $500 cash

Credit Limit

A credit limit is basically how much debt you are allowed to have outstanding at any point in time.

For example, if you have a $10,000 credit limit, you can have $10,000 worth of debt to your name.

$10,000 Limit

If you've maxed this out, and then pay back $100 of the debt, that opens up $100 of debt which you can take back on. It's what we to call revolving debt.

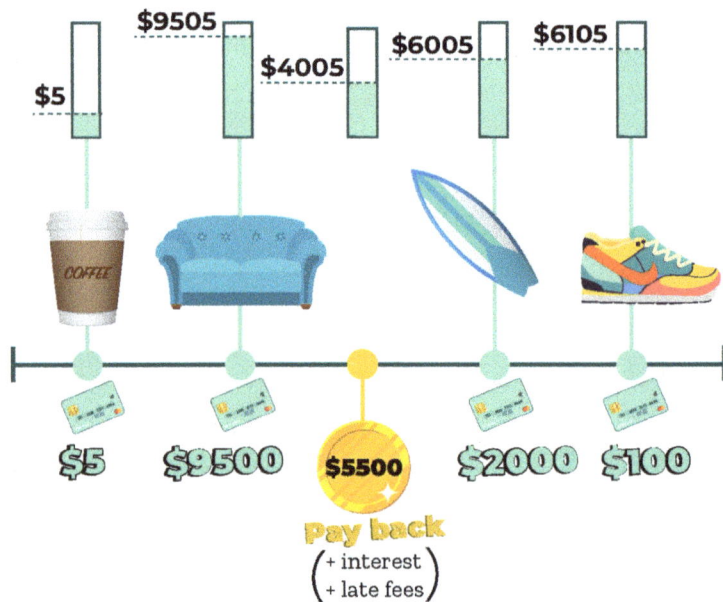

$5 · $9505 · $4005 · $6005 · $6105

$5 · $9500 · $5500 pay back (+ interest + late fees) · $2000 · $100

Unfortunately, Credit Cards come with a whole series of red flags. These are the key ones to look out for!

1 High Interest Rates

Red flag number one is that credit cards can have exceptionally high interest rates. Usually, they will provide you with an interest-free period. This is the time after the purchase you have to repay the balance *before* interest starts being applied. After that time has finished, interest will start compounding (often daily) and can range from around 9% up to an well beyond of 20%. This interest can stack up scary fast!

2 Expensive Fees

Credit Card Fees can include registration, annual and late fees (to name a few). Accidentally forget a payment? hello late fee!

3 Minimum Repayment Rates

A minimum repayment rate is the absolute minimum percentage of your credit card balance you are allowed to repay, to avoid late fees. These rates can be as low as 2%. The catch? The remaining 98% of your credit balance that you don't repay each month sticks around to accrue interest. Ouchie.

Depending on the size of debt and your minimum repayment rate, you could end up paying it off for years and years... Just because you *can* get a credit card, doesn't mean you *actually* can. Make sure your temptation to spend big on a credit card doesn't overtake what you can actually afford!

D8.6.1 Consider this Credit Card scenario...

- You have a credit limit of $10,000 (This is the total amount of credit you can have outstanding, including interest and fees).
- After you buy the couch, you have an additional $20 worth of interest and late fees applied.

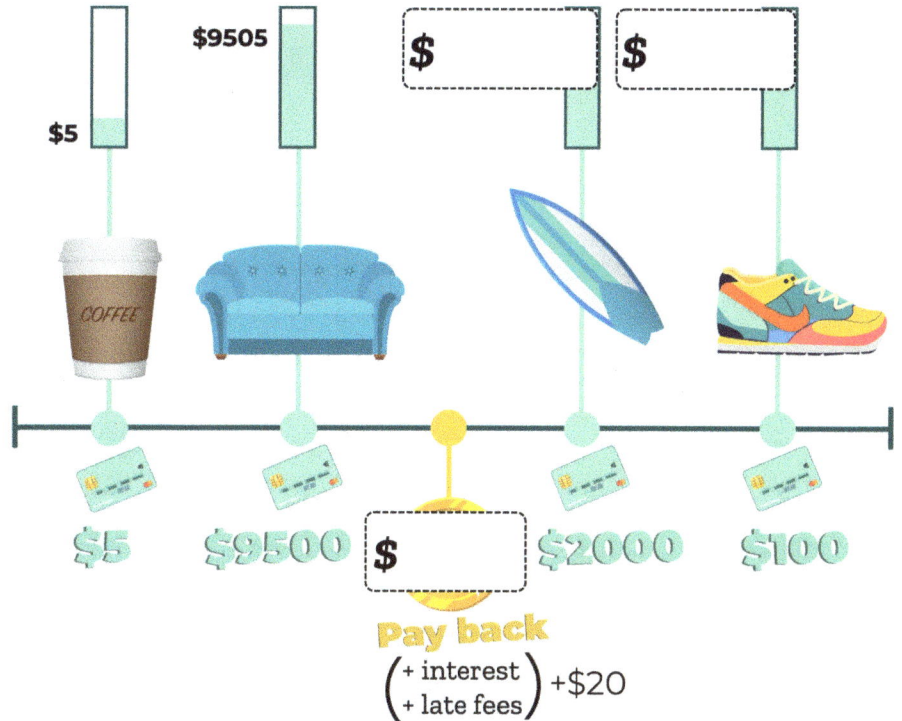

What is the minimum you would need to repay to be able to afford the $2000 surfboard and $100 shoes?

$5

$9505

$

$

$5 $9500 $ $2000 $100

Pay back

$\left(\begin{array}{l}+\text{ interest}\\+\text{ late fees}\end{array}\right) + \$20$

If a credit card requires you to repay a minimum of 2% of your outstanding credit balance, what are two reasons you might want to repay more than this?

Just because you can use a credit card, should you? Why / Why not?

Just because you can max out your credit card, should you? Why / Why not?

Red Flags When Using Buy Now Pay Later

'You're telling me that I can take this new phone today, and I don't have to pay you for another six weeks?' Does that sound too good to be true? Sometimes, it can be... in this chapter, we'll focus on the uses and dangers of Buy Now Pay Later.

Buy Now Pay Later is one of the newer and more abstract forms of debt on the market. It means you get the product or service now, and you pay for it in instalments over time instead of paying it in total upfront. Sound good? Well, it definitely can be! It's technically interest-free, and the cost of the service is paid by the business you're buying from.

The catch? If you miss a payment, you're in for late fees. True, there is no interest, BUT! When you compare the typical interest rate of a similar loan, you're looking at a pretty similar cost of debt.

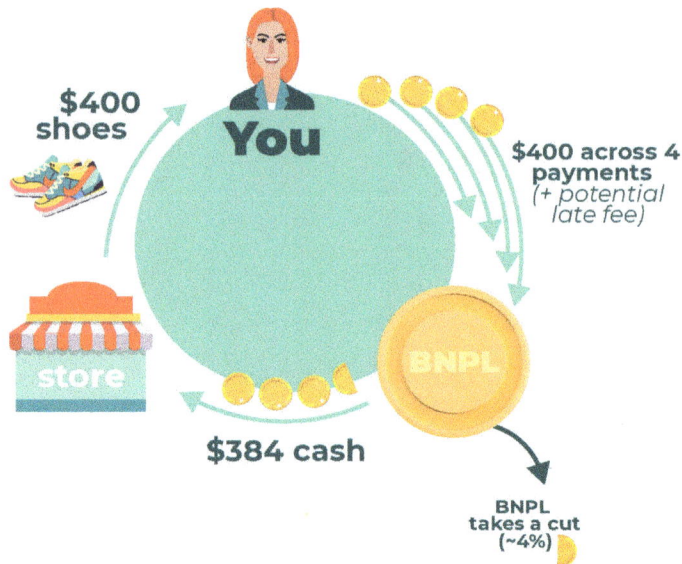

$400 shoes

You

$400 across 4 payments *(+ potential late fee)*

BNPL

store

$384 cash

BNPL takes a cut (~4%)

Don't let the gift wrap and bow on top fool you. Sure, it's super accessible and efficient to the naked eye; but nonetheless, it's still debt and could cost you.

Here are some red flags to keep an eye out for...

1 Ethical Gap

Red flag number one is the ethical gap. Most Buy Now Later providers don't properly check whether the person they're loaning can pay it back. This means it's all on you to make sure you can afford what you're buying.

Ethical gap

2 Accessibility Trap

Red flag number two is the accessibility trap. Just because you can, doesn't always mean you should! If you spend all your money on day 1 of the month, what's going to get your through the other 29 days?

3 Consumer Protection

The last red flag is the fact that there's minimal consumer protection (at least at this stage). BNPL providers are much less regulated than other providers. This means that you have much less power as a consumer if things go sideways.

Other red flags which might set off mini alarm bells in your head are potential hidden fees, and any impact on your credit score if you end up missing payments. So, BNPL can be a great too when making a considered purchase; just make sure you can stay on top of your dues and pay it back on time!

D8.7.1

Your advice!
Your friend is desperate to buy a pair of shoes using Buy Now Pay Later. What are three things you could tell them to convince them that to save up for the shoes rather than use a loan?

Convincing argument Number 1

Convincing argument Number 2

Convincing argument Number 2

If you've spent most of your **May** salary in **April** using BNPL... What are your two options to be able to afford life in May? Why is this a problem?

Red Flags When Taking Out A Pay Day Loan

Have you ever found yourself counting down the days until payday? In this chapter, we'll help you identify the uses and dangers of payday loans.

Payday Loans are...
- Small loans up to a few thousand dollars
- Provided mostly by private lenders
- Available on pretty short notice

Typically, you'll have anywhere from two weeks all the way up to a whole year to pay it back. Sounds pretty good? Well, all may not be as it seems: that small loan usually comes with some serious strings attached, and astronomical fees.

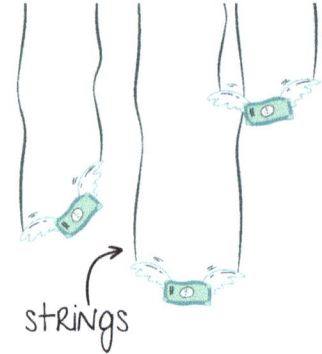

strings

The Fees

Establishment Fee
20% of loan $

Monthly Fee
4% of loan $

- Payday lenders often start with an establishment fee, which is typically around 20% of the amount you borrowed.
- Next is the monthly fee, which can be around 4% of what you borrowed.

These percentages are unique depending on the provider. Make sure you know the terms of the loan inside-out before taking it on!

An Example

You decide to go for a payday loan of $2,000. You're up for a $400 loan establishment fee and then $80 for each month your debts are outstanding.

Let's say you take out this loan for $2,000 and pay it back within a year. That's a $400 establishment fee and then $80 for each month the debt is outstanding. That makes added fees of over $1,300, and a total of $3,360. Even though the 'establishment fee' and the 'monthly fee' sounded pretty innocent, you'll end up paying more than 50% extra than the amount you initially borrowed.

Establishment Fee
$400 $

Monthly Fee
$80 per month $

= $1,300 fees

The B.I.G Red Flag

Pay day loans are masters of disguise. On the surface, they seem like harmless, quick and easy ways to get your hands on a bit of cash. They advertise fast loan approvals, low or no interest rates, flexible repayments, no credit checks. But before you know it, you've got a growing bill on your hands.

0% Interest
Flexible Repayment
Instant Cash

Pay day loans can be really (really) hard to spot. Whenever you see an offer for quick or instant cash... you're likely looking at a pay day loan of some kind.

As with all debt and financial decisions, before taking out a payday loan, do your research and make sure you're aware of the true cost.

Depending on your situation, you could consider a government emergency loan, which allows you to borrow up to $2000 for essentials such as appliances or furniture, car repairs or rego, a new phone or laptop, or medical, dental or vet expenses. Borrow up to $3000 for housing-related expenses such as bond or rent-in-advance, or for recovery from a natural disaster.

Pay Day Loan Maths...
Figure out how much each of this payday loan could cost you.

Establishment Fee
20% of loan $

+

Monthly Fee
4% of loan $

- You've just taken out a loan of $1000
- You will pay it back at the end of 12 months.
- There is a loan establishment fee of 20%
- There is a monthly fee of 4%

How much in fees will you be owe?	How much in total will you need to pay back?	If you repay that total in 12 equal monthly payments, how much will you pay each time?

What are some loan shark "promises" you might see when payday loans are advertised?

Hint: Google "Emergency loans"

When And When (Not) To Use Debt

Despite the red flags, debt can be a very useful tool (when used correctly). In this chapter, we'll help you decide when and when not to used debt. As a general rule of thumb, begin by considering whether your reason for taking out debt is Good, Ok or Bad...

✓ Appropriate

✗ Inappropriate

Good Debt	OK Debt	Bad Debt
Debt that helps you leverage money making opportunities (investments etc)	Debt that helps you better your position in life (HECS)	Debt that is the result of poor cashflow management

Let's use debt as a tool to manage our money better

Let's use debt to buy things we can't afford

"Good Debt"

Sometimes debt can be useful to reaching long term lifestyle or investment goals. For example, starting a business or buying a home or investment property. Typically, the only way you would be able to buy a house or business outright is by saving up, which can take well over 20 years.

Today — 20 Years

Here's where a **mortgage** (a loan specifically for property purchases) comes into play: for a minimum deposit percentage, you can own and live in your house... When you actually need it! And in the case of starting a business, debt is called 'leverage' for a reason!

"OK" and "Bad" Debt

For forms of debt that aren't obviously beneficial to your long term goals (for example, buying a pair of shoes or a holiday)... It's time to question yourself if going into debt is really the answer here. A great way to do this is to ask yourself, **'Do I NEED it?'**

NO

If not, it's time to put some work into your savings and practice patience.

YES

If the answer is yes, the next question to ask is, what's the smartest loan available to you?

- Is it an interest-free emergency loan from the government?
- Is it a more formal bank loan with a repayment plan?
- Is it a credit card with an interest-free period but steep interest rates once that period is over?
- Is it a small buy-now-pay-later product with a friendly repayment plan but a scary set of late fees?
- Is it something else?

Not all debt is bad debt, but it's always helpful to remember: you're technically taking money from 'future you' when you take out a loan. Will 'future you' be happy with your decision to use their money?

D8.9.1

When is the right time for debt?
Brainstorm examples of what you believe are
appropriate vs inappropriate reasons for using debt...

'Appropriate' uses of Debt

'Inappropriate' uses

Do you think it's possible to go your entire life without debt?
Why / Why not?

The Technicalities Of Repaying Debt

Ok, so you've taken out a loan, and now you're figuring out what you're on the hook for in terms of payments. In this chapter, we will explore how debt repayment works. The first thing to understand is that your debt repayment requirements are dependent on the kind of debt you take on. While each is unique, there are two broad buckets that we can organise them into (always with nuance and exceptions of course!)....

Informal Repayment

On the more straightforward end of the scale, you might be in a situation where your total debt balance grows or shrinks, depending on how much you pay off and the interest or late fees that accumulate into the total amount owed.

Mixture of Principal + Interest + Fees

Total Debt

Grows X — As interest + Fees get added

Shrinks ✓ — As you pay it back

Debt Balance

Principal: $100
Interest: $20
Fees: $5

Total: $125

PayDay Loan

Your total balance is regularly reported to you, and you have to pay that balance in accordance with the terms. Maybe it's a minimum percentage of that balance, the full balance, or anywhere in between. This could be a credit card, maybe a Buy-Now-Pay-Later product, or even a Payday loan balance.

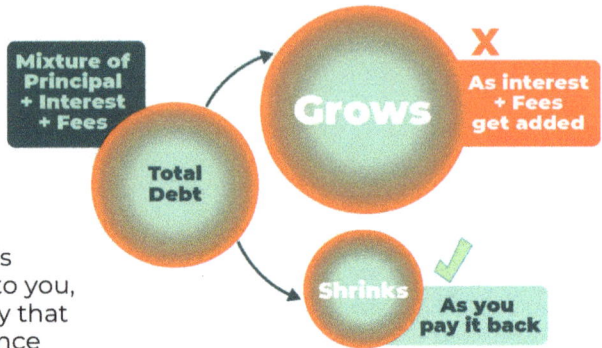

Formal Repayment Plan

Maybe you have a loan that is slightly more involved and formally set out - for example, a bank loan. What happens here is that the lender figures out the total amount you'll be owing throughout the loan, between day one and the end of the loan period. This is based on the assumption that things will be smooth sailing and you'll stay on top of all your repayments.

So, they bundle up your total predicted debt owed (the principal + the total interest you're going to be paying over the lifetime of your debt). Next, they break down this hefty total figure into equal recurring payments. This works because the same amount of money is taken out of your account for each payment.

Getting into technical speak, the ratio of principal versus interest within this amount is constantly changing. In the beginning, the majority of your repayment is interest, with only tiny bits of the principal loan amount being paid off. The ratio gradually inverts until the majority of the payment is the principal.

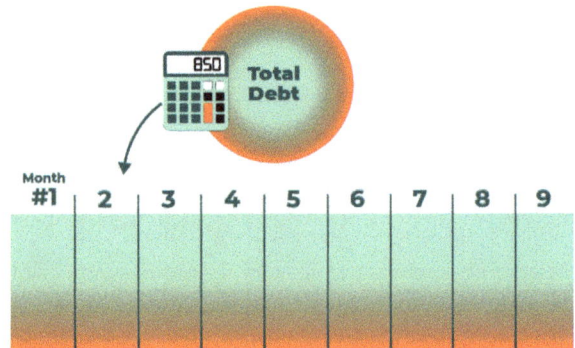

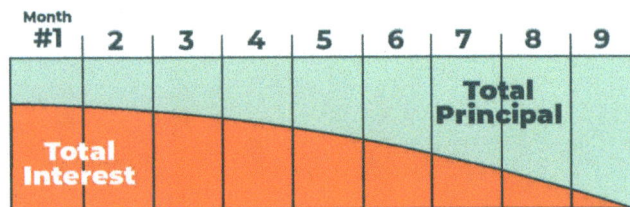

850 **Total Debt**

Month #1 2 3 4 5 6 7 8 9

Total Principal

Total Interest

Month #1 2 3 4 5 6 7 8 9

Why does it matter? There are a few technical reasons, but the most relevant one is that interest and principal are treated quite differently in the land of taxes. Try to think of it in the context of paying off an investment property. Under current tax laws, interest can be a useful tax deduction if you own an investment property.

Whichever route you're going down, it's best to avoid any unwanted surprises - so knowing your debt repayment schedule is key to building it into your budget.

Repayment Term Types!
Match these types of debt with their (typical) repayment terms!

Bank Loan

PayDay Loan

PayDay Loan

Buy Now Pay Later

Credit Card

1 Scheduled repayments (including fees) automatically deducted from your bank account

2 Combined principal & total interest over loan broken up into equal repayments

3 Revolving debt where the total debt figure grows or shrinks depending on how much debt you take on or repay.

4 Total loan divided into 4 equal payments to repay at set dates. Fees added to your debt balance.

At what stage in a person's life might formal debt be tricky to take on?

How To Build Debt Into Your Budget

Perhaps you've got a bit of debt, or perhaps you're thinking about taking some out. How will you manage it? Incorporating your debt repayment into your budget is key to keeping organised and staying on track. In this chapter, we'll help you figure out how to comfortably manage debt within your budget.

The experts say to always pay yourself first before tending to your bills when budgeting (in other words, prioritise your savings above all else). We're going to add a condition to that... If you've got debt, it's really important to prioritise paying your repayments on time!

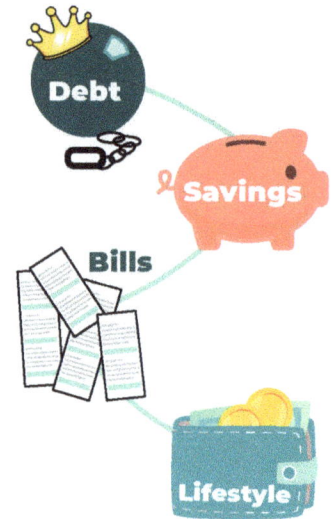

> Whether you invest or pay your debt off first depends on the maths! Head back to the interest chapter to see how you can make these decisions.

Debt
Savings
Bills
Lifestyle

Budgeting Logistics

To start, figure out how much debt you'll be due to repay each budgeting period. This could be a constant figure or a number you'll need to adjust each time. Check your debt repayment terms!

I owe Bank $1000 total
$88 a month
Jun '22 - Jul '22

Next, input this into a dedicated section for debt repayment in your budget plan, or simply record it as an expense to make things easier! The thing to focus on here is to plan for it within your budget as a regular "outflow".

Income

Spending
Debt
$88

Savings
Rainy Day

But here's the thing: a budget shouldn't just be to help you repay your debts. It's best if you also consider how you can use your budget in ways that prevent you from falling into debt in the future.

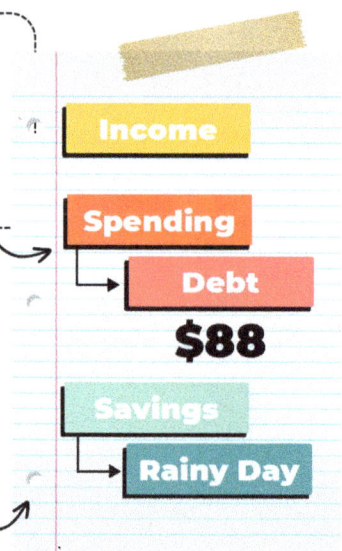

Debt Prevention

1 First, putting aside money for a rainy day fund can make a difference down the track when the only other option would be debt.

Can't get into debt...

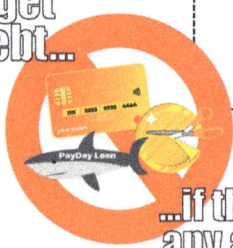

...if there isn't any available

2 Second, get rid of any debt temptation. Close down any unused buy-now-pay-later accounts, credit cards or Payday loan accounts.

3 Third, use the power of tech. Set up bills predictors, automatic debt payments, payment reminders.

Debt can be a scary thing to get into; that's why it's essential to always stay on top of it. Once you've got it embedded as part of a regular plan, though, managing it becomes much less stressful.

D8.11.1 Consider the following scenario...
Complete the budget!

- You have 3 (of 4) monthly payments left for the $80 pair of shoes you purchased using Buy Now Pay Later.
- The next payment is due in July.
- You also have a $100 monthly mortgage repayment due each month.

	Jul	Aug	Sep	Oct	Nov
Income	$550	$550	$550	$550	$550
Spending	$230	$230	$230	$250	$250
Bills	$150	$150	$150	$150	$150
Food	$80	$80	$80	$100	$100
Debt	$120	$120	$120	$100	$100
BNPL Payment					
Mortgage Repayments					
	$350	$350	$350	$350	$350
Saving	$200	$200	$200	$200	$200
Surfboard Goal	$30	$30	$30	$50	$50
Emergency Fund	$150	$150	$150	$150	$150
	$200	$200	$200	$200	$200
Total	$550	$550	$550	$550	$550

Are there any steps you can take in your financial life to make debt less tempting or accessible?

Recovering From Debt

So you've let yourself slip, and debt is controlling you, not the other way around. In this chapter, we'll work through an action plan to get yourself upright again. Debt recovery can be a short-term exercise in discipline, or it can be an entire restructure of your financial situation. Let's start with a few quick wins you could aim for.

Quick Debt Recovery wins!

1 Firstly, you could try paying off the loan with savings if you have this option available.

2 Secondly, talk to your current lender about an extension of payment deadlines. After all, they're also interested in getting their money back!

3 Thirdly, you could explore the snowball, avalanche or dominos debt repayment methods. These simply explore different ways to tackle debt repayment within your budget. Research these online for more information.

If those options aren't going to cut it, it's time to delve into the more complex land of debt 'refinancing'.

Debt Refinancing

It's a word and big concept, but we got this. Debt refinancing is simply where you replace existing debt with another debt which has better terms or conditions. It could involve...

- Consolidating multiple loans into one that you work towards paying off. The aim here is to make sure that the new combined loan is 'cheaper' than all of the individual sources of debt. This is quite a maths heavy exercise and can be quite a significant step to take. Consider speaking to an advisor to help you make this decision.

- Or, refinancing could involve getting in touch with your lender to rearrange a better interest rate or fee structure.

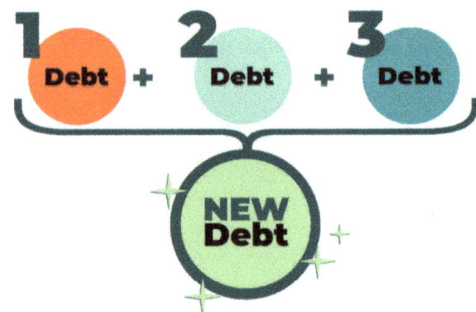

1 Debt + **2** Debt + **3** Debt → **NEW Debt**

Beyond simply a debt recovery exercise, why would debt refinancing be worth the effort?

A few reasons...
- Maybe national interest rates have decreased, and you want to make the most of these lower rates.
- Perhaps you've had an extreme clean-up of your credit score and want to cash in on your upgraded creditworthiness.
- Perhaps you're looking for a longer loan with lower repayments to reflect your decreased income.
- Perhaps you just want to change from a fixed to a variable rate, or vice versa.
- Perhaps you're looking to simplify your repayments into one regular payment every month, for simplicity!

Whatever your reasoning, debt refinancing could be one option to explore to lower your debt or make it more approachable. In Australia, we're pretty lucky to have various free resources to assist with debt recovery. If you feel like you need a hand, you can always reach out to a professional or a government help service to get advice about your debt.

For example, the National Debt Helpline **1800 007 007**

D8.12.1

Design an action plan!
Imagine a friend of yours is suffering from being in a large amount of debt. Assuming they don't have any savings, what is a three-step action plan you could recommend?

Step 1

Step 2

Step 3

DEBT

A space for your notes, questions, plans!

LIFE ADMIN

Explore key milestones ahead of you, essential products you'll interact with, and key admin tasks

Lesson 1
Life Milestones

1 Understanding HECS Debt
2 Cost Of Moving Out
3 Logistics Of Moving Out
4 Cost Of A Car

Lesson 2
Real World Essentials

1 Insurance Fundamentals
2 How Does Medicare And PHI work?
3 Phone Plan Basics
4 Scams, Fraud And Consumer Rights

Lesson 3
Money Admin

1 Basic Banking Tasks
2 Admin Essentials
3 Technical Admin To-Do list
4 Accessing Financial Support

Understanding HECS Debt And Its Repayment

Getting to true financial independence is a long journey, and the journey becomes increasingly complex as you dive deeper into it. Think buying a car, moving out of home, starting to take responsibility for your own bills... and how does that 'insurance' thing work?

If you're in tertiary education, one of the biggest costs you might be worried about is tuition. The good news is that for Aussie citizens, approved courses are covered by HECS, also known as the Higher Education Contribution Scheme! It's not just limited to universities, there are many approved higher education providers that qualify for HECS!

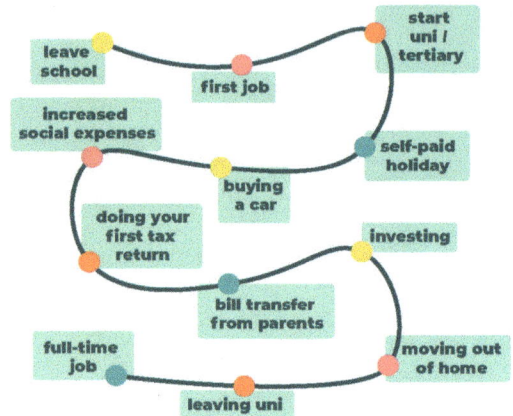

How does HECS work?

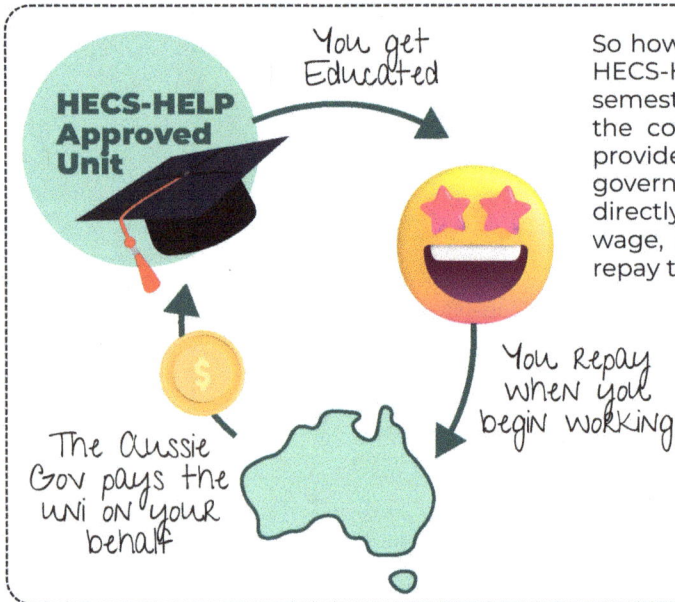

HECS-HELP Approved Unit

You get Educated

The Aussie Gov pays the uni on your behalf

You Repay when you begin working

So how does it work? Each time you enrol into a HECS-HELP unit and pass the census date of that semester or term, you'll be officially charged for the course. However, instead of the education provider invoicing you, they send the bill to the government, who then fronts the cost of the loan directly. Over the course of life, as you earn a wage, salary or any other taxable income, you repay the government in small increments.

Random HECS facts!
- There's typically a discount on your units if you pay up-front.
- You can try up to 5 weeks of a unit before the 'census date' when HECS debt is officially triggered for that unit.
- HECS debt doesn't charge interest, it only grows with inflation.
- You have a limit on the amount of HECS you can take on (roughly $110,000 for most students).
- Most post-grad degrees aren't covered by FEE-HELP, only some are.
- You can head to MyGov to see how much of your HECS loan is left.

How does repayment work?

1 First, they're collected as an an additional component as part of your income tax, instead of their own separate payment.

2 Secondly, this repayment only happens once you earn above a certain threshold. For example, a hypothetical threshold of $50,000 per year means that if you're earning anywhere below that number, repayments aren't made. As soon as you hit $50,000, you're up for HECS repayment.

3 Thirdly, the rate of repayment increases in proportion to the amount you make. If you land in a high tax bracket, you'll be paying a higher percentage of income off your loan.

Do some research around the qualification criteria of HECS, and keep in mind it doesn't provide anything except core course fees. Books, living costs, and a social life are not covered by HECS.

Doing study after school and getting an education is just one of the life milestones you might want to throw yourself into. HECS can be an awesome tool to help you on your way with this one.

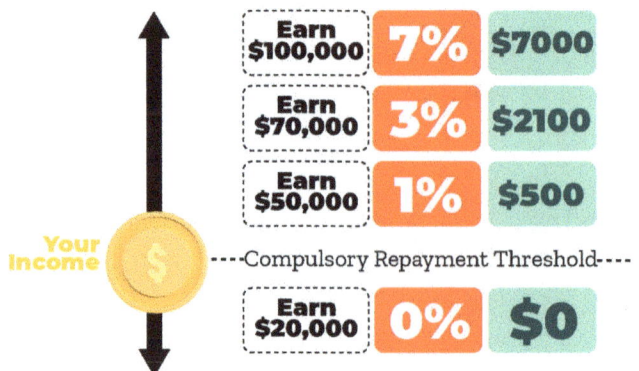

Earn $100,000	7%	$7000
Earn $70,000	3%	$2100
Earn $50,000	1%	$500

Your Income

----Compulsory Repayment Threshold----

| Earn $20,000 | 0% | $0 |

These figures are illustrative only

Thinking about your own situation...
Brainstorm the following two questions.

What are you planning on doing after school? Is your planned study route covered by a HELP loan such as HECS or VET Student Loans?

If not, what's your plan B to be able to afford your studies?

This payslip is actually inaccurate... It's missing HECS deductions!

Hint: You are welcome to research current HECS contribution percentages to use, instead of the illustrative percentages given here.

Earn $100,000	7%	$7000
Earn $70,000	3%	$2100
Earn $50,000	1%	$500

Your Income $

----Compulsory Repayment Threshold----

| Earn $20,000 | 0% | $0 |

Payslip

Employer:	Mandy Money
ABN:	123456789
Employee Name:	Mandy
Employment Status:	Part Time

Earnings

	Unit	Rate	Total
Hours Worked Week 1	40	$30	$1200
Hours Worked Week 2	40	$30	$1200
Hours Worked Week 3	40	$30	$1200
Hours Worked Week 4	40	$30	$1200
Gross monthly payment		**$ 4800**	

Super Contribution

Superannuation <10% additional>	$ 480

Deductions

Taxation (PAYG)	$ 766

Net Payment	$ 4034

How much HECS repayment will be deducted from this monthly payslip, and where will this be written on the payslip?

What will the new Net Payment be?

The True Cost Of Moving Out Of Home

Flying the nest is a life milestone everyone gets to at some stage, but how expensive is it really? Let's break down the costs of moving out. We'll split these into one-off costs and recurring costs.

You, getting too big for the Nest

1 One-Off Costs

These are the things you'll be paying once - before, during and right after you move.

- The most obvious one, we have the actual moving expenses, including van rental or professional help.
- Next, a rental bond is required in most Aussie states, which is typically **four weeks rent**. While you should get this back at the end of your tenancy, treating it as a sunk cost means that when you do get it back, you can then use it towards your next rental bond. Or, worst case scenario, if you damage the property, the landlord might decide to keep it!
- Next, in your new place, utilities companies often require a connection fee upfront to secure things like power, gas and internet services.
- Finally, most first-time renters will forget that the house you rent usually comes empty, you'll need to supply everything inside: beds, appliances, homeware, linen and everything in between. While you may already have some of these, and others are available second hand, fully kitting out a bare home can add up to a pretty penny.

Moving Costs

Rental Bond

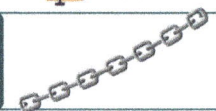
Utilities Connection

Furniture & Supplies

2 Recurring Expenses

Our second category, we have recurring expenses... All the things used through the course of daily life.

For the home and your belongings...
- Rent
- Utilities
- Phone bills
- Maintenance

For personal expenses...
- Clothes
- Self-Care
- Transport
- Food
- Social activities
- Gifts

> There are two types of recurring expenses to be aware of:
>
> **Fixed Expenses:** Expenses that are the same each month/quarter and don't change each budget period. For example, your phone bill.
>
> **Variable Expenses:** Expenses that are flexible each period, like your grocery bill.

House & Health Bills

Clothes & Self-Care

Food & Transport

Social & Lifestyle

Extras

Finally, it's not a bad idea to have a serious **emergency fund** within reach to soften the blow of unexpected expenses. You can run into the most bizarre expenses that you'd never have dreamt of after moving out, like spending $100 to fix the washing line, or maybe your cat needs a trip to the vet because it ate a balloon! An amount to aim for is to have three months of expenses at the ready. This will cover you for any shortfalls and generally give you a good safety net for anything you might encounter.

All in all, there are plenty of hidden costs when it comes to moving out. It's useful to be aware of what these could be. If you're currently at home, taking an interest in household expenses such as the grocery shop or utilities bills may give you an idea on the numbers behind everyday life. Make sure you have a really detailed and realistic budget plan before you jump into the deep end.

> Experts (generally) recommend spending <25% of your income on accomodation.

L9.2.1

You and your best friends are moving out together!
Research your rental property and put together an individual budget about how much your first month will cost you. Make sure to include your emergency fund!

Monthly Costs

Rent	
Utilities	
Insurance	
Transport	
Food	
Essentials	
Fun	

Total Monthly Cost =

Remembering that you still have savings to account for, how much will you be need to earn per month to afford this?

What needs to happen to make this realistic?

Moving Out Day

Bond	
Furnishing	
Moving Costs	

Total (*without* Emergency) =

This is how much you'll actually be spending

Emergency Fund

Total (*with* Emergency) =

This is ideally, how much you'll want to have saved up

How much will you need to save up between now and your ideal moving out date, and how much a month / week will you have to save to make that happen?

Moving out Date_____

Number of months / weeks until then _____

Total to save up (including your emergency fund) $_____

Amount to save per month / week _____

What do you need to change about your earning / spending / saving to make this happen?

Moving Out, What You Need To Know

Moving out of home is a big step! There are many things to plan for and consider. Here's the run-down.

One Year Before

Saving up

(Referring to the chapter on moving out costs) Once you've decided your monthly budget, moving costs and your emergency fund goal, now it's time to get to it!
- Build and execute a strong savings strategy.
- Make any changes in your life you'll need to be able to support your new monthly budget.

1-6 months before

Choosing a place

Choosing a place can be the hardest part. There are many different factors (and a bit of luck) involved. There are two common ways to go about finding a place to rent.

Taking out a Lease

Taking out a Lease is a very formal process. It involves finding a place advertised by a real-estate agency, doing an official application, providing references plus whatever the agency needs to verify that you're a responsible renter. You are also financially responsible at the end of the leasing term.

Joining an existing Lease (Subletting)

Subletting is slightly less formal, where you join an existing lease. You can often find these through friends, apps or social media. Subletting is a legally binding agreement, but you aren't financially responsible at the end of the lease term, and don't have all the formal lease obligations.

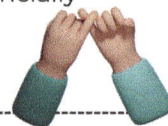

One month before

Packing and Prep

Depending on whether you're taking out a new lease and starting from scratch, or moving out into an existing house, your packing job can vary from tiny to HUGE. Here are a few things to remember...

Packing
- ☐ Clothes, Shoes, Toiletries
- ☐ Kitchen & Bathroom
- ☐ Electronics & Cleaning
- ☐ Bedroom & Bedding
- ☐ Basic Furniture

Prep
- ☐ Signing the (sub)lease
- ☐ Paying the bond
- ☐ Setting up Electricity & Gas
- ☐ Setting up Wifi & TV cable
- ☐ Address Updates

On the day!

Moving in

Even if you've prepped everything, moving day can still be a bit stressful and can involve lots of little hiccups. All part of the fun! *A few things to remember:*
- Getting the right vehicle to move your things. Do you need to rent a van, or find a moving company?
- Make sure you have budget for takeaway meals the first few days. You might not have the energy or kitchen supplies yet. Or maybe there's a delay in your electricity or gas set-up.
- Getting your essentials set-up first. Bed, kitchen, bathroom. The artwork can wait!
- Remember that everything is temporary! Any hiccups or problems will get sorted out in time.

Paying (and splitting) Bills

Paying bills (Gas, Electricity and Water) can seem scary, especially if you don't plan for them or expect them. If you are subletting, you might simply have a monthly utility charge.

Bill Cycles

Bill cycles are often quarterly (every 3 months). Make sure to split the predicted cost and save up each month. This helps you not get caught out when they arrive.

Usage guage

For your first cycle of bills, take very careful note of how you are using electricity, water and gas. After your first bill, you'll have a better gauge about much utilities cost.

Splitting Bills

Splitting bills can get complicated. Make sure to set clear expectations about who's paying how much and any relevant usage rules (especially heating & aircon!)

You're planning for your first round of bills.
Build these quarterly bills into your budget plan!

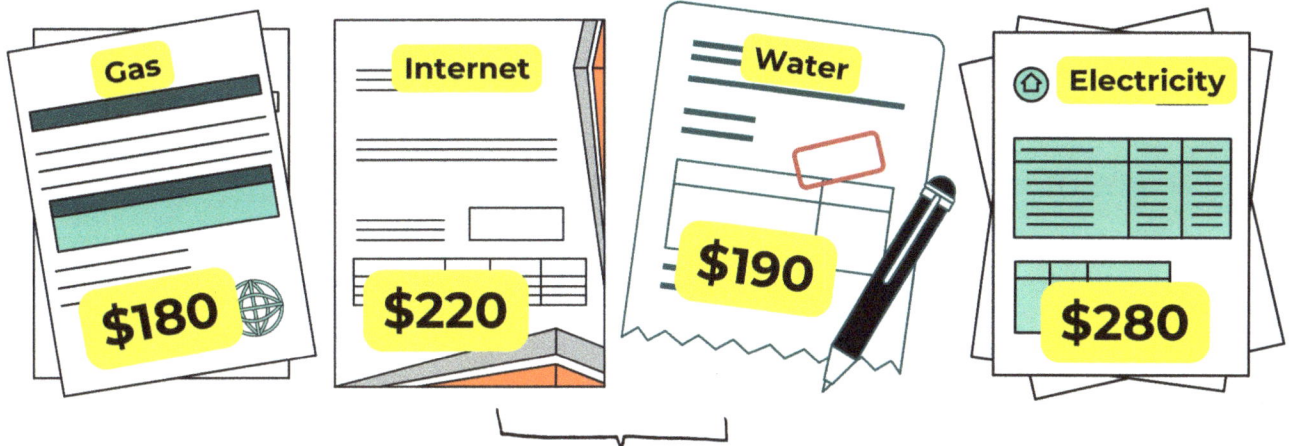

Gas **$180**

Internet **$220**

Water **$190**

Electricity **$280**

Quarterly Utility Bills that arrive at the end of month 3

Using the below budget template, prepare for these bills by recording down how much you will save each month.

	Month 1	Month 2	Month 3
Income	**$4000**	**$4000**	**$4000**
Spending			
Rent	$960	$960	$960
Utilities	$0	$0	**$870**
Insurance	$150	$150	$150
Transport	$300	$300	$300
Food	$800	$800	$800
Essentials	$400	$400	$400
Fun	$300	$300	$300
Saving			
Bills			
Emergency Fund	$400	$400	$400
Investments	$400	$400	$400
Total	**$4000**	**$4000**	**$4000**

At the end of the month, the electricity bill is almost double what you expected as your room mate has been absolutely pumping the aircon. What are two suggestions you talk through with your room mate to avoid paying for their excess usage in the future?

The True Cost Of Buying And Owning A Car

Depending on who you ask, a car can either be a liability, an asset, or a big headache on wheels. The true cost of owning a car might be more than you think...

1 Price of the Car

Firstly, the obvious one: the price of the car. This is the biggest cost by far, and as such it's sometimes hard to save up the upfront cost all at once. Because of this, people find the money for cars in many ways: Paying cash, borrowing money from Mum and Dad, or taking out a loan are all legitimate options to be considered. Remember that getting a loan from a third party will also cost you money. Let's say a $10,000 car is bought with an 8 percent loan over a five year period. You'd pay $2,166 extra in interest, which is almost a quarter of the car's value, simply for the privilege of using that money.

2 Registration

Ok, you've got the keys, now you have to register and insure it. Registration can be more expensive than you'd expect, and is paid annually. These costs vary by state and where you live, so jump online to look yours up.

3 Insurance

Insurance is the next cost, and unfortunately this topic is very deeply nuanced with long winded policies of what they do and don't include. To keep it simple, there are two main types of car insurance: Comprehensive and third party.

- **Comprehensive** insurance will cover all parties in an accident. It does however have the downfall of being expensive, especially for new drivers.

- **Third party**, on the other hand, only covers other drivers you cause damage to, but will be a lot cheaper - and can be useful if you have a bad habit of bumping into expensive cars. Read your specific policy to make sure you know exactly what yours covers.

Comprehensive

Third Party

You

The Other Party

4 Day-to-day costs

Next on our list of car costs are what can be considered day-to-day costs. These include everything from fuel to servicing, and toll roads to cleaning. Of course, if you're a bit forgetful, remember that parking tickets can also come with the territory!

Lifetime Cost

Considering all 4 costs listed here, the total lifetime cost of a car can be calculated by adding up all of the expenses you'll pay over its life, and subtracting the price you expect to get for the car should you sell it one day.

Sometimes the bus or train doesn't look like too bad of an option after all!

Minus

Insurance

FINE

Eventual Sale Price

L9.4.1

Research your dream first car...

Put together a budget about how much your first three years will cost you. To keep things simple, let's imagine you're buying it in cash (not a loan).

One-Off Costs

Cost Of Car	
Roadworthy	

Total Upfront Cost =

How much will you need to save up between now and your ideal purchase date?

Purchase Date_____

Number of months / weeks until then...

_____

Amount to save per month / week...

_____

Annual Costs

Registration	
License	
Insurance	
Servicing	
Cleaning	
Fines + Toll	
Fuel	
Moving Costs	
Furnishing	

What do you need to change about your earning / spending / saving to make this happen?

Total Annual Cost =

This is how much your annual car costs are

Total 3 Year Cost (Including Car) =

This is how much you've spent on the car over 3 years

Assuming your car sells for 70% of its initial value, how much was its lifetime cost?

Hint: 3 year total cost including car, minus re-sale value

How does the lifetime cost compare to using public transport or ride-share alternatives?

This is unique depending on preferences, where you live, what you do for work!

How Does General Insurance Work?

The 'I' word, insurance, an unavoidable cost, can't live with it, can't live without it. There are many types of insurance that might become necessary over the course of your life. Many of these won't be relevant until later in life, but some are already relevant, even in high school. Here are some of the most common insurances you'll interact with over your life journey...

Car Insurance	Health Insurance	Travel Insurance	Pet Insurance
Life Insurance	Property Insurance	Income Protection	Contents Insurance

How does insurance work?

Every type of insurance is slightly unique, but here's how some of the most common ones work! For example, car insurance. Step 1: your insurer determines how to price your insurance. They weigh up...

- The likelihood of a specific event happening to you,
- Potential costs if this event actually happens.

For example, you lose your phone while travelling and need a new one, or you forget to pull the hand brake and your car ends up in the river.

These events might be unlikely, but their risk can be assessed using hundreds of factors unique to you. The more likely, or the more costly an event, the more expensive your insurance.

Likelihood of event ↑ Cost of event ↑ Price of insurance ↑

There are two parts to your insurance costs...

The 'Premium'

A **premium** is the regular amount of money you pay to stay insured, whether that's monthly or annual. If your risk level goes up, so does your premium.

For example, if you crash your car, you've demonstrated that you're a riskier driver, and that means your premiums might go up.

Premium more expensive after

+

The 'Excess'

As part of taking out insurance, you are also given an **excess** amount. What this means, is that if you need to claim your insurance, you pay your excess amount, and your insurer will cover the rest.

So let's say your car crash cost $6000 in damage, and your excess is $1000... You only pay that $1000, and your insurer pays the rest.

Fixing Cost $6000

You pay $1000 "the Excess"

Your insurance pays $5000

You can often customise how your insurance is priced. If you choose a cheaper premium, your excess may be larger. If you choose a higher premium, your excess may be smaller.

Do you need insurance? The short answer is no... However, insurance is the barrier that sits between unpredictable problems and catastrophic financial outcomes. It may feel expensive and unnecessary, but having the right kind of insurance can quite literally save your life. As you hit certain life milestones, consider the types of insurances relevant to your situation and make a decision with the facts at hand.

Insurance Choices...
Match the different kinds of car insurance with different individuals based on their needs. Justify your decisions!

I'm a Lawyer: with high income, medium risk

A

I'm a teacher: with medium income, low risk

B

I'm a Student with low income, high risk

C

Comprehensive insurance, high excess.	Comprehensive insurance, low excess.	Third party insurance, low excess.

Recap: Two types of car Insurance

- **Comprehensive** insurance will cover all parties in an accident. It does however have the downfall of being expensive, especially for new drivers.
- **Third party**, on the other hand, only covers other drivers you cause damage to, but will be a lot cheaper - and can be useful if you have a bad habit of bumping into expensive cars. Read your specific policy to make sure you know exactly what yours covers.

Comprehensive

Third Party

You **The Other Party**

Insurance Budgeting...
You've just signed up to a new car insurance policy. *You're paying a $100 monthly premium and have a $600 excess.* In month three, you get into an accident with has $2000 worth of repairs. Reflect this information in the budget below.

	Month 1	Month 2	Month 3
Income	**$1000**	**$1000**	**$1000**
Spending			
Essentials	$500	$500	$500
Fun	$100	$100	$100
Car Insurance			
Saving			
Emergency Fund			
Bills	$100	$100	$100
Total	**$1000**	**$1000**	

How Does Health Insurance Work?

Health insurance is slightly unique in Australia. As an Australian citizen, you are automatically enrolled into public (government-owned) health insurance. It's called Medicare!

How does Medicare work?

Working Aussie Tax payers pay a 'Medicare levy'. This is a small tax you begin paying when you earn over a certain amount. You are covered by Medicare even if you don't pay this tax yet.

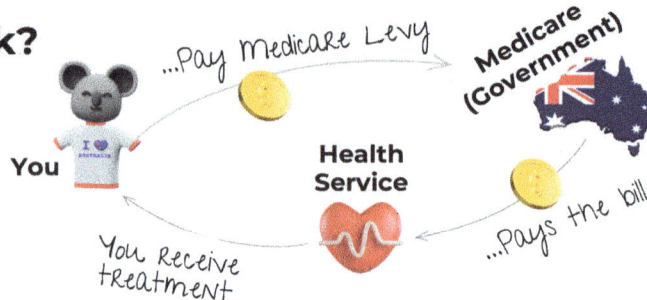

...Pay Medicare Levy

You

Medicare (Government)

Health Service

...Pays the bill

You receive treatment

Hospital Cover

You have free access to essential hospital treatments via Australia's **Public Hospital** system. The catch? You can't choose your doctor or your admittance date. You can opt for a private hospital, which gives you more flexibility. However, Medicare will only cover a certain percentage of the cost of certain procedures. The rest is for you or your private health insurance to cover.

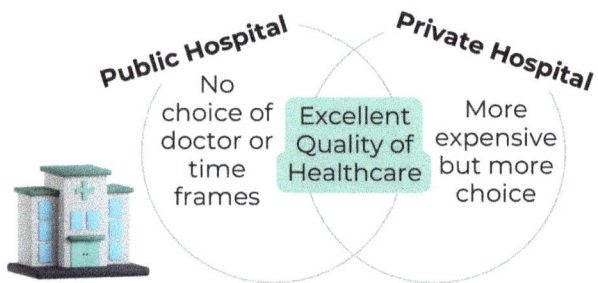

Public Hospital
No choice of doctor or time frames

Excellent Quality of Healthcare

Private Hospital
More expensive but more choice

General Services

You are entitled to many low- or no-cost basic medical services and prescription medication. This could be visiting the GP, getting an eye-test or a psychology session. You can opt for a "Bulk-Billing" GP Clinic which is covered by Medicare. Or, you might choose a private clinic which may charge a **"Gap Payment"**. This means that a part of the cost is not covered by Medicare, and must be paid by you. Your private insurer may or may not cover this Gap payment.

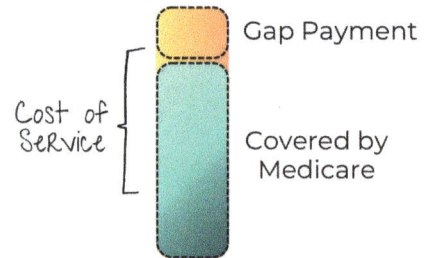

Gap Payment

Cost of Service

Covered by Medicare

Here's what is NOT included in Medicare...	• Ambulance • Dental	• Physio • Osteo / Chiro	• Hearing Aids • Glasses	• Non-Essential Surgery

What about Private Insurance?

Private insurance, on the other hand, pays for some or all of your treatment costs at private hospitals, and gives you access to more choices, such as choice of hospital, or choice of doctor. It may also get you quicker access to some medical services. But, Private insurance still has its limits! For example, depending on your cover, the service and provider you choose, your insurer might not cover your gap payment. When you sign up with a private insurer, you can select from a range of cover options. Similar to car insurance, choosing a cheaper premium might result in less coverage when things do go wrong.

> *It can be complicated!* Simply ask the admin staff at the GP or hospital to clarify how much medicare is paying, how much your private insurer is paying, and how much you will have to pay.

Which is better?

The choice comes down to your preferences and budget. There isn't a huge difference between the quality of care between private and public hospital systems, except for the fact that you might have to wait much longer in the public system. Private Health insurance can give you access to quicker healthcare and more freedom of choice, however, it is expensive and doesn't automatically cover the gap amount for general services and private hospital treatment. There are three key factors to consider:

- Your budget
- Your health situation and foreseeable needs
- Your age (private insurance premiums become more expensive if you haven't signed up by age 30)

Considering each of these scenarios...
Answer the below questions, True or False!

	A I'm going to the Dentist	B I'm having surgery at a public hospital	C I'm having surgery at a private hospital	D I'm visiting the GP
Medicare Only	Gap Payment	Covered by Medicare	Gap Payment Covered by Medicare	*Potential* Gap Payment Covered by Medicare
Medicare + Private Health Insurance	*Potential* Gap Payment Covered by Private Health Insurance	Covered by Medicare	*Potential* Gap Covered by Private Insurance Covered by Medicare	*Potential* Gap Payment Covered by Medicare

1. Going to the Dentist is covered by Medicare... **True or False?**
2. Going to a public hospital is free, even if you don't have private Health Insurance... **True or False?**
3. Medicare doesn't cover your surgery unless you go to a public hospital... **True or False?**
4. Gap Payments at the GP are covered by Private Health Insurance... **True or False?**

Payslip

Employer:	Mandy Money
ABN:	123456789
Employee Name:	Mandy
Employment Status:	Part Time

This payslip is actually inaccurate... It's missing Medicare Levy deductions!

Let's assume that if you earn between $24,000 and $93,000 annually, **your medicare levy is 2% of your entire salary!** *Check up-to-date figures if you are curious.*

Earnings

	Unit	Rate	Total
Hours Worked Week 1	40	$30	$1200
Hours Worked Week 2	40	$30	$1200
Hours Worked Week 3	40	$30	$1200
Hours Worked Week 4	40	$30	$1200
Gross monthly payment		*$ 4800*	

Super Contribution

Superannuation <10% additional>	*$ 480*

Deductions

Taxation (PAYG)	*$ 766*

Net Payment	*$ 4034*

How much medicare will be deducted from this monthly payslip, and where will this be written on the payslip?

What will the new Net Payment be?

How Do Phone Plans Work?

Our little hand computers (also known as phones) are by-and-large a necessary expense for anyone wishing to function in today's world.

There are two parts to a phone purchase: the phone itself, and the plan. Buying first-hand, second-hand, a top-end phone or a sturdy flip phone will see wide varieties in price.

Secondly, the sometimes confusing, and always complex world of phone plans. A phone plan is a paid agreement with a mobile carrier allowing your phone to call, use the internet and text. The complicated part comes in the inclusivity of each plan, balancing functionality with price. There are two main options you might think about: prepaid and SIM-only plans.

The Handset

The little thing that makes the handset, handy

Prepaid Plan

Prepaid plans are the simplest, and work much like the fuel tank in your car. You pay in advance for what you use through buying a certain amount of credit. When your credit is used, your phone is out of gas.

SIM-only Plan

Secondly, SIM-only plans – for these, you'll agree on a certain set of monthly limits for your texts, calls, and data. Your provider will send you a bill at the end of each month, which will usually be the same amount... unless you've gone over your allowance, in which case it could be much steeper.

So what happens when you accidentally take your phone for a swim and you need a new one stat, but you haven't got the cash? That's when a mobile phone plan comes in handy!

Mobile phone plans come with the handset and sim included as part of the deal, giving you access to a phone on a payment plan. These phone plans have a fixed term which often span 12 or 24 months. You don't technically own the phone until your last payment has been made.

If you want to exit the contract early, there's likely to be extra fees for you.

Month One
Month Two
Month Three
Month Four
Month Five

The Phone is now yours!

In general, when comparing plan types...

If you buy a phone outright, you pay the full cost of the phone upfront, then choose a prepaid or SIM only plan for calls, text and data. This option costs more at the outset, but makes it easier to switch plans or providers when you want.

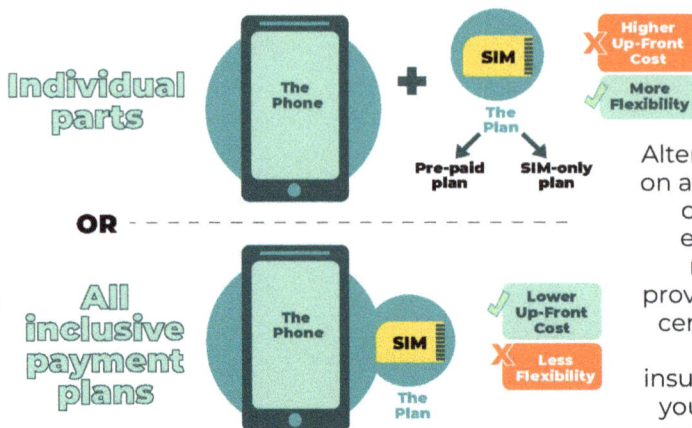

Individual parts

The Phone

SIM

The Plan

Pre-paid plan
SIM-only plan

Higher Up-Front Cost
More Flexibility

OR

All inclusive payment plans

The Phone

SIM

The Plan

Lower Up-Front Cost
Less Flexibility

Alternatively, buying a phone on a plan can spread the cost out, but can make it more expensive overall, and can make it difficult to switch providers. However, there are certain perks you can opt to tap into, like phone insurance... Should you break your phone, you could get a new one as part of the plan.

Different options will work better for different situations, but as always, it's well worth shopping around and talking to different providers about what they might have that can work for you!

Consider these scenarios...
Match the different kinds of phone plans with different individuals based on their needs. Explain your decisions!

Lawyer: high income, lives in the city, needs a high amount of data

A

Student: low income, lives in the city, needs a high amount of data

B

Teacher: medium income, lives rurally, needs a average amount of data

C

- Phone + Sim monthly payment contract plan
- Large network coverage
- Average amount of data available.

- Newest Phone model bought with full upfront cost
- Sim Only plan bought separately
- Limited network coverage
- high amount of data available

- Prepaid plan
- Second hand phone bought separately
- Limited network coverage
- High amount of data available.

Scams, Fraud & How You're Protected By The Law

Navigating the world of money can have its ups and downs. It's important to be aware of what you're entitled to as a consumer, how to stay safe, and where to find help! Here are two key concepts to learn.

Consumer protection laws

As a consumer (someone who buys something!), there are certain laws and rules created to protect you from unfair situations. These are called Consumer guarantees. Here are a few of them...

✅ **Quality and Acceptability Guarantee**
Goods and services must be of acceptable quality, which means they should be safe, durable, and free from defects.

✅ **Guarantee of No Hidden Charges**
Consumers should not be subjected to any hidden costs or charges that were not disclosed at the time of purchase.

✅ **Guarantee of Repair or Replacement**
If a good or service has a major defect or does not meet the consumer guarantees, you have the right to a repair, replacement, or refund, depending on the nature of the problem.

If you find yourself in a position where you believe your consumer rights aren't being respected, and you've tried (unsuccessfully) to resolve with problem with the business, you can call the **Australian Competition and Consumer Commission on 1300 302 502**

Often the trickiest part of a refund is the courage to ask for one. Remember that you are allowed to request one - it's a normal part of everyday business! In fact, even if the store says that no refunds or exchanges are allowed... If the product doesn't meet one of the consumer guarantees (for example it's faulty), you are entitled to a refund, repair or replacement. It pays to know your consumer rights!

Scams & Fraud

Scams have been around since the beginning of the time, but really found their footing when the internet became a thing (research the Nigerian prince scam!). Here's a quick run down on what a scam might look like, how to avoid one, and what to do if you've been scammed!

Examples of what a scam might look like...

- **Online Shopping Scams:** Price too good to be true? Weird looking checkout?
- **Phishing Emails:** Is an email asking for personal information? Is it asking you to pay something you don't know anything about? Does it come from an unknown email address?
- **Social Media Scams:** Is someone you don't know asking for personal info? Or asking for money? Or promising something that seems to good to be true?
- **Online Gaming Scams:** Is someone offering you cheats, game currency, or rare items for a fee?
- **Job Offer Scams:** Is someone you don't know offering you a part-time job online? Are they asking you for personal information or bank account details?
- **Identity theft:** Someone could use your identity to buy things, set-up phone plans, or take out debt.
- **Lottery and Prize Scams:** Is someone telling you you've won the lottery but need to pay a tax?
- **Travel and Vacation Scams:** Is someone offering you a holiday or flight that is too good to be true?
- **Texting Scams:** Have you received a text that's out of context, has weird links or has a weird request?

Victim of a scam?
You're not alone! Talk to your bank, any relevant people or businesses involved, and call Australia's Cyber Hotline on **1300 292 371**

What can you do to avoid a scam?

- Protect private details using an app or program
- Looks fishy? Ask friends or family for opinions
- Call Australia's Cyber Hotline on 1300 292 371
- Search the business, account, number or email

Card Details
Tax File Number
Identity documents
Passwords

Your rights as a consumer...
Look at each of these examples below and explain why or why not each person is eligible to return / exchange their purchase.

A

You've just bought a pair of earrings, but when you put them on for the first time later that day, they fall apart. The tag says "Not eligible for returns or exchanges".

Are you eligible for a refund / exchange / repair? Why / Why not?

B

You've just bought a pair of shoes on a final sale. You've tried them on at home and they are too small. The shop signs says, "No returns or exchanges for final sale items".

Are you eligible for a refund / exchange / repair? Why / Why not?

C

You bought a new jacket 3 weeks ago from a big department store, which has a 14 day returns policy. You've just realised there's a big hole in the sleeve.

Are you eligible for a refund / exchange / repair? Why / Why not?

You've just stumbled upon something that seems like it could be a potential scam... What are three steps you could take to double check whether it is or not?

Step 1

Step 2

Step 3

Banking Functions And Choosing A Bank For You

Banks are a core part of the world's financial systems, and your financial journey! You'll be interacting with them countless times over your life. It's worth understanding how you can make the most of them.

Why are banks actually useful?

Banks are more than just big businesses that store your money. Banks have many different functions which you can choose to take advantage of (or not!). Note that not all banks have all these features!

Storing Money
You can keep your money in one or multiple different bank accounts. Putting your money in a bank is called 'depositing' your money.

Cashflow Management
Banks allow you to set up many different accounts, and transfer money between those accounts. This enables you to create a functional money ecosystem!

Boosting Your Savings
Many offer interest-earning products like Savings accounts and Term Deposits. These allow you to earn interest for keeping your savings in the bank!

Recieving Money
Unless your employer pays cash, they'll need somewhere to send your pay! Providing your employer with bank account details is the most common way to do this.

Sending Money
Whether you're sending money to a friend who paid for your lunch, or overseas relatives, or to another bank you have an account with... Banks make this easy.

Paying for things
Whether you're paying for something in-store or online...Using a banking debit (or credit) card will allow you to do this easily.

Cash-Out (or exchange)
You can 'withdraw' your money in the form of cash. Many big banks also offer foreign exchange services so that you can access foreign cash for your travels!

Loans
Most banks will have loan products of some shape or size. Whether it's a credit card, small personal loan, or mortgage... Banks are one option to consider.

Insurance, Advice, Support Etc
Banks often have many other services that you can use to support your financial needs. Each bank is different, so make sure to do your research!

Two types of banks to choose from

Beyond consider a product, you also want to think about the bank offering the product. Depending on your banking preferences (online, on your phone, in person), different banks offer different benefits.

Traditional Banks
Traditional banks are what you are most likely to hear your parents and older generations talk about. They're the classic, large, banking institutions which offer everything from basic banking services to mortgages and multi-million dollar loans for businesses.

Neo-Banks
Neo-banks are newer to the scene and provide only digital-banking. Because they don't operate physical branches, they can often have lower fees and higher interest on savings. They are often very user-friendly, but only offer a basic set of banking products.

Placing your money in a bank isn't essential, but it's exceptionally difficult to avoid it in today's world. There are three reasons keeping your money "Under the mattress" isn't a realistic idea in the long-term.
- **Safety**. What happens if someone robs your retirement stash?
- **Practicality**. Will you need to buy a bigger mattress to keep your cash?
- **Inflation**. Any savings that aren't invested, lose buying power over time.

Choosing the right bank for you...

Consider the fictional profiles of banks and their products and match them up to each person according to their needs, explaining your choice!

Bank A

I'm a large bank that has been around for literal *centuries*. I offer every service and product under the sun, but I'm a bit slow and only have a very old app that you can use.

Everyday Account
- $0 annual fee
- 1% International Fees*
- $0 ATM fee

Savings Account
- 3% Annual Interest
- 1% Bonus interest if you deposit $100 each month

Bank B

I'm a small local bank, relatively new compared with bigger banks. I don't offer all the products, but I have great customer service and a good banking app for you!

Everyday Account
- $5 annual fee
- No International Fees*
- $0 ATM fee

Savings Account
- 4% Annual Interest, only if you deposit $100 each month into the account

Bank C

I'm a Neo-Bank and only three years old! I only have a few key products, but have an incredible app with heaps of features, so that you hardly have to use customer service.

Everyday Account
- $0 annual fee
- No International Fees*
- $2 ATM fee

Savings Account
- 3% Annual Interest
- No rules to unlock this interest rate

International fees describe the cost to use the card in a different country

A

I'm 18, work part-time and m looking for an everyday account. I'm planning on travelling overseas next year!

B

I'm a working professional and will be travelling overseas for 8 months next year. I like using cash in foreign countries.

C

I am a pensioner and my travel days are done. I only pay in cash, so withdraw from the ATM weekly.

D

I'm a young professional that earns a reliable wage. I want a savings account that has the highest interest rate possible.

E

I'm a freelancer that has an unpredictable income. I want a savings account that allows for this flexibility.

F

I am a student and have a very tiny income. I want a savings account that I can use for any extra cash.

Admin Tasks To Get Your Money Organised

Being a financially fit adult means many things, but mostly, it means getting organised. In this chapter, we'll go over some financial building blocks. Let's get started!

1 Collate your important details

Firstly, you want to start collecting and keeping all your important financial details and passwords in one place. Things like: bank account numbers, tax file numbers, passport details, and MyGov details. On top of this, passwords are more valuable than your house keys, so accurately keeping tabs of passwords to everything is integral. This could be in a phone app or a cloud-based storage system that you lock and encrypt.

> Security is key! Wherever you choose, make sure it's a safe place with encryption and high protection against data theft.

» Passwords
» Usernames
» Bank client N°
» Card Details
» Account Details
» Banking Pin
» PayID
» Passport Details
» MyGov details
» Centrelink number

» Tax File Number
» Super Details
» Medicare N°
» License Details
» Student Number
» Frequent Flyer #
» Personal ABN
» RSA number
» Working with Children's check

2 Create a "Life Admin" folder to organise & store documents

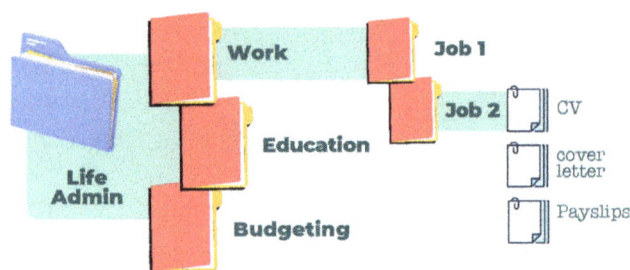

Life Admin
- Work
  - Job 1
  - Job 2
    - CV
    - cover letter
    - Payslips
- Education
- Budgeting

The second task is setting up a big 'life admin' folder for all your digital documents. Doing this on a cloud platform can help protect you against your computer having a bad day. How you organise the internals of this folder is up to you, but ideally you would want a set of subfolders for things like work, education, budgeting, and tax. From there, you can get as specific as you like. So what goes in our life admin folder? ID documents, tax declarations, payslips and everything in between.

3 Collect Identity Documents

In today's world, you will encounter identity checks at every corner! The basic aim of the ID game is to provide a combination of ID documents - each worth a certain number of metaphorical 'points' - to add up to at least 100 points. There are three categories of documents to get you to this score.

- Firstly, primary documents. These are the most trusted forms of ID. You'll need at least one of these to even play the game, and they include your passport or birth certificate.
- Next, your secondary documents. For example, your working with children's check. Finally, tertiary documents. This is the weakest form of ID, for example, your medicare or bank card.

When you have documents totalling 100 points, this gives organisations such as power companies, banks and government bodies enough reassurance that you are who you say you are. So, scan the above documents, saving them in your well-encrypted folders, and add any relevant ID details into your newly set-up storage app or platform.

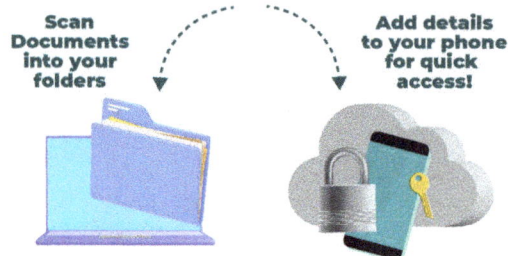

40 points
2 Secondary documents
DRIVERS LICENSE
WORKING WITH CHILDREN'S CHECK

70 points
1 Primary documents
PASSPORT
BIRTH CERTIFICATE

25 points
3 Tertiary documents
MEDICARE CARD
BANK CARD

Scan Documents into your folders

Add details to your phone for quick access!

L9.10.1 Make an action plan!
Answer these questions to get your money life organised!

Important Detail Collation

Where will you set up your storage note? Which App/location?	What are the first three things you will list there?

Life Admin Folder

What will your main folder and first layer of sub-folders be called?	What are the first three documents you'll drop there?

Identity Documents

How will you get your documents scanned into the right folder?	Do you have 100 points of ID ready to go? Which documents?

Technical To-Do's To Get Your Money Organised

There are several digital resources you'll need to have set up as a young person. 5 key task include: The MyGov portal, the ATO app, your tax file number, your super fund, and your banking set-up.

1 MyGov

First cab off the rank is getting set up on MyGov. MyGov is an online portal that gives you access to many of your government services which help you with things like your Tax return, Super consolidation and Centrelink.

It's packed with useful features and information to help you navigate your financial journey.

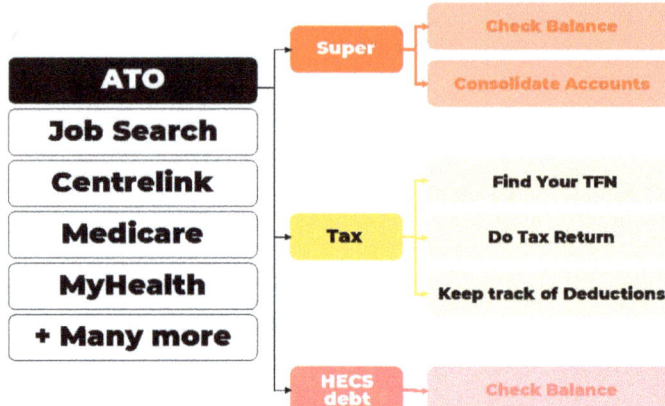

| ATO |
| Job Search |
| Centrelink |
| Medicare |
| MyHealth |
| + Many more |

Super → Check Balance, Consolidate Accounts

Tax → Find Your TFN, Do Tax Return, Keep track of Deductions

HECS debt → Check Balance

2 The ATO App

The second is downloading the ATO app. While this isn't necessarily an essential task, the app does have some fairly handy calculators and features to help you collect tax return information and keep you organised throughout the year.

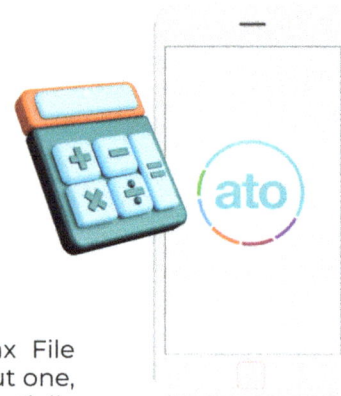

3 Tax File Number

The third is getting a Tax File Number. Funnily enough, a Tax File Number is not actually compulsory to work in Australia, but without one, whatever you earn will get taxed at the highest tax rate - potentially costing you lots of money! Getting a TFN is a fairly quick process; simply jump onto the Australian Tax Office website and go from there.

4 Superfund

The fourth is choosing and setting up your Superfund, if you haven't already. There's a fair bit of research and decision making that goes into choosing one. They'll be responsible for managing your retirement money, which, with the help of time, could turn into a pretty significant retirement fund, so it's worth putting in the research to choose one you're happy with!

Set-up your super fund so your employer knows where to send your retirement money!

5 Online Banking

The fifth task is to set up your online and mobile banking environments. Depending on which bank or types of accounts you might use, being savvy at accessing and managing your money on your phone or your laptop will make it much easier to manage and make your budgets. This can take the form of both browser-based websites and mobile applications, depending on where you spend your time.

Life admin is a non-glamorous part of the financial journey, but will make it all so much smoother.

Go through this list of technical to-do's...
Figure out which you have done, and are still yet to do! Next, of those you haven't done, order them according to your priority.

		Done?	Priority?
MyGov	*Have you set up an account?*	☐	☐
The ATO App	*Have you downloaded it?*	☐	☐
Tax File Number	*Have you got one?*	☐	☐
Superfund	*Have you chosen and set-up one?*	☐	☐
Online Banking	*Can you access your banking online / App?*	☐	☐

True or False: MyGov is an online portal that gives you access to many of your government services which help you with things like your Tax return, Super consolidation and Centrelink.

True or False: Choosing a Superfund doesn't really matter since they are all essentially the same.

True or False: While a Tax File Number is not compulsory to work in Australia, without one, whatever you earn will get taxed at the highest tax rate.

Where To Find Help And Support With Your Money

Asking for support as a young person can be daunting, but knowing how to access financial support can be the difference between two very different kinds of futures. In this chapter, we'll break down the types of support you might need into four categories.

1 Technical Support

Firstly, technical support. Let's say you need to get your tax return done by a professional, or need specific accounting help. There's likely a local accountant whom your family or friends could introduce you to, (or one you can find via google). Whichever way you go, make sure the accountant is a member of a professional body who has the the right qualifications and complies with professional standards. In Australia, there are countless types of technical support professionals, including: Financial Advisors, Accountants, Financial advisors, Mortgage Brokers, Stock Brokers, Insurance Agents.

Local professional   **Online providers**

Most professionals will provide you with a free intro session for you to ask questions and check it's a good fit!

2 Advice & Guidance

Secondly, advice and guidance. Unfortunately the old adage that 'free help isn't good, and good help isn't free' does play a role here. Advice from a financial advisor in Australia can be extremely expensive. However, it's not uncommon to find free or discounted support through your university, local council, or a charity. These services can be an excellent starting place, even if they're a little harder to find. Your bank or superfund might also be able to provide you with counsel or a recommendation.

University, local council, charity   **Bank or superfund**

3 Education

If you're not ready to reach out for help yet, get educated and upskill yourself, giving you power to make many of the decisions on your own. There are many free resources on the Internet and on social media. Read the news, watch YouTube videos, listen to podcasts, read articles - every little bit helps. It's important to note, though - not all information is created equal. Watch for biases, and make sure of the reputability of the advice you find by cross-checking across multiple sources.

Gift yourself the power of decision-making!

4 Financial Support

Finally, financial support. You might find yourself in a tricky situation and need extra help to support yourself. While there can be a variety of grants or charity support you could lean on, the key government resource to explore is Centrelink. Centrelink has a long list of payments you could be eligible for - ranging from one-off crisis payments, to continued support, to interest-free emergency loans. These can take a while to get processed, and you do need to tick all the eligibility criteria, but they can be a great first port-of-call.

Sometimes, your financial journey can be about momentum: a wrong turn along the way, and you might need a hand to get the ball rolling again. This list should help you find the right support!

Help out a friend!
What support would you recommend in these scenarios?

Scenario #1: Jerry has had a busy financial year working as a contractor, but needs to submit a tax return which they have never done before. Where might you send them for assistance?

Scenario #2: Taylor has had trouble recently paying her rent and utility bills, they seem to always have trouble managing their money. What advice might you offer?

Scenario #3 Sammy has taking out a few loans to fund their recent holiday, and has since gone into debt. They are struggling to work out how to best repay. Could you offer any guidance?

LIFE ADMIN ✨

A space for your notes, questions, plans!

Congrats!

You've completed the...

SMART FOUNDATIONS
micro-credential

- Interest
- Debt
- Life Admin

To collect your certificate and resume badge...

1 Complete this knowledge quiz

2 Email **microcredential@mandymoney.com.au** with your **quiz ID number** and a photo of this page!

tinyurl.com/22wdb7cj

Get a parent, teacher or librarian to complete this!

I,_____, can confirm that
(First and last name of teacher)

_____ has completed the activities for
(First and last name of student)

this micro credential, to the best of their ability.

Signed:_____ Date: _____ Email:_____
(In case we need to check that you're real!)

Answers

To access answers and
suggested responses,
visit this link!

tinyurl.com/
22wdb7cj

Thank you and
Acknowledgments

It really does take a village!

Ben Toohey, Kellie Bailey, Gabrielle Hurrel, Harry Robertson, Paul Ikin, Lisa Fraumano-Braddy, Lisa Thomas, the Haileybury Community & Alumni, Ben Seater, Cameron Ensor, Michael Strauss, Kenwa Seong, Daniel Lopez, Riley Cahill, Rayan Shergill, Seb Andreassen, GoodOne (and friends), Thyme Studio and Lizzie Hedding, Tim Grogan, Zoe Nolan, Finn Cole-Adams, Merrymen and the Cafes of Hampton, the van der Merwe family, the Toohey family, Oliver Krasny, Isy Paton, Taylor Jackson, Chloe Smith, Chai Ng, Sabine Partington, Annelise McCarthy, Janey Martino, Seve Jones, Carla Tobin, Connie Gamble, Joey Moshinsky, Mary Tsipis, Jasmine Cheruvankalayil, Olivia Smith, Jack Spittle + Tony O'Donnell and the generous team at Deloitte, Exo Digital, Zane Davidson, Kate Butterworth, Richard Mathieson, Andrew Duncan, Grace Gibson, Connie Zhang, Jack and Rachel Doughty, Tom McLeod, Olivia Spanos, the Kit Team, Casper Bjarnason, Khai Ling Chan, Trianna Valdes, Hannah Pikkat, Di Fleming, Andrew Loh + Rory McNiece and the team at MAP, Damien Meunier, Matt (Davo) Davidson, ANdrew Dexter, Ben Sze. Mandy Money friends, family, schools and education partners.